BRADFORD'S HISTORY

Of Plymouth Colony

Of Plimoth Plantation

And first of ye occasion, and ynducments ther unto; the which that y^t may truly unfould, y^t must begine at ye very roote & rise of ye same. The which I shall endevor to manefest in a plaine stile; with singuler regard unto ye simple truth in all things, at least as near as my slender Judgmente can attaine the same.

1. Chapter

It is well knowne unto ye godly, and judicious, how ever since ye first breaking out of ye lighte of ye gospell, in our Honourable Nation of England (which was ye first of nations, whom ye Lord adorned ther with, after ye grose darknes of popery which had covered & overspred ye christian world) what warrs & oppossions ever since Satan hath raised, maintained, and continued against the saints, from time, to time, in one sorte, or other. Some times by bloody death & cruell torments, other whiles ymprisonments, banishments, & other hard usages; As being Loath his kingdom should goe downe, the trueth prevaile; and ye churches of God reverte to their anciente puritie; and recover, their primitive order, Libertie & bewtie. But when he could not prevaile by these means, against the maine truths of ye gospell, but that they began to take rooting in many places; being watered with ye blood of ye martires, and blesed from heaven with a gracious encrease. He then begane to take him to his anciente Stratagemes, used of old against the first christians. That when by ye bloody & barbarous persecutions of ye Heathen Emperours, he could not stoppe, & subverte the course of ye Gospell; but that it speedily overspred, with a wounderfull celeritie, the then best known parts of ye world. He then begane to sow errours, heresies, and wounderfull disentions amongst ye professours them selves (working upon their pride, & ambition, with other corrupte passions, yncidente to all mortall men; yea to ye saints them selves in some measure) By which wofull effects followed; as not only bitter contentions, & hartburnings, Schismes, with other horrible confusions. But Satan tooke occasion & advantage therby to foyst in a number of vile ceremoneys, with many unproffitable Cannons, & decrees which have since been as snares, to many poore & peacable souls, even to this day. So as in y^e anciente times, the persecuti-

---

The first page of Bradford's history "Of Plimoth Plantation."

THE HISTORY

Of Plymouth Colony

BY WILLIAM BRADFORD

A MODERN ENGLISH VERSION

WITH AN INTRODUCTION BY

GEORGE F. WILLISON

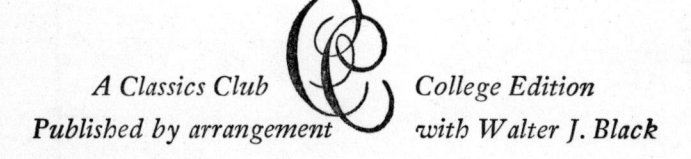

A Classics Club   *College Edition*
Published by arrangement   *with Walter J. Black*

D. VAN NOSTRAND COMPANY, INC.
TORONTO   NEW YORK   LONDON

Copyright 1948 by Walter J. Black.

Printed in the United States of America

INTRODUCTION

O̧f Plimoth Plantation, as Governor William Bradford modestly styled his now famous history of the Pilgrims, tells one of the great American stories. And Bradford, who was the ruling spirit in the Plymouth Colony during its first thirty years, had the wit and skill to tell it well, with rare eloquence and power. A fascinating record of high adventure in the realm both of the flesh and the spirit, of profound human interest from first page to last, his engaging chronicle is a towering monument in American history and in American literature as well.

Most Americans, recalling their days in school, think they know that story well. The simple and demonstrable fact is, most of us do not know it half as well as we should—at least, not in authentic and significant detail, and even less in its larger historical context, so that we fail to appreciate the great reach of the story and its meaning for us today. Our ideas about the Pilgrims, unfortunately, have been shaped far more by the pale fictions of uninspired mythmakers than by the clear and luminous facts left us by the Pilgrims themselves. As a consequence, the latter are still extravagantly praised for accomplishing what they never attempted or intended, and are even more foolishly abused for attitudes and attributes quite foreign to them. In the popular mind, to complicate matters further, the Pilgrims are still generally confused—to their disadvantage—with the Puritans who later came to settle north of them around Boston Bay.

It is time, I think, to go back to the record and see for ourselves who the Pilgrims really were and what they were about.

For that purpose Bradford is indispensable. Indeed, he is unique, for without him there would have been no Pilgrim history worthy of the name, and the ghosts raised by the mythmakers could never be laid.

It was in 1630, ten years after the landing at Plymouth, that Governor Bradford sat down amid the distractions of office to begin what he called his "scribled Writings." Of necessity, these were "peeced up at times of leisure afterwards," for to the end of his days almost forty years later Bradford led a busy life at the center of affairs. By 1650, when he laid down his pen, he had compiled a manuscript of 270 folio pages, all patiently inscribed in his own neat hand. Here, in fine full-bodied prose spiced with a grim kind of humor and lighted occasionally by a flash of malicious wit, was the story of the Pilgrims from its beginning at Scrooby in 1606 to the year 1647, through the most critical and eventful period of their always eventful career.

As is clear from Bradford's pages, the Pilgrims were not the people that legend has represented them to be. They were not pale plaster saints, resigned to practicing the merely negative virtues. On the contrary, they were red-blooded and self-assertive rebels, in conscious and deliberate revolt against the existing order. Having boldly declared their independence of the Church of England at a time when Church and State were one, they were prepared to sacrifice much for their principles, even their very lives, as many of them were called upon to do. But they were armed, in Bradford's memorable phrase, with always "answerable" courage. Having set their course, they were resolved to go on, cost them what it might—and "that it cost them something, this ensewing historie will declare," as Bradford remarked.

It should not be forgotten, as it often is, that the Pilgrims, far from being genteel and rather anemic Victorians, were children of the Elizabethan Age and shared to the full the robust qualities of that amazing age. They were restless and impatient with old ways, scornful of precedent and tradition, daring in their speculations, passionate in their enthusiasms, eager for change, bold and even reckless in action. Not once, but many times, they embarked on desperate adventure and nothing could stop them or divert them from their course. Far from being meek and mild and soft-spoken, they were always stout and sometimes savage fighters in their own defense. Fond of controversy and sharp of tongue, they indulged in many strident quarrels with foes, with friends, and even among themselves, as Bradford tells us in describing many such incidents—including the mutiny on the *Mayflower* to which we are indebted for the celebrated Mayflower Compact.

In their acceptance of the simpler joys of life the Pilgrims were likewise Elizabethan. They were not ascetics, practicing no torments of self-denial. They liked the pleasures of the table and the comforts of the bottle, being fond of "strong waters" and beer, especially the latter, and at Plymouth never complained more loudly of their hardships than when, in their extremity, they were reduced to drinking water. Good Elizabethans suspected water in all its uses, a bath being regarded as a very dangerous thing, exposing the body to every imaginable ill, a view the Pilgrims shared.

In their dress, too, the Pilgrims mirrored their times. Only on the Sabbath did they go about in funereal blacks and grays. Ordinarily they wore the bright Lincoln green and the rich russet browns common among the English lower classes from which they sprang, for it should be remembered that the Pilgrims were simple and plebeian folk. Farmers and artisans, for the most part, they were "from the cottages and not the castles of England," as has been well said. Whatever else may have been shipped on the *Mayflower*—and there has been much violent dispute about furniture and other items—one thing at least is certain. There was not a drop of blue blood on board that vessel or any of the Pilgrim ships that followed.

In more important and vital respects the Pilgrims reflected their age, which, like our own, was one of great contention and confusion. All of Europe had been seething since 1517 when Martin Luther, "that stubborn monk," kicked over the traces and nailed his ninety-five theses to the door of Wittenberg Cathedral. His bold defiance of the Pope, still the King of Kings, both the temporal and spiritual overlord of Europe, had shaken Christendom to its foundations, fanning long-smoldering discontents into a bright blaze that soon swept the Continent in the great revolutionary movement known as the Reformation. In England the Pilgrims stood with their fellow-Separatists in the vanguard of that movement.

England had broken with Rome in 1529 and established

a national church of her own. Henry VIII's resolve to divorce Catherine of Aragon was the occasion rather than the cause of the conflict, and high politics rather than religion were involved. As envisaged by Henry, his new Anglican church was to be a "purified" Catholic church with little change in doctrine or ritual. To quiet reformers and for purposes of his own, the King forbad the worship of "idols," ordering the destruction of shrines and images throughout the land. Also, it was ordered that every church should install a Bible for public use. And the Bible was not to be in Latin, but in English—a revolutionary innovation with consequences that have come thundering down the centuries. For the first time Englishmen could examine Holy Writ for themselves and come to their own conclusions about it, without benefit of clergy. Here was born the right to independence of judgment, to liberty of conscience, which the Pilgrims so vehemently demanded—if not for all, at least for themselves. Here was the birthplace of the Pilgrim tenet that no doctrine or ritual was "lawful" unless specific warrant could be found for it in Scripture. All else, in Bradford's phrase, was "human invention," or "priestcrafte."

The English church first assumed a Protestant character under Edward VI, with the repeal of many of Henry's religious edicts and the publication of the first *Book of Common Prayer* (1549) and Edwardian *Service Book* (1552). But reform abruptly ceased when Edward died and was succeeded by Mary, daughter of Henry and Catherine of Aragon.

A zealous Catholic, Mary reinstituted the Roman rite throughout the realm. Again the Pope was recognized as the spiritual and temporal overlord of Europe. Hundreds of Protestants—men, women, and small children—were sent to the stake or hanged. But the days of "bloody" Mary were few, for she died of malignant inherited disease in the fourth year of her reign.

Under Queen Elizabeth, Anne Boleyn's spirited daughter, there was another sharp reversal of policy. Again England broke with Rome and proscribed its rites. But in all else Elizabeth pursued a wary and devious policy from the first. On the one hand, she had reason to fear the Papists in the land, for England was still largely Roman in sympathy and belief, as it was to remain down to the defeat of the Spanish Armada thirty years later, in 1588. On the other hand, she thoroughly disliked the more zealous reformers, particularly the radicals of the Calvinist school, fearing that they might precipitate civil war. Under the circumstances, she adopted the tactic of now favoring one side and now the other, adroitly playing one against the other to keep both within bounds.

Elizabeth might swing back and forth in her official credo, but of her subjects she demanded absolute uniformity of belief. No one could preach without a license. Above all, there was to be no unlicensed printing, for that would surely lead to "seditious and hellish errours." Machinery to test and enforce orthodoxy already existed in the Court of High Commission, which, as has been well said, was merely the Court of the Holy Inquisition under another sky. Two "heretics" were burned in 1575. Hundreds of people were jailed at the order of the bishops, who derived their authority not from statutory law but the limitless royal prerogative. They could summon and examine anyone at all for his opinions. They could—and did—condemn suspects upon no other evidence than their own frightened and confused replies to some malicious bit of gossip. But in spite of everything they could do,

Elizabeth and her bishops failed to silence the champions of the essentially democratic new order being so painfully born.

Reform centered at the University of Cambridge, where many distinguished scholars and earnest students were increasingly distressed by the state of the church. True radicals in seeking the root of things, they dug into Scripture to discover just where "disorder" had first crept in. The more they dug and explored, the less warrant they could find for much current belief and observance. The simplicity of the early Christian faith, they declared, had been corrupted by time and "human invention." The need of the hour was to restore that faith to its "ancient puritie" —or, as Bradford and his brethren later phrased it, "to its primative order, libertie, & bewtie."

These views angered the orthodox and those holding them were denounced by the Archbishop of Canterbury as "these precise men." It was a graphic phrase, and the reformers were soon known as the Precisians, somewhat later as the Puritans—so named, it should be noted, for their theological doctrine and not their moral code.

The Puritans had many sharp and well-founded criticisms of the church, anticipating Bradford's later remark that it was "a pache of popery, and a pudle of corruption." Certainly, the church stood badly in need of reform, as even some of the orthodox were willing to grant, but now was never the time for reform. All in all, critics made little progress and the authorities began more and more insistently to demand that all hold their tongues and strictly conform. Under increasing pressure many of the Puritans, especially those more comfortably situated, resigned themselves to a nominal conformity and fell silent from fear of jeopardizing their pleasant stations in life.

But some few were made of sterner stuff, and Robert Browne was their leader. A prosecuted and persecuted minister of the "forward" Puritan school, he had finally decided that it was impossible to reform the church from within. Abandoning the reformist Puritan position, he surveyed the ground and laid the foundations for a new and very different kind of church. So great was his influence that all religious radicals, regardless of creed, were soon known as Brownists.

The kingdom of God, said Browne, was "not to be begun by whole parishes, but rather by the worthiest (in each), were they ever so few." In every parish these people should withdraw from the church. They should secede, separate, as they had warrant to do by Scripture (Paul: "Come out from among them, and be ye separate, saith the Lord, and touch not the unclean thing"). Having withdrawn, they should organize themselves under a covenant "to forsake & denie all ungodliness and wicked fellowship, and to refuse all ungodlie communion with Wicked Persons." Every congregation so organized was to elect its pastor and other officers in a democratic manner, with all communicants having a vote. However many congregations were formed, each was to remain quite independent. They might cooperate in a purely voluntary fellowship, but there were to be no bishops, no archbishops, no central organization or authority of any kind, for there was no warrant for that in Scripture.

The "Holy Discipline," as Browne called his practice and credo, was well named. It was only for the holy, only for the devout, only for those who led unblemished lives. The "true" church, Calvin had declared, should embrace the entire baptized population. No, said Browne, that was too inclusive. His was to be a religious élite, a "priesthood of believers," a church of "saincts," from which the irreligious and even the passively religious were to be excluded, whether baptized or not.

In such a church, naturally, the lives of all were to be subject to the closest scrutiny and continuous review, for every act, every word, and even every thought had to be weighed in the balance. Sharp and constant criticism of oneself and others became a positive religious duty, which led to much fruitful searching of soul. It also led to that mean-spirited prying into the most intimate details of one another's lives which marked all the Separatist churches and caused many of them to founder—even that so hopefully established by Browne, who soon returned to live out a long life in the bosom of the Church of England, despised by Puritans and Separatists alike. But he had planted seeds that were to sprout and flourish, and one would grow into the Pilgrim church. Though they were Brownists in all essential respects, the Pilgrims always disliked being called so, and with good reason, for to be known as a Brownist in those days invited prosecution by the authorities and ruthless persecution on every hand.

With the death of Queen Elizabeth in 1603, the hope of reformers bounded up, for they expected great things of her successor, James VI of Scotland, who became James I of England. Surely he would put the hated Anglican bishops in their place, for he had been raised among the doughty Scots who had already overthrown the episcopacy and established their own Presbyterian kirk. But hopes of reform were quickly dashed.

"Away with all your snivelling!" cried the King when some Puritans approached him to advocate a few moderate reforms. Turning to his ministers, he announced his resolve to put down such "malicious spirits," even at the cost of his crown.

"I will *make* them conform," he thundered, "or I will harry them out of the land!" Drastic new decrees were issued to enforce conformity, and for their refusal or reluctance to obey these more than three hundred Anglican clergymen were deprived of office within a year, including "that famous & worthie man," John Robinson, later the Pilgrims' beloved pastor during their pleasant years in Leyden.

But there was one small group in and around the hamlet of Scrooby, in the narrow northern tip of Nottinghamshire, who were not to be frightened or intimidated. For "sundrie years, with much patience" they had borne the silencing of "godly & zealous preachers." Now their patience was exhausted. The time for half measures had passed. Plainly, there was just one thing to do and this, as Bradford tells us, they did. Following Browne's lead, they shook off the "yoake of antichristian bondage, and as ye Lord's free people joyned themselves (by a covenant of the Lord) into a church estate, in ye felowship of ye gospell, to walke in all his wayes made known or to be made known unto them, according to their best endeavors, whatsoever it should cost them, the Lord assisting them."

Thus the Pilgrim church was born, and Bradford picks up the story of the "Lord's free people" here and carries it forward forty years through all the vicissitudes of fortune—persecution, poverty, death, hunger, disease, Indian alarms, misunderstandings with the merchant adventurers and among themselves, abysmal ignorance of the ways of the wilderness, costly miscalculations, and an almost incredible run of just plain bad luck—as epic a tale as has ever been told.

Bradford enjoyed two great advantages usually denied the historian. First, he had been an actor in all the scenes he described. Second, as chief of the inner council at Plymouth almost from the day of the landing, he knew what had been going on behind the scenes as well, and his pages reflect this. Bradford could be disingenuous at times, as will appear, not being above suppressing whole chapters in his brethren's history or distorting facts to place the fairest possible face upon some very dubious action, as in the liquidation of Wessagusset and the brutal killing of many Indians there, which drew a sharp rebuke from their pastor, the great John Robinson. And it should be said that he was always savage in his remarks about those who crossed him or his brethren in any way. There is nothing in the earlier or the later careers of Thomas Weston, John Oldham, or the Reverend John Lyford to bear out Bradford's unpleasant and often scandalous reports about them. And his characterization of Thomas Morton of Merry Mount must be taken with more than a grain of salt. It is simply not true, as Bradford declared, that Morton was locked up for months in Exeter Gaol on suspicion of murder. Even so, Bradford's history is usually a safe and always an informative guide in threading what would otherwise be a hopeless maze.

Bradford knew the Pilgrim story from the beginning, having lived their brave and hazardous adventure from the start. He was born in the hamlet of Austerfield, a few miles north of Scrooby, in 1589. Early left an orphan, he went to live with uncles "who devoted him, like his ancestors, unto the affairs of husbandry." He appears to have had a very unhappy childhood, perhaps the cause of the "soon and long" sickness he suffered in early life, which seems to have been psychological in character, passing away as he grew older. In his amazingly active later life he came to regard his early sickness as a blessing in disguise, saying that it had kept him "from the vanities of youth." By the age of twelve he was deep in Scripture, consorting with the Puritans in the neighborhood, and had begun his "holy, prayerful, watchful, and fruitful Walk with God, wherein he was very exemplary."

All of his family violently opposed his course, warning him that if he went on associating with "heretics," he would lose everything he prized—his good name, the broad acres he had inherited from his father, even his very soul. But Bradford felt sure that he was on the right path, "nor could the wrath of his uncles, nor the scoff of his neighbors, now turned upon him as one of the Puritans, divert him from his pious inclinations."

Fortunately, the boy soon fell under the gentle and knowing hand of William Brewster, then bailiff of Scrooby manor and local postmaster, later the Pilgrims' respected ruling elder, the most lovable of all the Plymouth "Saincts," as the Pilgrims often called themselves. Brewster virtually adopted Bradford as his son and led him into Separation, for it was Brewster who organized the Scrooby congregation. It was not a large group, probably having some fifty to sixty members, who managed to meet secretly every Sabbath at Brewster's, in the rather imposing manor house, and all must have enjoyed the irony that their secret meeting house was the property of an arch-enemy, the Archbishop of York.

Harassed on all sides, the congregation decided to flee to Holland where they had heard there was "freedome of religion for all men." After several near disasters, about half the company managed to get across to Amsterdam and Bradford was among the first to arrive, with only the shirt on his back, quickly apprenticing himself to a French silk-maker to keep from starving. His brethren got what jobs they could in the least skilled and most miserably paid operations of the textile, metal, leather, and other handicraft trades, for all were simple country folk, skilled only as farmers. That training was of no use to them now in the city, and it was not long before they saw "ye grimme & grisly face of povertie coming upon them like an armed man."

It was a boon to the bewildered exiles to have friends to welcome them to Amsterdam—notably, another group of Separatist exiles, largely from London, who had fled to Holland about ten years before and were now known as the Ancient Brethren. This congregation, then the largest and most renowned of the Separatist movement, had just built a new meeting house in the *Bruinistengange* (Brownists' Alley), as a narrow street in the heart of the old city is still known, and here Brewster and his brethren worshiped for more than a year before they thought of moving on again, because of doctrinal disputes among the Ancient Brethren and for "some other reasons," as Bradford reticently remarks in his history.

Bradford could be disingenuous at times, and he was here. His "some other reasons" included the always quarrelsome temper, the bitter spirit of contention, the petty personal animosities, and the many lurid scandals that soon united in a violent explosion to shatter the Ancient Brethren, once the pride of the Separation. The Ancient Brethren's antics brought shame to Separatists everywhere and when Bradford sat down to write his history, he simply dropped the Amsterdam chapter from his annals, fail-

xvii

ing even to note that in moving to Leyden he and his brethren lost their pastor, the Reverend Richard Clyfton, who chose to remain with the Ancient Brethren.

The small Scrooby group constituted only a minority in the exodus to Leyden. The majority consisted of Ancient Brethren who had resigned from their church in disgust, and many of these became prominent Pilgrims—notably, Deacon Samuel Fuller and Deacon Robert Cushman, to both of whom Bradford pays high tribute. Within a few years the Scroobyites and their new allies acquired a permanent place of worship in Bell Alley, in an old quarter of the city, with the purchase of a "spacious" old house known as the *Groenepoort*, or Green Gate. It served them both as a meeting house and a parsonage. Behind it lay a garden and a large lot where many smaller houses were built to shelter the poorer members of the congregation. Here, "under ye able ministrie and prudente governmente of Mr. John Robinson & Mr. William Brewster," now called upon to become their pastor and ruling elder respectively, the Saints were happy at last and lived together "in peace, & love, and holines; and many came unto them from diverse parts of England, so as they grew a great congregation," having perhaps some three hundred members.

Though the Saints were poor, suffering the disabilities and hardships of exiles in a strange land, these years at the Green Gate were the most contented and wholly satisfying of their lives, and they would never know any like them. Bradford had become a maker of fustian (corduroy, moleskin) and, with others, became a citizen of Leyden; only citizens could belong to the merchant guilds which controlled all business and skilled trades in the city. Now in his early twenties, Bradford was married in 1613 to his first wife, Dorothy May, a young girl of sixteen, daughter of one of the Ancient Brethren's deacons, who was later tragically drowned, falling or jumping off the *Mayflower* as it lay anchored off the tip of Cape Cod.

As for Brewster, he first became a tutor, offering private instruction in English to university students and others. Later, he established a publishing house, the celebrated Pilgrim Press, as it is now known. For politic reasons Bradford tells us nothing about this though it forms one of the most significant and interesting chapters in Pilgrim history. The primary purpose of the press was the printing of "subversive" literature—what the English ambassador to Holland soon loudly denounced as "atrocious and seditious libels"—which were smuggled into England to aid the Separatist cause. The matter came to the attention of King James himself, who commanded his ambassador at The Hague to "deal roundly" with the Dutch authorities and persuade them to arrest Brewster and smash his press. The press was seized and closed down, but Brewster took to his heels and escaped, going into hiding for more than a year, probably in the neighborhood of Scrooby, completely baffling the authorities who went on searching for him all over Holland.

By 1617 the Green Gate congregation was again restless and talking of moving on once more. As indicated by Bradford, there were two main reasons for this—first, their growing poverty in spite of hard and continual labor, even on the part of their children, who "bowed under ye weight of ye same, and became decreped in their early youth"; second, their fear of being absorbed by the Dutch, which, as things turned out, was not a groundless fear, for that was the ultimate fate of most of the congregation, not a third of whom ever reached the New World. They wished freedom of worship, of course, but they did not have to go seeking that in the wilderness. They enjoyed it to the full in Holland, without let or hindrance of any kind.

Then followed three years of tedious and involved negotiations in trying to find means of financing their migration to America. Agents were sent to England in 1617 to discuss possibilities with the merchant adventurers of the First (or London) Virginia Company, which had secured an English foothold in America at last with the founding of Jamestown ten years earlier. Like the Muscovy, East India, and other great joint stock corporations organized at this period to promote colonization and foreign commerce, the Virginia Company enjoyed a monopoly in the territory allotted it by the Crown under a royal charter defining the limits of the territory, the general pattern of government, and the authority of its officers. But it was the company, not the King, who appointed these officers, even the governor, and it also had the right to assess and collect taxes, maintain military forces, regulate trade, coin money, and dispose of its lands as it saw fit—being almost a sovereignty in itself, a state within a state, and its primary function was to pay the merchant adventurers as large a profit as possible on the money they had invested in company stock.

The agents from Leyden finally obtained a patent from the Virginia Company, but this was never used, for what the poor Leydeners most needed was free shipping, and this the Virginia Company was unable to provide, being already well on its way to the bankruptcy that overtook it in 1624. The Green Gate congregation then turned to a friend, Thomas Weston, an ironmonger of London, who succeeded in organizing a merchant adventurer group of his own. Bradford tells us the terms of the contract drawn with them, a more or less typical document of the time. But he did not note the most important point about the entire arrangement.

Weston's company was small and relatively weak, and it was never incorporated. It had none of the vast powers bestowed upon the Virginia Company by royal charter. The agreement was simply a business contract. Weston and his partners had no authority to promulgate ordinances and decrees or to appoint the governor of the colony, so that at Plymouth the Pilgrims could more or less go their own way from the start. And they made the most of this, electing their own governor and setting their own pattern of government, with the annual town meeting at its base. The true distinction of John Carver is not that he was the first Pilgrim governor, but rather that he was the first colonial governor in the New World, probably the first in history, to be named by the colonists themselves and chosen by democratic means in a free election.

At last, all things were ready, or as ready as they ever would be, and a group of Saints left Leyden—"they knew they were pilgrimes," they said, and from this phrase in Bradford came their name, first applied to them in 1793 but not commonly used till many years later. Crossing to England, they suffered vexatious delays and several near disasters before they finally embarked on September 6, 1620, upon what they called their "waighty Vioage," with the *Mayflower* packed to the gunnels, carrying 102 passengers—men, women, and children. There was a simply preposterous number of children on board, more than a third of the company, thirty-four in all, down to babes in arms—not to speak of those in embryo, two of whom, Oceanus Hopkins and Peregrine White, were born at sea.

Nothing is more deeply ingrained in the American mind than the notion that the *Mayflower* company was a homogeneous group, united by religious ties and the remembrance of hardships they had suffered together, all from Scrooby by way of Leyden. The fact is, only three were from Scrooby—William Bradford, William Brewster and his wife Mary—and little more than a third of the company were "Saincts" from Leyden. The majority on this ship, as on all the later Pilgrim ships, were "Strangers," in Bradford's phrase, who had been recruited at large in London and elsewhere by the merchant adventurers. So long as a man was willing to work hard and strive to turn a profit for the adventurers, the latter were not concerned how he prayed. In fact, as some of them soon complained, praying might interfere with more important business.

Far from being Separatists of any school, these "Strangers" were members of the hated Church of England. What they were seeking in the New World, like the tens of millions who followed them across the Atlantic for three centuries, was not spiritual salvation but economic opportunity, a chance to better their worldly lot, and for a time they stoutly resisted all efforts by the Saints to convert them to the "true" church. This generated considerable friction from the start and several head-on conflicts that almost wrecked New Plimoth, for the smaller Leyden group was in command and determined to impose its religious views upon the majority, whether the latter wished to accept the Holy Discipline or not. It was their common hardships and their fight against adversity together that finally united the two groups, under Separatist doctrine. The fight for religious tolerance, for real "freedom of conscience," was not won at Plymouth but elsewhere— first, in Rhode Island under the great Roger Williams, who had been at Plymouth and left because the Saints disapproved of his broader views.

Bradford is at his best in describing those first few awful years at Plymouth when men staggered in the street from hunger, scarcely able to go to and from the corn fields upon which their very lives depended. The Pilgrims had many difficulties to contend with, the chief being their utter ignorance of the ways of the wilderness. They had to learn the hard way, by trial and frequent error. But they learned fast, and by 1623 had securely established themselves on the inhospitable New England coast. The victory was their own, for, as Bradford declared, they had never had any substantial aid from any quarter.

Five years later, in 1628, the great Puritan migration to New England began with the arrival of John Endicott and his company at Salem, followed in 1630 by Governor John Winthrop's much larger company, which soon founded Boston, some forty miles north of Plymouth. Unlike the Pilgrims', this was a well-financed venture, with many rich and powerful sponsors having ample capital to equip and ship across a large number of colonists. In 1630 alone Puritan ships brought in more than 1,000 settlers, three times as many as Plymouth had received in its ten years of settlement. Also richer in resources and better situated, the Massachusetts Bay Colony soon overshadowed the Old Colony, as Plymouth now began to call itself, finally absorbing the latter in 1692.

But the Pilgrims had their triumph, too, and with far-reaching effects that are still felt today. On arrival these Puritans were still members of the Anglican church, though of its liberal left wing. They desired reform but still practiced a nominal conformity, partly because of ideological objections to "schisme," chiefly because they were trimmers without the courage of their convictions, fearing the heavy hand of the bishops and civil authorities. Once beyond the reach of the latter, they changed their course. They had been advised "to take advice of them at Plymouth"—and they did, embracing the Separation and adopting the Holy Discipline, largely through the persuasions of Deacon Samuel Fuller. And so, for good and all, "the Pilgrim saddle was on the Bay horse," as the phrase went.

The day on which these former Puritans—confusingly, their original name still sticks to them—took over the Pilgrim meeting house was a momentous one in our history. For the individualistic doctrines and the essentially democratic procedures of the meeting house, their influence radiating far and wide from Massachusetts, have been basic in shaping the ideas, philosophy, manners, customs, ways of life, and moral values of millions of Americans.

Active to the last, Governor Bradford died in 1657. Largely self-taught and rather widely read, as is evident from his pages, he had been blessed with a sharp mind and retained an eager intellectual curiosity to the end of his life. In his later years he somehow found time amid all the onerous responsibilities of office to turn to the study of philosophy and the ancient languages, Latin and Greek. But he was especially interested in Hebrew, for he had a great desire to see with his own eyes, he said, the language of God and the angels and "how the words and phrases lye in the holy texte, . . . and what names were given to things from the creation."

Gifted and indefatigable, passionately devoted to the welfare of Plymouth, Bradford was unquestionably the greatest of the Pilgrims, one of the greatest figures of seventeenth century New England—indeed, of our entire colonial era—and went to his grave honored and "lamented by all of the colonies of New England, as a common blessing and father to them all."

Bradford died the richest man in the colony. But his greatest treasure—*Of Plimoth Plantation*—was little appreciated and almost lost, going on many strange pilgrimages of its own. As Bradford had not written for publication, but rather to satisfy some inner need or desire, his manuscript history was handed down from father to son for several generations, with little or no appreciation of its unique worth. A few passages were copied into the church records by Nathaniel Morton, Bradford's nephew and secretary, who also used it in compiling his sketchy annals of the Pilgrims, *New England's Memorial*, published in 1669. Many years later the manuscript fell into the hands of another early New England chronicler, the Reverend Thomas Prince, who published a few excerpts from it and then placed it on the shelves of his library in the renowned Old South Church, Boston. Here it presumably remained until the American Revolution.

During the early years of that conflict the British occupied the Old South, using it as a riding rink and stable. When the Redcoats evacuated Boston, an inventory of Prince's library revealed that Bradford's history and other old documents were gone. A search was made for them, without success until 1793, when a manuscript volume of Bradford's letters suddenly turned up in Halifax, Nova Scotia, where its large folio pages were being used by a local grocer to wrap butter, cheese, and other small purchases. The letter book was rescued, and for a time there was lively hope that other missing treasures might turn up in the town. But as decade after decade passed without discovery of a single clue, that hope faded and died, and

Of Plimoth Plantation was written off as a casualty of the Revolution.

Then, in 1855, a student of Massachusetts history happened to borrow a book from a friend, a dull ecclesiastical work on the Episcopal Church in America, published in London in 1844. The work seems to have been rather widely studied and read, for it went into a second edition in 1849. But the startling clues it contained went unnoticed for eleven years, escaping detection until the Reverend John S. Barry, thumbing through his borrowed copy, suddenly came upon several long quoted passages attributed to an unsigned manuscript source and instantly recognized that they could have been written only by Bradford. This promising lead was quickly followed up, and the long-lost history was soon traced to its dusty hiding place, being found—and how the "Saincts" would have raged!—in the library of Fulham Palace, one of the episcopal seats of the bishops of London.

How this loot from the Old South came into their possession has never been explained. Nor was the manuscript immediately returned. But his then Lordship was gracious enough to allow a transcript to be made, and *Of Plimoth Plantation* was given to the world the next year. Its publication at Boston in 1856 marks, in a real sense, the beginning of Pilgrim history, which had largely been legend and myth before.

The question of returning the manuscript was raised in 1860 by the Massachusetts Historical Society. The legal authorities of the British government foresaw no difficulties in arranging this, but the Lord Bishop of London objected, saying that the "difficulty of alienating property of this kind could, I believe, only be got over by an act of Parliament." Seven years later, finding itself in possession of documents which did not properly belong to it, the Free Library of Philadelphia returned them to Britain, and it was tactfully suggested—but without result—that *Of Plimoth Plantation* might be sent back to us in exchange. The question was again raised in 1877 and once more in 1881. Finally, in 1896, many distinguished Americans petitioned our ambassador in Britain to explore every avenue that might possibly open a way for the return of Bradford's chronicle.

The church authorities, after much discussion, suggested a plea to the Consistory Court of the Diocese of London. One was drawn, with the usual legalistic abracadabra, and the chancellor of the court was much impressed.

"Had this mss. been solely of historical value," he would have found it very difficult indeed, he said, to see any reason for its removal. Fortunately, there was one sound argument for granting the plea—"the necessity of protecting the pecuniary interests of the descendants of the families named in it, in tracing and establishing their rights to succession of property."

And thus, as a mere title deed and not as a superlative historical document, a genuine American classic, Bradford's manuscript came back to our shores at last—but not home to Mother Plymouth. It went to Boston instead, where it was presented to the governor of Massachusetts and then placed in a glass case, in the State House, where its beautifully inscribed and fascinating pages are still to be seen.

GEORGE F. WILLISON

Editorial note: This book was put into modern English by Harold Paget. The quotations at the beginning of each chapter were selected from the text of that chapter, and are in Bradford's own phraseology and spelling. The chapter headings are in Bradford's wording, but modernized as to spelling. The occasional footnotes which Bradford added to his original text are distinguished from those supplied by the editor by the initial 'B.'

PART ONE

History of the

Pilgrims

1608-1620

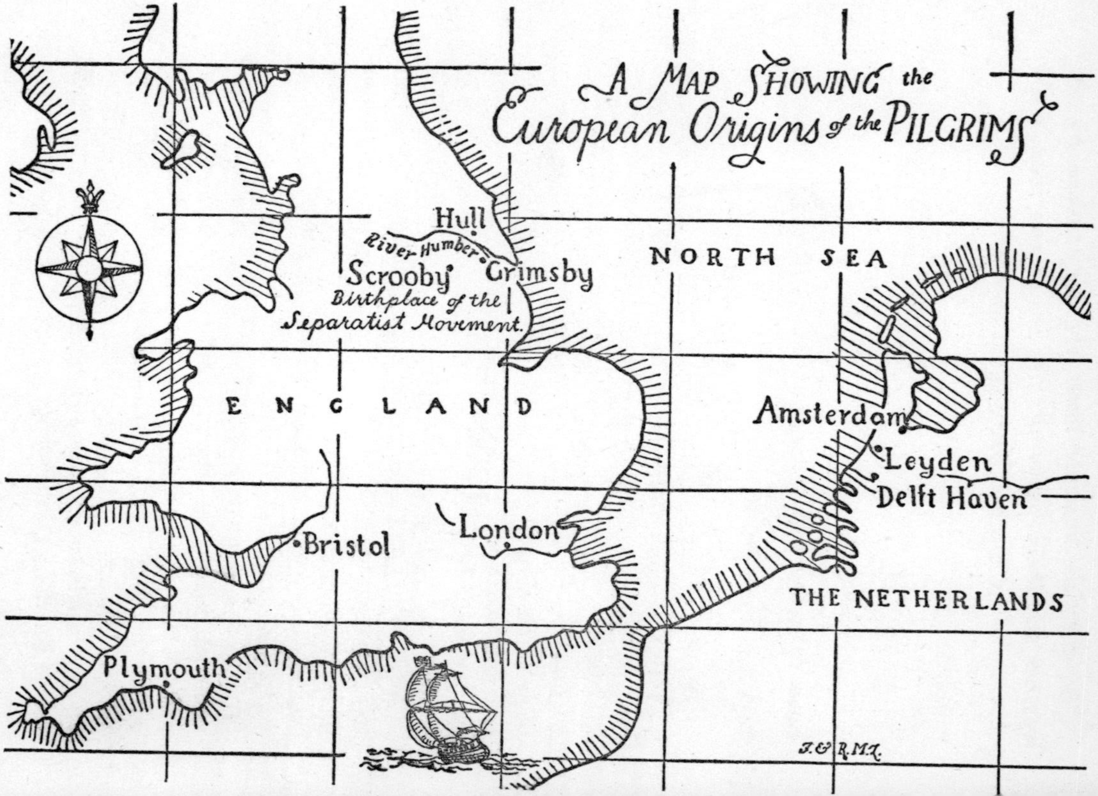
A MAP SHOWING the
European Origins of the PILGRIMS
Hull
River Humber
Grimsby
Scrooby
Birthplace of the
Separatist Movement.
NORTH SEA
ENGLAND
Amsterdam
Leyden
Delft Haven
London
Bristol
THE NETHERLANDS
Plymouth
J. & R.M.L.

"So as in the anciente times, the persecutions by the heathen and their Emperours was not greater then of the Christians one against another."

CHAPTER I

FIRST CAUSE OF THE FOUNDATION OF THE NEW PLYMOUTH PLANTATION.

First I will unfold the causes that led to the foundation of the New Plymouth Settlement, and the motives of those concerned in it. In order that I may give an accurate account of the project, I must begin at the very root and rise of it; and this I shall endeavor to do in a plain style and with singular regard to the truth—at least as near as my slender judgment can attain to it.

As is well known, ever since the breaking out of the light of the gospel in England, which was the first country to be thus enlightened after the gross darkness of popery had overspread the Christian world, Satan has maintained various wars against the Saints, from time to time, in different ways—sometimes by bloody death and cruel torment, at other times by imprisonment, banishment, and other wrongs—as if loth that his kingdom should be overcome, the truth prevail, and the churches of God revert to their ancient purity, and recover their primitive order, liberty, and beauty. But when he could not stifle by these means the main truths of the gospel, which began to take root in many places, watered by the blood of martyrs and blessed from heaven with a gracious increase, he reverted to his ancient stratagems, used of old against the first Christians. For when, in those days, the bloody and barbarous persecutions of the heathen emperors could not stop and subvert the course of the gospel, which speedily overspread the then best known parts of the world, he began to sow errors, heresies, and discord amongst the clergy themselves, working upon the pride and ambition and other frailties to which all mortals, and even the Saints themselves in some measure, are subject. Woeful effects followed; not only were there bitter contentions, heart-burnings, and schisms, but Satan took advantage of them to foist in a number of vile ceremonies, with many vain canons and decrees, which have been snares to many poor and peaceable souls to this day.

So, in the early days, Christians suffered as much from internal dissension as from persecution by the heathen and their emperors, true and orthodox Christians being oppressed by the Arians [1] and their heretical accomplices. Socrates [2] bears witness to this in his second book. His words are these: "Indeed, the violence was no less than that practiced of old towards the Christians when they were compelled to sacrifice to idols; for many endured various kinds of torment—often racking and dismemberment of their joints, confiscation of their goods, or banishment from their native soil."

Satan has seemed to follow a like method in these later

---

[1] The adherents of Arius held that Christ was not of the same divine substance as God; the doctrine was condemned by the Council of Nicaea, 325.
[2] Socrates was a fifth-century theologian who wrote a history of the early Christian church.

times, ever since the truth began to spring and spread after the great defection of that man of sin, the Papal Antichrist.[3] Passing by the infinite examples throughout the world as well as in our country, when that old serpent found that he could not prevail by fiery flames and the other cruel torments which he had put in use everywhere in the days of Queen Mary and before, he then went more closely to work, not merely to oppress but to ruin and destroy the kingdom of Christ by more secret and subtle means, and by kindling flames of contention and sowing seeds of strife and bitter enmity amongst the reformed clergy and laity themselves.

Mr. Foxe [4] records that besides those worthy martyrs and confessors who were burned and otherwise tormented in Queen Mary's days, as many as 800 students and others fled out of England, and formed separate congregations at Wesel, Frankfort, Basel, Emden, Marburg, Strasbourg, Geneva, etc.

Among these bodies of Protestant reformers—especially among those at Frankfort—arose a bitter war of contention and persecution about the ceremonies and the service book and other such popish and anti-Christian stuff, the plague of England to this day. Such practices are like the high places in Israel, which the prophets cried out against; and the better part of the reformers sought to root them out and utterly abandon them, according to the purity of the gospel; while the other part, under veiled pretenses,

---
[3] The Pope was given this appellation generally by Protestants at this time.
[4] John Foxe had fled to Germany to escape persecution during Queen Mary's reign. While in exile he wrote in Latin his famous history of Christian persecutions, commonly known as the *Book of Martyrs;* it was first published in English in 1563.

sought as stiffly to maintain and defend them, for their own advancement. This appears in the account of these contentions published in 1575—a book that deserves to be better known.[5]

The one party of reformers endeavored to establish the right worship of God and the discipline of Christ in the Church according to the simplicity of the gospel and without the mixture of men's inventions, and to be ruled by the laws of God's word dispensed by such officers as pastors, teachers, elders,[6] etc., according to the Scriptures.

The other party—the episcopal—under many pretenses, endeavored to maintain the episcopal dignity after the popish manner—with all its courts, canons, and ceremonies; its livings, revenues, subordinate officers, and other means of upholding their anti-Christian greatness, and of enabling them with lordly and tyrannous power to persecute the poor servants of God. The fight was so bitter that neither the honor of God, the persecution to which both parties were subjected, nor the mediation of Mr. Calvin and other worthies, could prevail with the episcopal party. They proceeded by all means to disturb the peace of this poor persecuted church of dissenters, even so far as to accuse (very unjustly and ungodly, yet prelate-like) some of its chief members with rebellion and high treason against the Emperor, and other such crimes.

---

[5] The work referred to is *A Brieff Discours off the Troubles begonne at Franckford in Germany, 1554*. William Whittingham, afterward dean of Durham, was probably the author.

[6] The duties of pastor, teacher, and elder varied considerably with place and period. Both the teacher and the elder were the pastor's assistants; among the elder's special duties were to act as moderator, keep watch over the conduct of members, and on occasion preach. The deacon was a lesser officer, usually having charge of such matters as the distribution of charity.

And this contention did not die with Queen Mary, nor was it left beyond the seas. At her death the episcopal party of the Protestants returned to England under gracious Queen Elizabeth, many of them being preferred to bishoprics and other promotions, according to their aims and desires, with the result that their inveterate hatred towards the holy discipline of Christ in his church, represented by the dissenting part, has continued to this day; furthermore, for fear it should ultimately prevail, all kinds of devices are used to keep it out, incensing the Queen and State against it as a danger to the commonwealth; arguing that it was most needful that the fundamental points of religion should be preached in these ignorant and superstitious times, and that in order to win the weak and ignorant it was necessary to retain various harmless ceremonies; and that though reforms were desirable, this was not the time for them. Many such excuses were put forward to silence the more godly, and to induce them to yield to one ceremony after another, and one corruption after another. By these wiles some were beguiled and others corrupted, till at length they began to persecute all the zealous reformers in the land, unless they would submit to their ceremonies and become slaves to them and their popish trash, which has no ground in the word of God, but is a relic of that man of sin. And the more the light of the gospel grew, the more they urged subjection to these corruptions—so that, notwithstanding all their former pretenses, those whose eyes God had not justly blinded easily saw their purpose. In order the more to cast contempt upon the sincere servants of God, they opprobriously gave them the name of "Puritans," [7] which

---

[7] The Puritans (first called "precisians") were so called not by reason of their strict moral code but because of their desire to

it is said the novations assumed out of pride. It is lamentable to see the effects which have followed. Religion has been disgraced, the godly grieved, afflicted, persecuted, and many exiled, while others have lost their lives in prisons and other ways; on the other hand, sin has been countenanced, ignorance, profanity, and atheism have increased, and the papists have been encouraged to hope again for a day.

This made that holy man, Mr. Perkins,[8] cry out in his exhortation to repentance, upon Zeph. ii. "Religion," said he, "has been amongst us these thirty-five years; but the more it is disseminated, the more it is condemned by many. Thus, not profanity, or wickedness, but religion itself is a byword, a mocking stock, and a matter of reproach; so that in England at this day the man or woman who begins to profess religion and to serve God, must resolve within himself to sustain mocks and injuries as though he lived among the enemies of religion." Common experience has confirmed this and made it only too apparent.[9]

---

purify the Church. The group of Puritans with which this chronicle is concerned soon became known as Separatists or Independents, for they made a complete break with the Church of England; only later were they known as Pilgrims. Novations means innovators.

See Introduction, pp. viii-xi, for a fuller treatment of this subject.

[8] William Perkins was a theologian of the period.

[9] Bradford inserted the following note many years later: "Little did I think that the downfall of bishops, with their courts, canons, and ceremonies had been so near, when first I began these scribbled writings—which was about the year 1630, and continued as leisure permitted—or that I should have lived to see and hear it. But it is the Lord's doing, and ought to be marvelous in our eyes. . . . Do you not now see the fruits of your labors, O all ye servants of the Lord that have suffered for his truth, and have been faithful witnesses of it, and ye little handful amongst the rest, the least among the thousands of Israel? You have not only had a seed-time, but many of you have seen the joyful harvest. Should you not

But to come to the subject of this narrative. When by the zeal of some godly preachers, and God's blessing on their labors, many in the north of England and other parts become enlightened by the word of God and had their ignorance and sins discovered to them, and began by His grace to reform their lives and pay heed to their ways, the work of God was no sooner manifest in them than they were scorned by the profane multitude, and their ministers were compelled to subscribe or be silent, and the poor people were persecuted with apparators and pursuants [10] and the commissary courts. Nevertheless, they bore it all for several years in patience, until by the increase of their troubles they began to see further into things by the light of the word of God. They realized

---

rejoice, then, yea, and again rejoice, and say Hallelujah, Salvation, and Glory, and Honor, and Power to the Lord our God, for true and righteous are His judgments (Rev. xix, 1, 2) . . . The tyrannous bishops are ejected, their courts dissolved, their canons forceless, their service cashiered, their ceremonies useless and despised; their plots for popery are prevented, all their superstitions discarded and returned to Rome, whence they came, and the monuments of idolatry rooted out of the land. Their proud and profane supporters and cruel defenders (the bloody papists and wicked atheists and their malignant consorts) are marvelously overthrown. And are not these great things? Who can deny it?

"But who has done it? Who, even He that sitteth on the white horse, Who is called faithful and true, and judgeth and fightest righteously (Rev. xix, 11). Whose garments are dipped in blood, and His name was called the Word of God, for He shall rule with a rod of iron; for it is He that treadeth the winepress of the fierceness and wrath of God Almighty. And He hath upon His garment, and upon His thigh, a name written: The King of Kings, and Lord of Lords.

"Anno Domini, 1646.   Hallelujah."

Bradford is of course here rejoicing at the temporary overthrow of episcopacy in England under Cromwell. It was restored with the restoration of the monarchy, in 1661.

[10] Officers of the ecclesiastical courts.

not only that these base ceremonies were unlawful, but also that the tyrannous power of the prelates ought not to be submitted to, since it was contrary to the freedom of the gospel and would burden men's consciences and thus profane the worship of God.

On this subject a famous author thus writes in his Dutch commentaries: "At the coming of King James into England, the new King found established there the reformed religion of Edward VI, but retaining the spiritual office of the bishops—differing in this from the reformed churches in Scotland, France, the Netherlands, Emden, Geneva, etc., whose reformation is shaped much nearer to the first Christian churches of the Apostles' times."

Those reformers who saw the evil of these things, and whose hearts the Lord had touched with heavenly zeal for His truth, shook off this yoke of anti-Christian bondage and as the Lord's free people joined themselves together by covenant as a church, in the fellowship of the gospel to walk in all His ways, made known, or to be made known to them, according to their best endeavors, whatever it should cost them, the Lord assisting them. And that it cost them something, the ensuing history will declare.

These people became two distinct bodies of churches and congregated separately; for they came from various towns and villages about the borders of Nottinghamshire, Lincolnshire, and Yorkshire. One of these churches was led by Mr. John Smith,[11] a man of able gifts, and a good

---

[11] Bradford here introduces the four outstanding leaders of the Separatist movement. John Smyth was one of their ablest preachers. Before his migration to Amsterdam in 1607, he had been the pastor at Gainsborough. When he died in 1612, his adherents were absorbed into other reform or Separatist churches in Holland. Richard

preacher, who was afterwards made pastor; but later, falling into some errors in the Low Countries, most of its adherents buried themselves and their names. To the other church, which is the subject of this discourse, belonged besides other worthy men, Mr. Richard Clyfton, a grave and reverend preacher, who by his pains and diligence had done much good, and under God had been the means of the conversion of many; also that famous and worthy man, Mr. John Robinson, who was afterwards their pastor for many years, till the Lord took him away; also Mr. William Brewster, a reverend man, who was afterwards chosen an elder of the church, and lived with them till old age.

But after the events referred to above, they were not long permitted to remain in peace. They were hunted and persecuted on every side, until their former afflictions were but as fleabitings in comparison. Some were clapped into prison; others had their houses watched night and day, and escaped with difficulty; and most were obliged to fly, and leave their homes and means of livelihood. Yet these and many other even severer trials which afterwards befell them, being only what they expected, they were able to bear by the assistance of God's grace and spirit.

Clyfton was pastor of the group which met in the manor house at Scrooby, famous as the birthplace of Separatism and as the home of the Brewster family. John Robinson, like Smyth, was a graduate of Cambridge, then a divinity school, and was persuaded by Smyth to join the movement. Beloved and brilliant pastor of the Leyden Separatists, Robinson was hindered from accompanying his flock to New England. The Scrooby postmaster, William Brewster, elder and spiritual leader of the Plymouth colony during its hardest years, devoted his long life to the cause. Young William Bradford, an orphan, came into contact with Brewster while still a boy, and their relationship continued close, almost that of father and son, until Brewster's death. See Introduction for a fuller description.

However, being thus molested, and seeing that there was no hope of their remaining there, they resolved by consent to go into the Low Countries, where they heard there was freedom of religion for all; and it was said that many from London and other parts of the country, who had been exiled and persecuted for the same cause, had gone to live at Amsterdam and elsewhere in the Netherlands. So after about a year, having kept their meeting for the worship of God every Sabbath in one place or another, notwithstanding the diligence and malice of their adversaries, seeing that they could no longer continue under such circumstances, they resolved to get over to Holland as soon as they could—which was in the years 1607 and 1608. But of this, more will be told in the next chapter.

> *"For by these so publick troubls, in so many eminente places, their cause became famouss, and occasioned many to look into the same; and their Godly carriage and Christian behaviour was such as left a deep impression in the minds of many."*

CHAPTER II

OF THEIR DEPARTURE INTO HOLLAND AND THEIR TROUBLES THERE, WITH SOME OF THE MANY DIFFICULTIES THEY FOUND AND MET.

For these reformers to be thus constrained to leave their native soil, their lands and livings, and all their friends, was a great sacrifice, and was wondered at by many. But to go into a country unknown to them, torn by war,[1] where they must learn a new language, and get their livings they knew not how, seemed an almost desperate adventure, and a misery worse than death. Further, they were unacquainted with trade, which was the chief industry of their adopted country, having been used only to a plain country life and the innocent pursuit of farming. But these things did not dismay them, though

---

[1] The War of Dutch Independence, begun in 1567, was being terminated by a truce which lasted from 1609 to 1621. The English had been helping the Dutch, then the most enterprising and progressive people in Europe, in their struggle against Spain. This friendly connection, the freedom of worship offered to all, and the nearness of Holland, all helped the Pilgrims to settle on this country as a haven.

they sometimes troubled them; for their desires were set on the ways of God, to enjoy His ordinances; they rested on His providence, and knew Whom they had believed.

But this was not all; for though it was made intolerable for them to stay, they were not allowed to go; the ports were shut against them,[2] so that they had to seek secret means of conveyance, to bribe the captains of ships, and give extraordinary rates for their passages. Often they were betrayed, their goods intercepted, and thereby were put to great trouble and expense. I will give an instance or two of these experiences.

A large number of them had decided to take passage from Boston in Lincolnshire, and for that purpose had hired a ship wholly to themselves, and made agreement with the captain to be ready at a convenient place on a certain day to take them and their belongings. After long waiting and great expense—he had not kept day with them—he came at last and took them aboard at night. But when he had secured them and their goods he betrayed them, having arranged beforehand with the searchers and other officers to do so. They then put them in open boats, and there rifled and ransacked them, searching them to their shirts for money—and even the women, further than became modesty—and took them back to the town and made a spectacle of them to the multitude that came flocking on all sides to see them. Being thus rifled and stripped of their money, books, and other property, they were brought before the magistrates, and messengers were sent to inform the Lords of the Council about them. The mag-

---

[2] No one at that time could leave the realm without permission. The authorities especially wished to prevent any from seeking sanctuary in the New World, unless they went as colonizers under a royal patent.

istrates treated them courteously, and showed them what favor they could; but dare not free them until order came from the council-table. The result was, however, that after a month's imprisonment, the majority were dismissed, and sent back to the places whence they came; but seven of the leaders were kept in prison,[3] and bound over to the Assizes.

Next spring there was another attempt made by some of the same people, with others, to get over from a different place. They heard of a Dutchman at Hull who had a ship of his own belonging to Zealand, and they made an agreement with him, and acquainted him with their plight, hoping to find him more reliable than the English captain had been; and he bade them have no fear. He was to take them aboard between Grimsby and Hull, where there was a large common a good way from any town. The women and children, with all their effects, were sent to the place at the time arranged in a small bark which they had hired; and the men were to meet them by land. But it so happened that they all arrived a day before the ship came, and the sea being rough, and the women very sick, the sailors put into a creek hard by, where they grounded at low water.

The next morning the ship came, but they were stuck fast and could not stir till about noon. In the meantime, the captain of the ship, seeing how things were, sent his boat to get the men aboard who he saw were ready, walking about the shore. But after the first boatful was got aboard and she was ready to go for more, the captain espied a large body of horse and foot, armed with bills and guns and other weapons—for the countryside had turned

---

[3] Brewster was among them.

out to capture them. The Dutchman, seeing this, swore his country's oath, "Sacramente!" and having a fair wind, weighed anchor, hoist sail, and away! The poor men already aboard [4] were in great distress for their wives and children, left thus to be captured, and destitute of help—and for themselves, too, without any clothes but what they had on their backs, and scarcely a penny about them, all their possessions being aboard the bark, now seized. It drew tears from their eyes, and they would have given anything to be ashore again. But all in vain, there was no remedy; they must thus sadly part.

Afterwards they endured a fearful storm at sea, and it was fourteen days or more before they reached port, in seven of which they saw neither sun, moon, nor stars, being driven near the coast of Norway. The sailors themselves often despaired, and once with shrieks and cries gave over all, as if the ship had foundered and they were sinking without hope of recovery. But when man's hope and help wholly failed, there appeared the Lord's power and mercy to save them; for the ship rose again, and gave the crew courage to manage her. If modesty permitted, I might declare with what fervent prayers the voyagers cried to the Lord in their great distress—even remaining fairly collected when the water ran into their mouths and ears; and when the sailors called out, "We sink, we sink!" they cried (if not with miraculous, yet with sublime faith): "Yet Lord, Thou canst save! Yet Lord, Thou canst save!" Upon which, the ship not only righted herself, but shortly afterwards the violence of the storm began to abate, and the Lord filled their afflicted minds with such comfort as but few can understand, and in the end brought

---

[4] The eighteen-year-old Bradford was on board this vessel.

them to their desired haven, where the people came flocking, astonished at their deliverance, the storm having been so long and violent.

But to return to the rest where we left them. The other men, who were in greatest danger, made shift to escape before the troops could surprise them, only sufficient staying to assist the women. But it was pitiful to see these poor women in their distress. What weeping and crying on every side: some for their husbands carried away in the ship; others not knowing what would become of them and their little ones; others again melted in tears, seeing their poor little ones hanging about them, crying for fear and quaking with cold! Being thus apprehended, they were hurried from one place to another, till in the end the officers knew not what to do with them; for to imprison so many innocent women and children only because they wished to go with their husbands seemed unreasonable and would cause an outcry; and to send them home again was as difficult, for they alleged, as was the truth, that they had no homes to go to—for they had sold or otherwise disposed of their houses and livings. To be short, after they had been thus turmoiled a good while, and conveyed from one constable to another, they were glad to be rid of them on any terms; for all were wearied and tired of them. Though in the meantime, they, poor souls, endured misery enough. So in the end, necessity forced a way for them.

But not to be tedious, I will pass by other troubles which they endured in their wanderings and travels, both on land and sea. I must not omit, however, to mention the fruit of it all. For by these public afflictions, their cause became famous, and led many to inquire into it; and their Christian behavior left a deep impression on the minds of many. Some few shrank from these first conflicts, and no wonder; but many more came forward with fresh courage and animated the rest. In the end, notwithstanding the storms of opposition, they all got over, some from one place, some from another, and met together again with no small rejoicing.

"Being thus setled they continued many years in a comfortable condition, injoying much sweete and delightfull societe and spirituall comforte together in the ways of God."

CHAPTER III

OF THEIR SETTLING IN HOLLAND AND THEIR MANNER OF LIVING AND ENTERTAINMENT THERE.

Having reached the Netherlands, they saw many fine fortified cities, strongly walled, and guarded with troops of armed men; and they heard a strange and uncouth language, and beheld the different manners and customs of the people, with their strange fashions and attire—all so far differing from their own plain country villages wherein they were bred and had lived so long, that it seemed they had come into a new world. But these were not the things they gave much attention to. They had other work in hand, and another kind of war to wage. For though they saw fair and beautiful cities, flowering with abundance of all sorts of wealth and riches, it was not long before they saw the grim and grisly face of poverty coming upon them like an armed man, with whom they must buckle and encounter, and from whom they could not fly; but they were armed with faith and patience against him and all his encounters; and though they were sometimes foiled, yet, by God's assistance, they prevailed and got the victory.

When Mr. Robinson, Mr. Brewster, and the other principal members had arrived—they were among the last, having stayed to help the weakest over—such things were deliberated as were necessary for their settling and for the best ordering of the church affairs. When they had lived at Amsterdam about a year, Mr. Robinson, their pastor, together with the most discerning of the others, seeing that Mr. John Smith and his followers had already fallen out with the church which was there previously, and that nothing could avail to end the quarrel, and also that the flames of contention were likely to break out in the parent church itself (as afterwards, alas, came to pass); they thought it best to move, before they were in any way involved, though they knew it would be to their worldly disadvantage, both at present and probably in the future—as indeed it proved to be.

For these and other reasons, then, they removed to Leyden, a fair and beautiful city, of a sweet situation, made famous by its university, in which recently there had been so many learned men. However, lacking seafaring trades, which Amsterdam enjoys, it was not so favorable in providing means of livelihood. But being settled here, they fell to such trades and employments as they best could, valuing peace and their spiritual comfort above any other riches whatever; and at length they came to raise a competent and comfortable living, though only by dint of hard and continual labor.[1]

---

[1] Bradford's restrained account gives but a faint idea of the hardships and stresses endured. Most of the Pilgrims had to work as day laborers, as weavers, carders, and bakers, at a subsistence wage. A few of the better off were able to establish small businesses. Bradford, when he came of age, converted his inheritance into cash, and engaged in making fustian, a ribbed cloth. William Brewster

Thus, after numerous difficulties, they continued many years in good circumstances, enjoying together much sweet and delightful intercourse and spiritual comfort in the ways of God, under the able ministry and prudent government of Mr. Robinson, and Mr. William Brewster, who before had been his assistant in place of an elder, to which position he was now called and chosen by the church. So they grew in knowledge and other gifts and graces of the spirit of God, and lived together in peace and love and holiness; and many came to them from different parts of England, so that there grew up a great congregation. And if any differences arose or offenses broke out—as cannot but be even amongst the best of men—they were always so met with and nipped in the head betimes, that love, peace, and communion continued; or, in some instances, the church was purged of those who were incurable and incorrigible, when, after much patience used, no other means would serve.

Indeed, such was the love and respect that this worthy man, Mr. John Robinson, had to his flock, and his flock to him, that it might be said of them, as it once was of the famous Emperor Marcus Aurelius and the people of Rome, that it was hard to judge whether he was more delighted in having such a people or they in having such a pastor. His love was great towards them, and his care was always bent to their best good both for soul and body; for, besides his singular ability in divine things (wherein he excelled), he was also very able in directing their civil affairs and foreseeing dangers and troubles; so he was very helpful to their material well-being, and was in every way a common father to them. None offended him more than

---

taught English as a private tutor, and later published books proscribed in England. Edward Winslow became a printer.

those who kept apart from the rest, and neglected the common good; or those who were rigid in matters of outward order and would inveigh against the evil of others, and yet were remiss themselves and not too careful to maintain virtuous conversation. The congregation, too, ever had a reverent regard for him and held him in precious estimation, as his worth and wisdom deserved; and highly as they esteemed him whilst he lived and labored amongst them, it was even more so after his death, when they came to feel the want of his help, and saw by woeful experience what a treasure they had lost; a loss that grieved their hearts and souls and could not be repaired, but left them orphaned. But to return. I know not but it may be spoken to the honor of God, and without prejudice to any, that such was the true piety, the humble zeal, and fervent love, of this people, whilst they thus lived together, towards God and His ways, and the single-heartedness and sincere affection of one towards another, that they came as near the primitive pattern of the first churches as any other church of these later times has done.

It is not my purpose to treat of what befell them whilst they lived in the Low Countries—which would require a large treatise of itself—but to show the beginnings of the New Plymouth Settlement. But since some of their adversaries, upon their departure from Leyden of their own free will, uttered slanders against them, as if the country had been weary of them and had driven them out, as the heathen historians asserted of Moses and the Israelites when they went out of Egypt, I will mention a particular or two to show the contrary, and the good acceptation they had in the place where they lived.

First, though many of them were poor, there were none so poor but that if they were known to be of that congregation, the Dutch (either bakers or others) would trust them to any reasonable extent when they lacked money to buy what they needed. They found by experience how careful they were to keep their word, and saw how diligent they were in their callings, that they would even compete for their custom, and employ them in preference to others.

Again, about the time of their departure, or a little before, the magistrates of the city, gave this commendable testimony of them in the public place of justice in reproof to the Walloons,[2] who were of the French church there. "These English," said they, "have lived among us these twelve years, and yet we never had any suit or accusation against any of them; but your strifes and quarrels are continual."

At this time occurred the great trouble with the Arminians,[3] who molested the whole state, and this city in particular, where the chief university was situated. So there were daily hot disputes in the schools thereabouts, and the students and other learned people were divided in their opinions between two professors of divinity, the one daily teaching in favor of the Arminian faction, and the other against it. Things grew to such a pass, that few of the followers of the one professor would hear the other teach. But Mr. Robinson, though he preached thrice a week himself and wrote several books, besides his many other duties,

---

[2] The Walloon Church had been established by Protestant refugees from France about 1581.
[3] Followers of the Dutch Protestant theologian, Jacobus Arminius, founder of an anti-Calvinistic school of theology. The Arminians stood against the doctrine of predestination, believing that Christ had made atonement for the sins of all mankind, both Christian and non-Christian, and that all had freedom of will enough to enable them to accept that salvation.

went constantly to hear their readings, the one as well as the other; so he became well-grounded in their controversy and saw the force of all their arguments, and knew the shifts of the opponent, and being himself very able, none was fitter to buckle with them than himself—as appeared by various disputes. In fact, he began to be a terror to the Arminians, so that Episcopius,[4] the Arminian professor, put forth his best strength and advanced various theses which he asserted he would defend against all comers in public dispute.

Now Poliander, the other professor, and the chief preachers of the city, requested Mr. Robinson to take up his challenge, but he was loath to do so, being a stranger. However, the others importuned him, and told him that such was the ability and nimbleness of the opponent, that the truth would suffer if he did not help them. So he acquiesced and prepared himself accordingly; and when the day came, the Lord so helped him to defend the truth and foil his adversary, that he put him to an apparent nonplus in public audience. And he did the same thing two or three times upon similar occasions. This, while it made many praise God that the truth had so famous a victory, procured him much honor and respect from those learned men and others who loved the truth. So far from being weary of him and his people, or desiring their absence, had it not been for fear of giving offense to the government of England, they would have conferred upon him some public honor. Indeed, when there was talk of their departure to America, several men of prominence in the country tried to induce them to become naturalized, and

---

[4] Simon Episcopius became successor to Arminius at Leyden on the latter's death in 1609.

even made them large offers to do so. Though I might mention many other similar examples to show the untruth of this slander, these suffice, for it was believed by few and was raised in malice.

"All great and honorable actions are accompanied with great difficulties, and must be both enterprised and overcome with answerable courages."

CHAPTER IV

SHOWING THE REASONS AND CAUSES OF THEIR REMOVAL.

After they had lived here for some eleven or twelve years—the period of the famous truce between the Low Countries and Spain—several of them having died, and many others being now old, the grave mistress, Experience, having taught them much, their prudent governors began to apprehend present dangers and to scan the future and think of timely remedy. After much thought and discourse on the subject, they began at length to incline to the idea of removal to some other place; not out of any new-fangledness or other such giddy humor, which often influences people to their detriment and danger, but for many important reasons, the chief of which I will here briefly touch upon.

First, they saw by experience that the hardships of the country were such that comparatively few others would join them, and fewer still would bide it out and remain with them. Many who came and many more who desired to come could not endure the continual labor and hard fare and other inconveniences which they themselves were satisfied with. But though these weaker brethren loved the members of the congregation, personally approved their cause, and honored their sufferings, they left them, weeping, as it were—as Orpah did her mother-in-law, Naomi,[1] or as those Romans did Cato at Utica, who desired to be excused and borne with, though they could not all be Catos.[2] For, though many desired to enjoy the ordinances of God in their purity, and the liberty of the gospel, yet, alas, they preferred to submit to bondage, with danger to their conscience, rather than endure these privations. Some even preferred prisons in England to this liberty in Holland, with such hardships. But it was thought that if there could be found a better and easier place of living, it would attract many and remove this discouragement. Their pastor would often say that if many of those who both wrote and preached against them were living where they might have liberty and comfortable conditions, they would then practice the same religion as they themselves did.

Secondly, they saw that though the people generally bore these difficulties very cheerfully and with resolute courage, being in the best strength of their years; yet old age began to steal on many of them, and their great and continual labors, with other crosses and sorrows, hastened it before their time; so that it was not only probable, but certain, that in a few more years they would be in danger of scattering by the necessities pressing upon them. Therefore, according to the divine proverb (Prov. XXII, 3), that

---

[1] Book of Ruth, I, 8-14.
[2] Plutarch, in his *Life of Cato the Younger*, tells how the three hundred Romans with Cato at Utica, when Julius Caesar by his victory over Pompey made himself master of the Roman world, begged Cato's indulgence for their weakness in deciding to submit to Caesar instead of joining him in a desperate resistance. Plutarch's *Lives*, translated from French into Elizabethan English, was familiar to every educated Englishman at this time.

a wise man seeth the plague when it cometh, and hideth himself; they, like skillful and hardened soldiers, were wary of being surrounded by their enemies, so that they could neither fight nor flee, and thought it wiser to dislodge betimes to some place of better advantage and less danger, if any such could be found.

Thirdly, as necessity was a taskmaster over them, so they themselves were forced to be, not only over their servants, but in a sort over their dearest children; which not a little wounded the hearts of many a loving father and mother, and produced many sad and sorrowful effects. Many of their children, who were of the best disposition and who had learned to bear the yoke in their youth and were willing to bear part of their parents' burden, were often so oppressed with their labors, that though their minds were free and willing, their bodies bowed under the weight and became decrepit in early youth—the vigor of nature being consumed in the very bud, as it were. But still more lamentable, and of all sorrows most heavy to be borne, was that many of the children, influenced by these conditions, and the great licentiousness of the young people of the country, and the many temptations of the city, were led by evil example into dangerous courses, getting the reins off their necks and leaving their parents. Some became soldiers, others embarked upon voyages by sea and others upon worse courses tending to dissoluteness and the danger of their souls, to the great grief of the parents and the dishonor of God. So they saw their posterity would be in danger to degenerate and become corrupt.

Last and not least, they cherished a great hope and inward zeal of laying good foundations, or at least of making some way towards it, for the propagation and advance of the gospel of the kingdom of Christ in the remote parts of the world, even though they should be but stepping stones to others in the performance of so great a work. These, and some other similar reasons, moved them to resolve upon their removal, which they afterwards prosecuted in the face of great difficulties, as will appear.

The place they fixed their thoughts upon was somewhere in those vast and unpeopled countries of America, which were fruitful and fit for habitation, though devoid of all civilized inhabitants and given over to savages who range up and down, differing little from the wild beasts themselves. This proposition when made public found many different opinions, and raised many fears and doubts. The hopeful ones tried to encourage the rest to undertake it; others more timid objected to it, alleging much that was neither unreasonable nor improbable. They argued that it was so big an undertaking that it was open to inconceivable perils and dangers. Besides the casualties of the seas, they asserted that the length of the voyage was such that the women, and other weak persons worn out with age and travail, could never survive it. Even if they should, they contended that the miseries which they would be exposed to in such a country would be too hard to endure. They would be liable to famine, nakedness, and want. The change of air, diet, and water would infect them with sickness and disease. Again, all those who surmounted these difficulties, would remain in continual danger from the savages, who are cruel, barbarous, and treacherous, furious in their rage, and merciless when they get the upper hand—not content to kill, they delight in tormenting people in the most bloody manner possible; flaying some alive with the shells of fishes, cutting off the members and joints of others piecemeal, broiling them on the coals, and eating collops of their flesh in their sight whilst they live—with other cruelties too horrible to be related.

And the very hearing of these things could not but move the very bowels of men to grate within them and make the weak to quake and tremble. It was further objected that it would require greater sums of money to prepare for such a voyage, and to fit them with necessaries, than their diminished estates would amount to. Many precedents of ill success and lamentable miseries befallen others in similar undertakings were alleged, besides their own experience in their removal to Holland, and how hard it was for them to live there, though it was a neighboring country and a civilized and rich commonwealth.

It was replied that all great and honorable actions are accompanied with great difficulties, and must be both met and overcome with answerable courage. It was granted the dangers were great, but not desperate; the difficulties were many, but not invincible. For many of the things feared might never befall; others, by provident care and the use of good means, might in a great measure be prevented; and all of them, through the help of God, by fortitude and patience, might either be borne or overcome. True it was that such attempts were not to be undertaken without good ground and reason, rashly or lightly; or, as many had done, for curiosity or hope of gain. But their condition was not ordinary; their ends were good and honorable; their calling, lawful and urgent; therefore they might expect the blessing of God on their proceedings. Yea, though they should lose their lives in this action, yet might they have the comfort of knowing that their endeavor was worthy.

They were now living as exiles in poor circumstances; and as great miseries might befall them here as there, for the twelve years' truce was now over, and there was nothing but beating of drums and preparation for war. The Spaniard might prove as cruel as the savage of America, and the famine and pestilence as sore in Holland as across the seas. After many other things had been alleged on both sides, it was fully decided by the majority to undertake the enterprise, and to prosecute it by the best means they could.

"It is not with us as with other men, whom small things can discourage, or small discontentments cause to wish themselves at home againe."

CHAPTER V

SHOWING WHAT MEANS THEY USED IN PREPARATION FOR THIS WEIGHTY VOYAGE.

After humble prayers to God for His protection and assistance, and a general conference, they consulted what particular place to pitch upon. Some had thought of Guiana; some of those fertile places in hot climates; others were for some parts of Virginia, where the English had already made entrance. Those for Guiana alleged that the country was rich, fruitful, and blessed with a perpetual spring, where vigorous nature brought forth all things in abundance and plenty, without need of much labor, and that the Spaniards, having much more than they could possess, had not yet settled there, or anywhere very near.

To this it was objected that though the country was fruitful and pleasant, and might yield riches and easy maintenance to the possessors, other things considered, it would not be so fit for them. First, such hot countries are subject to horrible diseases and many noisome pests, which other more temperate places are free from, and they would not agree so well with our English bodies. Again, if they lived there and did well, the jealous Spaniards would never leave them in peace, but would dispossess them as they did the French in Florida [1]—and the sooner because they would have no protection, and their own strength would be insufficient to resist so potent an enemy and so near a neighbor.

On the other hand, against Virginia it was objected that if they lived among the English who had settled there, or so near them as to be under their government, they would be in as great danger of persecution for their religion as if they lived in England—and it might be, worse; while, if they lived too far off, they would have neither help nor defense from them.

At length the conclusion was reached that they should live as a separate body, by themselves, under the general government of Virginia; and that through their friends they should sue His Majesty to be pleased to allow them freedom of religion. That this might be granted they were led to hope by some prominent persons of rank and influence, who had become their friends.

Whereupon, two members of the congregation [2] were sent to England at the expense of the rest, to arrange the matter. They found the Virginia Company [3] anxious to have them, and willing to grant them a patent, with as

---

[1] The settlement of the Huguenots at Port Royal had been wiped out by Menendez in 1565.
[2] It was late in the summer of 1617 that Deacon Robert Cushman and Deacon John Carver, men of unusual abilities, who were to play important parts in the history of Plymouth, went to England on this mission. The difficult negotiations and preparations were to cover a span of three years.
[3] James I, in 1606, set up two Virginia companies, one to settle the northern and the other the southern section of the coast. The Pilgrims' original patent was from the southern company, but this was not used; another was granted them later by the Council for New England, successor to the northern Virginia Company.

ample privileges as they themselves had or could grant and to give them the best assistance they could. Some of the principal officers of the Virginia Company did not doubt that they could obtain the King's grant of liberty of religion, confirmed under his broad seal. But it proved a harder piece of work than they expected; and, though many means were used to accomplish it, it proved impossible. Many of high standing used their influence to obtain it—one of the King's chief secretaries, Sir Robert Nanton, was for them—and others urged the Archbishop [4] to give way to it; but it proved all in vain. They succeeded, however, in sounding His Majesty's mind, and found that he would connive at them, and not molest them, provided they behaved peaceably. But to allow or tolerate their claim to religious freedom by his public authority, under his seal, was found to be impossible. This was all the leading officials of the Virginia Company or any of their best friends could do; though they persuaded the congregation at Leyden to proceed with the undertaking, believing that they would not be troubled. With this answer the messengers returned.

This damped their enthusiasm, and caused some distraction. Many feared that if they should unsettle themselves and count upon these hopes, it might prove dangerous and be a sandy foundation. Indeed it was thought they might better have taken this understanding for granted, without making suit at all, than to have it thus rejected. But some of the chief members thought otherwise, and that they might well proceed, and that the King would not molest them, even though, for other reasons, he would not confirm it by any public act. And it was further contended

---

[4] George Abbot, Archbishop of Canterbury.

that if there was no security in the promise thus intimated, there would be no great certainty in its further confirmation; for if, afterwards, there should be a desire to wrong them, though they had a seal as broad as the house floor, it would not serve their turn, for means would be found to reverse it. With this probability of success they urged that they should trust to God's providence for the outcome, as they had done in other things.

Upon this resolution other messengers were despatched to close with the Virginia Company as well as they could and to procure a patent with as good and ample conditions as possible; also to arrange with such merchants and other friends as had manifested interest, to participate in the accomplishment of this voyage. For these ends they were instructed upon what lines to proceed—otherwise to conclude nothing without further orders.

Here it will be necessary to insert a letter or two bearing on these proceedings.

Sir Edwin Sandys [5] in London to John Robinson and William Brewster at Leyden:

After my hearty salutations. . . . The agents of your congregation, Robert Cushman and John Carver, have been in communication with some of the more important members of His Majesty's Council for Virginia; and by presentation of the seven articles subscribed with your names have given them such satisfaction as has decided them to further your wishes as well as possible, for your

---

[5] Sir Edwin Sandys, son of the Archbishop of York, was an influential member of Parliament. As treasurer of the Virginia Company he took a leading part in its affairs. The elder Sandys had given Brewster his post as bailiff-receiver of Scrooby Manor. The personal connection undoubtedly helped the Pilgrims' cause at this initial stage.

own and the public good. Several particulars we will leave to the faithful report of your agents, who have carried themselves here with a discretion that is as creditable to themselves as to those they represent. Having requested time to confer with those who are interested in this undertaking about several particulars, it has been very willingly assented to and so they now return to you. If, therefore, it may so please God to direct you that on your parts there occur no just impediments, I trust by the same direction it shall appear, that on our part all reasonable assistance will be given. And so I leave you, with your undertaking (which I hope is indeed the work of God), to the gracious protection and blessing of the Highest.

Your very loving friend,
EDWIN SANDYS.

London, Nov. 12th, 1617.

John Robinson and William Brewster at Leyden to Sir Edwin Sandys in London:

Right Worshipful,
Our humble duties, with grateful acknowledgment of your singular love, especially shown in your earnest endeavor for our good in this weighty business about Virginia. We have set down our request in writing, subscribed as you wished by the majority of the congregation and have sent it to the Council of the Virginia Company by our agent, John Carver, a deacon of our church, whom a gentleman of our congregation accompanies.

We need not urge you to any more tender care of us, since, under God, above all persons and things in the world, we rely upon you, expecting the care of your love, the counsel of your wisdom, and the countenance of your authority. Notwithstanding, for your encouragement in the work we will mention these inducements to our enterprise:

1. We verily believe and trust that the Lord is with us, unto Whom and Whose service we have given ourselves in many trials; and that He will graciously prosper our endeavors according to the simplicity of our hearts therein.

2. We are well weaned from the delicate milk of our mother country, and inured to the difficulties of a strange and hard land, which by patience we have largely overcome.

3. The people are for the most part as industrious and frugal, we think we may safely say, as any company of people in the world.

4. We are knit together as a body in a most strict and sacred bond and covenant of the Lord, of the violation whereof we make great conscience, and by virtue whereof we hold ourselves straitly tied to all care of each other's good.

5. Lastly, we are not like some, whom small things discourage, or small discontents cause to wish themselves at home again. We know what we can expect both in England and in Holland, and that we shall not improve our material well-being by our departure; whereas, should we be forced to return, we could not hope to regain our present position, either here or elsewhere during our lives, which are now drawing towards their periods.[6]

---

[6] O sacred bond—whilst inviolably preserved! How sweet and precious were its fruits! But when this fidelity decayed, then their ruin approached. Oh, that these ancient members had not died (if it had been the will of God); or that this holy care and constant faithfulness had still remained with those that survived. But, alas, that still serpent hath slyly wound himself to untwist these sacred bonds and ties. I was happy in my first times to see and enjoy the blessed fruits of that sweet communion; but it is now a part of my misery in old age to feel its decay, and with grief of heart to lament it. For the warning and admonition of others, and my own humiliation, I here make note of it.

(This note was inserted by Bradford in his manuscript at a later date.)

These motives we have been bold to put to you, and, as you think well, to any other of our friends of the Council. We will not be further troublesome, but with our humble duties to your Worship, and to any other of our well-willers of the Council, we take our leaves, committing you to the guidance of the Almighty.

Yours much bounden in all duty,
JOHN ROBINSON.
WILLIAM BREWSTER.

Leyden, Dec. 15th, 1617.

For further light on these proceedings, here follow some other letters and notes.

Mr. John Robinson and Mr. William Brewster at Leyden to Sir John Wolstenholme in London:

Right Worshipful,

With due acknowledgment of our gratitude for your singular care and pains in the business of Virginia, we have sent enclosed, as is required, a further explanation of our judgments in the three points specified by some of His Majesty's Honorable Privy Council; and though we are grieved that such unjust insinuations are made against us, we are glad of the opportunity of clearing ourselves before such honorable personages. The declarations we have enclosed. The one is more brief and general, which we think fitter to be presented; the other is somewhat more comprehensive, expressing some small accidental differences, which if you think well you can send instead of the former. Our prayer to God is, that your Worship may see the fruit of your endeavors, which on our parts we shall not fail to further. And so praying you, as soon as convenient, to give us knowledge of the success of the business with His Majesty's Privy Council, and accordingly what your further pleasure is, so we rest,

> Your worshipful in all duty,
> JOHN ROBINSON.
> WILLIAM BREWSTER.

Leyden, Jan. 27th, 1617.[7]

The first brief declaration was this:

As regards the ecclesiastical ministry, namely of pastors for teaching, elders for ruling, and deacons for distributing the churches' contribution, as also for the two sacraments—baptism and the Lord's supper—we agree wholly and in all points with the French Reformed Churches, according to their public Confession of Faith.

The Oath of Supremacy [8] we shall willingly take, if it be required of us, and if it be not sufficient that we take the Oath of Allegiance.

> JOHN ROBINSON.
> WILLIAM BREWSTER.

The second and ampler declaration was this:

As regards the ecclesiastical ministry, etc., as in the former declaration, we agree in all things with the French Reformed Churches, according to their public Confession of Faith; though some small differences may be found in our practices—not at all in the substance of the things, but only in some accidental circumstances.

---

[7] At this time the year was still reckoned as beginning on March 25 instead of on January 1. So by a modern calendar the date of this and the following letter would be 1618 instead of 1617.

[8] The Oath of Supremacy, first instituted by Henry VIII, was an oath acknowledging the king as the "Supreme Head of the Church in England." The Oath of Allegiance was merely a pledge of civil obedience.

1. Their ministers pray with their heads covered; ours uncovered.

2. We choose none for governing elders but such as are able to teach; which ability they do not require.

3. Their elders and deacons are annual, or at most for two or three years; ours perpetual.

4. Our elders deliver admonitions and excommunications for public scandals, publicly, before the congregation; theirs more privately, in their consistories.

5. We administer baptism only to infants of whom one parent, at least, is of some church, which some of their churches do not observe; though in this our practice accords with their public confession, and with the judgments of the most learned amongst them.

Other differences worth mentioning, we know of none. Then about the Oath of Supremacy, as in the former declaration.

Subscribed,
JOHN ROBINSON.
WILLIAM BREWSTER.

Part of a letter from the messenger in England who delivered the foregoing, to Mr. John Robinson and Mr. William Brewster at Leyden:

Your letter to Sir John Wolstenholme I delivered into his own hands almost as soon as I received it, and stayed with him whilst he opened and read it. There were two papers enclosed, which he read to himself, and also the letter; and while reading it he asked me: "Who will make them?" (viz., the ministers). I answered that the power of making ministers rested with the church; that they were ordained by the imposition of hands,[9] by its fittest mem-

---

[9] Ordaining a minister "by imposition of hands, by its fittest members" showed the trend away from central church authority, as embodied in bishops and presbyters, to invest it in the local group.

bers; that it must rest either with the church or with the Pope, and the Pope is Antichrist. "Ho!" said Sir John, "what the Pope holds good—as the Trinity—we do well to assent to; but we will not enter into dispute now." As for your letters, he said he would not show them, lest he should spoil all. He had expected that you would be of the Archbishop's mind in regard to the appointment of ministers; but it seems you differed. I could have wished to know the contents of your two enclosures, at which he stuck so much—especially the larger.

I asked his Worship what good news he had for me to write tomorrow. He told me very good news, for both the King's majesty and the bishops had consented. He said he would go to the Chancellor, Sir Fulk Greville, this day, and next week I should know more. I met Sir Edwin Sandys on Wednesday night; he wished me to be at the Virginia Court [10] next Wednesday, where I purpose to be. I hope next week to have something certain to communicate. I commit you to the Lord.

Yours,
S. B.

London, Feb. 14th, 1617.

These things being lengthily discussed, and messengers passing to and fro about them, they were long delayed by many rubs. At the return of the messengers to England they found things far otherwise than they expected. The Virginia Council was now so disturbed with quarrels among themselves, that no business could well go forward. This will appear in one of the messenger's letters which follows:

The conception of the people and not the ecclesiastical courts and high dignitaries as "the church" was central in Separatist thinking, and was to become the basic tenet of Congregational church polity.
[10] Meeting of the Virginia Company.

Robert Cushman in England to the congregation at Leyden:

I intended long since to have written to you, but could not effect it; but I doubt not that Mr. B. [11] has written to Mr. Robinson. The main hindrance to the Virginia business is the dissensions in the Council of Virginia. The cause of the trouble is, that, recently, Sir Thomas Smith, weary of his many offices, wished the Company of Virginia to relieve him of being its treasurer and governor—he having 60 votes, Sir John Wolstenholme 16 votes, and Alderman Johnstone 24. But Sir Thomas Smith, finding his honors diminished, was very angry, and raised a faction to contest the election, and sought to tax Sir Edwin Sandys, the new Governor, with many things which would both disgrace him and deprive him of his office as Governor. In these contentions they still stick, and what will result we are not yet certain. Most likely Sir Edwin will win, and if he does, things will go well in Virginia; if otherwise, they will go ill. We hope in some two or three courtdays things will be settled. Meanwhile I intend to go down to Kent, and come up again about 14 days or three weeks hence unless these contentions or the ill tidings from Virginia (of which I will now speak) should wholly discourage us.

Captain Argoll came home from Virginia this week. Upon receiving notice of the intentions of the Council, he left before Sir George Yeardley had arrived there; so there is no small dissatisfaction. But his tidings are ill. He says Mr. Blackwell's [12] ship did not reach there till March

---

[11] "Mr. B." was William Brewster, who had fled from Leyden in fear of arrest when the English authorities began to search for the publisher of certain controversial books and pamphlets which had begun to circulate surreptitiously in England. He remained in hiding for more than a year, but contrived to get aboard the *Mayflower* when it sailed in 1620.

[12] Francis Blackwell, formerly an adherent of the Separatist church

owing to northwest winds, which carried them to the southward beyond their course. The captain of the ship and some six of the sailors dying, it seems they could not find the bay till after long beating about. Mr. Blackwell is dead, and Mr. Maggner, the captain; in fact Captain Argoll says 130 persons on that ship died out of a total of 180. There were so many that they were packed together like herrings. They were ill with the flux, and they lacked fresh water; so here it is rather wondered at that as many are alive, than that so many are dead. The merchants here say it was Mr. Blackwell's fault for packing so many in the ship. There was much grumbling at the time, and Mr. Blackwell was blamed for his disposition of them and his insults to them. They say the streets of Gravesend rang with their quarreling, crying out at each other: "Thou hast brought me to this!" and, "I may thank thee for this!" Heavy news it is, and I wonder how far it will discourage our project.

No one here is much discouraged; they seem only to wish to learn by other men's misfortunes. As we desire to serve one another in love, so take heed of being enthralled by any imperious persons—especially if they seem to have an eye to their own advantage. It often troubles me to think that in this business all of us must learn, and none can teach; but better so, than to depend upon such teachers as Mr. Blackwell was. He once laid a similar trap for Mr. Johnson and his people at Emden—which was their ruin. But though in that instance he managed to pluck his neck out of the collar, at last his foot is caught. No letters have arrived yet, as the ship Captain Argoll came in is still on the west coast; all that we hear is his report; it seems he came away secretly. The ship that Mr. Blackwell went in will be here shortly. What Mr. Robinson once

---

at Amsterdam, had returned to the Church of England before organizing this disastrous expedition.

said has come true: that we should hear no good of them.

Mr. B. is not well; whether he will return to you or go north, I do not know. For myself I hope to see an end of this business ere I come, though I am sorry to be away from you. If things had gone straight forward, I should have been with you within these 14 days. I pray God direct us, and give us the spirit which is fitting for such a business. Thus having summarily pointed at things which Mr. Brewster I think has more largely written of to Mr. Robinson, I leave you to the Lord's protection.

Yours in all readiness, etc.,
ROBERT CUSHMAN.

London, May 8th, 1619.

A word or two, by way of digression, about this Mr. Blackwell. He was an elder of the church at Amsterdam —a man well known to most of them. He declined from the truth with Mr. Johnson [13] and the rest, and went with them when they parted from the congregation in that woeful manner, which brought such great dishonor to God, scandal to the truth, and ruin to themselves in this world. But, I hope, notwithstanding, through the mercies of the Lord, their souls are now at rest with Him in the heavens, and that they have reached the haven of happiness; though some of their bodies were thus buried in the terrible seas, and others sank under the burden of bitter afflictions.

He, with some others, had prepared to go by way of London to Virginia. At a private meeting—I take it a fast —in London, being discovered, many of them were arrested, Mr. Blackwell being one; but he so glozed with

---

[13] The Rev. Francis Johnson was pastor of the Ancient Brethren, a Separatist group at Amsterdam, whose settlement there had preceded that of the Pilgrims. See Introduction, pp. xvii-xviii.

the bishops, and either dissembled or flatly denied the truth which he had formerly maintained, and very unworthily betrayed another godly man who had escaped, so that he might slip his own neck out of the collar, that he won the bishop's favor (but lost the Lord's) and was not only acquitted, but in open court the Archbishop praised him highly, and gave him his solemn blessing to proceed on his voyage. But if such events follow the Archbishop's blessing, happy are they that miss it; it is much better to keep a good conscience and have the Lord's blessing, whether in life or death.

But to return to the concerns of the congregation at Leyden. At last, after all these occurrences, and their long waiting, they had a patent granted them and confirmed under the Virginia Company's seal. But these divisions had alienated many of their less constant supporters, and they were thus disappointed of much of their hoped for and proffered means. By the advice of some friends the patent was not taken out in the name of any of their own members, but in the name of Mr. J. Wincot (a religious gentleman then in the service of the Countess of Lincoln), who intended to go with them. But God so disposed things that he never went, nor did they ever make use of this patent, which had cost them so much labor and expense, as will appear. The patent being sent over for those at Leyden to consider, and also the propositions of such merchants and friends as would go with them or participate in the adventure—and especially those (Mr. Thomas Weston, etc.), on whom they chiefly depended for shipping and stores—they were requested to prepare with all speed. And this matter of the patent is a true emblem of the uncertain things of this world, which, when men have toiled to acquire them, vanish into smoke!

"It was also agreed on by mutuall consente and covenante, that those that went should be an absolute church of themselves."

CHAPTER VI

CONCERNING THE AGREEMENTS AND ARTICLES BETWEEN THEM, AND SUCH MERCHANTS AND OTHERS AS RISKED MONEY; WITH OTHER PREPARATIONS.

Upon the receipt of these papers through one of their messengers, they had a solemn meeting and a day of humiliation to seek the Lord's direction; and their pastor took this text, I Sam. xxiii, 3, 4: "And David's men said unto him, see, we be afraid here in Judah; how much more if we come to Keilah against the host of the Philistines? Then David asked counsel of the Lord again." From this text he taught things very aptly and befitting the present occasion, strengthening them against their fears and perplexities, and encouraging them in their resolutions.

Afterwards they decided what number and which of the members should prepare to go first; for not all that were willing to go could settle their affairs in so short a time; nor if all could have been ready, would there have been means of transport for them. Those that stayed, being the greater number, required the pastor, Mr. Robinson, to stay with them; and for other reasons he could not well go, and so it was the more easily conceded. The others then desired the elder, Mr. Brewster, to go with them, which was agreed to. It was also decided by mutual consent that those who went should be a separate church, distinct from those who stayed, since, with such a dangerous voyage before them, and removal to such a distance, it might happen that they should never meet again, as a body, in this world. But there was this proviso: that when any of the members at Leyden came over to join the others, or when any of the others returned, they should be received as members without any further testimonial. It was also promised by the rest to those that went first, that if the Lord gave them life and opportunity, they would come to them as soon as they could.

About this time, while they were troubled at the proceedings of the Virginia Company, and the ill news about Mr. Blackwell and his fellow colonists, and were busily inquiring about the hiring or buying of shipping for their voyage, some Dutchmen made them offers about going with them. Also, Mr. Thomas Weston,[1] a merchant of London, came to Leyden about the same time, being well acquainted with some of them, having assisted them in their former proceedings, and after much conference with Mr. Robinson and other chief members, he persuaded them to go on, and not to join with the Dutch, or to depend too much on the Virginia Company; for if that failed them, he and some of his merchant friends would supplement their means and set them forth. He advised them to prepare and fear neither want of shipping nor of money; what they needed should be provided. And, not so much for

---

[1] Weston was an entrepreneur who figures importantly in the chronicle. He was treasurer of the original group of merchant adventurers who backed the colonists, and came later with a colony of his own.

himself as for the satisfaction of his friends, they were to draw up articles of agreement, and make a proposition such as would be likely to incline his friends to the venture. Upon which an agreement was drawn up, and was shown to and approved by him, and was afterwards sent to England by their messenger, Mr. John Carver, who, together with Robert Cushman, were to receive the money and make provision both for shipping and other things for the voyage. They were charged not to exceed their commission but to proceed according to the agreement. Others at Leyden were chosen to proceed with similar arrangements which were to be made there. Those that were to go prepared with all speed and sold their estates, putting their money into the common stock, which was in charge of those appointed to make the general provisions.

About this time they heard both from Mr. Weston and others that sundry honorable lords had obtained a large grant from the King, of the more northerly parts of the country, arising out of the Virginia Company's patent, but wholly separated from its government, and to be called by another name, viz., New England.[2] To these parts, Mr. Weston and the chief members began to feel that it was best for them to go—amongst other reasons, chiefly because of the profit to be made from the fishing there.

But in all business the executive part is most difficult—

---

[2] This new royal patent incorporated a group of forty men—gentlemen and aristocrats—as the Council for New England, a territory defined as from 40° to 48° north latitude. The group, headed by Sir Ferdinand Gorges, was interested less in commercial enterprise in the New World than in establishing the proprietary or seignorial land system of England. Their patent was not officially signed until Nov. 3, 1620, a few days before the Pilgrims landed on Cape Cod.

especially where the concurrence of many agents is necessary. And so it was found to be in this undertaking; some of those in England who were to have gone, changed their minds and would not go; other merchants and friends, who had offered to invest their money in the project, withdrew, making many excuses. Some wished them to go to Guiana; others again would risk nothing if they did not go to Virginia; some again—indeed those they had most relied on—utterly disapproved of Virginia, and would do nothing if they went there. In the midst of these distractions, those at Leyden who had disposed of their property and expended their money were in great straits and feared disastrous results; but at length the majority inclined to New England.

But now another difficulty arose. Mr. Weston and some of his friends (either for their own advantage, or, as they pretended, to make further inducements for others to join them) insisted on altering some of the conditions that had been agreed upon at Leyden. To these alterations the two agents sent from Leyden (or at least one of them who is most to be blamed for it) consented, fearing that otherwise it would all be thrown up. They presumed to agree with the new terms, in some particulars overstepping their authority and commission, and without giving due notice. Indeed, the fact that it was concealed for fear of any further delay, afterwards caused much trouble and contention.

I will here insert a copy of these new conditions, as follows.[3]

---

[3] On the organization of private joint stock companies at this period for trading and colonization in distant lands, see Introduction, p. xx.

July 1st, 1620.

1. The adventurers and planters agree that every person who goes, of sixteen years and upwards, be rated at £10; £10 to be reckoned as a single share.

2. That he who goes in person, and furnishes himself with £10, either in money, or provisions, be accounted as having £20 in stock; and in the division shall receive a double share.

3. The persons transported, and the adventurers, shall continue their joint stock and partnership together for seven years (unless some unexpected impediment cause the whole company to agree otherwise), during which time all profits and benefits go by trade, traffic, trucking, working, fishing, or any other means, by any persons or person, shall remain in the common stock until the division.

4. That on their arrival there, they shall choose out such number of fit persons as may man their ships and boats at sea; employing the rest in their several faculties upon the land, such as building houses, tilling and planting the ground, and making such commodities as shall be most useful for the colony.

5. That at the end of seven years, the capital and profits, viz., the houses, lands, goods and chattels, shall be equally divided among the adventurers and planters; which done, every man shall be free of any debt to any other of them, arising from this adventure.

6. Whosoever shall come to the colony hereafter, or shall contribute to the stock, shall at the end of the seven years be allowed proportionately to the time of his doing so.

7. He who shall take his wife and children, or servants, shall be allowed for every person now aged sixteen years and upwards, a single share in the division; or if he provide them with necessaries, a double share; or if they be be-

tween ten and sixteen, two of them be reckoned as one person, both in transportation and division.

8. That such children as now go, and are under the age of ten years, have no other share in the division, but fifty acres of unmanured land.

9. That such persons as die before the seven years be expired, their executors to have their part or share at the division, proportionately to the time of their life in the colony.

10. That all such persons as are of this colony, are to have their food, drink, clothing, and all provisions, out of the common stock and goods of the said colony.

The principal difference between this and the former agreement consisted of these two points: that the houses and improved lands, especially gardens and home lots, should remain undivided, and should belong wholly to the planters at the seven years' end; secondly, that they should have two days a week for their own private employment, for the greater comfort of themselves and their families. But as letters are considered the best part of history by some wise men, I will show their grievances on the score by their own letters.

Mr. John Robinson at Leyden to Mr. John Carver in England:

My dear Friend and Brother,

Whom, with yours, I always remember in my best affection, and whose welfare I shall never cease to commend to God, by my best and most earnest prayers.

You thoroughly understand by our general letters the state of things here, which indeed is very pitiful; especially the want of shipping, and not seeing means of providing it; though, in addition, there is great want of money for other needful things. Mr. Pickering, you know before this, will not defray a penny here; though Robert Cushman reckoned upon I know not how many hundred pounds from him, and I know not whom else. But it seems strange that we should be asked to take the risk of his and his partners' enterprise—and yet Mr. Weston writes to him that he has drawn upon him for £100 more. There is some mystery in this, as indeed there seems to be in the whole affair. Besides this, those who were to pay in such of their money as is yet in arrears, refuse to do it till they see shipping provided, or steps taken for its provision. Indeed, I think there is not a man here who would pay anything, if he had his money in his purse again. We depended on Mr. Weston alone, and upon such means as he would procure; and when we had in hand another project with the Dutchmen, we broke it off at his instance and upon the conditions propounded by him shortly after. He had our interests sincerely at heart, I know; but he has not fulfilled his pledges thus far.

That he ought first to have put in his money is the opinion of many; but that I can well excuse, he being a merchant, and having uses for it in the meantime to his benefit; whereas, others, if it had been in their hands, would have expended it. But that he should not have had shipping ready before this, or at least definite provision for it, duly made known to us, cannot in my conscience be excused. I have heard that when he has been urged about the business, he has put it off and referred it to others; or would go to George Morton [4] and enquire news of him about things, as if he himself had scarcely been even an accessory to it. Whether some of his friends

---

[4] George Morton, a merchant of York, had accompanied the Pilgrims to Leyden; in 1622 he published the first account of their adventures in the New World under the title of *Mourt's Relation;* see footnote 11, p. 109. The following year he was to join them at Plymouth.

have failed him, and so he is not able to go through with things; or whether he fears it will be ready too soon and so increase the charge of shipping; or whether he thought by holding back to put us in straits, thinking that thereby Mr. Brewer [5] and Mr. Pickering would be induced to do more; or what other mystery is in it, we know not. But certain we are that the arrangements made do not accord with the requirements.

Mr. Weston makes himself merry with our endeavors to buy a ship; but we have done nothing about this without good reason, nor about anything else that I know of, except two. The one is that we employed Robert Cushman, who though a good man and of special ability in his way is known to be most unfit to deal for others, because of his singularity and too great indifference to the circumstances—for as a matter of fact, we have had nothing from him but terms and suggestions. The other is that we have relied too much by implicit faith as it were, upon generalities, without having the details of ways and means for so important an affair settled between us. For shipping, Mr. Weston, it seems, is set upon hiring, which I hope he may soon accomplish. Of Mr. Brewer you know what to expect. I do not think Mr. Pickering will take part except to buy, as specified in former letters.

About the conditions, you have our reasons for what is agreed upon. And let this specially be borne in mind; that the greatest part of the colony is likely to be employed constantly not upon cultivating their own particular land, and building houses, but upon fishing, trading, etc. So, though the land and houses would be but a trifling advan-

---

[5] Brewer and Pickering were merchant adventurers, members of the joint stock company organized by Weston. The former, a Separatist, had been with the Pilgrims at Leyden, furnishing capital for Elder Brewster's printing business. Later, after his return to England, he was subjected to persecution and died in prison.

tage to the adventurers, the ultimate division of them would be a great discouragement to the settlers who would tend them with singular care, to make them comfortable, with borrowed hours from their sleep. The same consideration of common employment, constantly by the majority, is good reason not to deny to the planters the two days a week for private use. Consider how unfitting you would find it that you and your likes should serve a new apprenticeship of seven years, and not a day's freedom from task.

Send me word what others are going; who that are possessed of useful faculties; how many; and particulars of everything. I know you do not lack a mind. I am sorry you have not been in London all this while. Time will suffer me to write no more; fare you and yours well, always in the Lord, in Whom I rest.

Yours to use,
JOHN ROBINSON.

June 14th, 1620.

Several of them at Leyden to John Carver and Robert Cushman in England:

To their loving friends John Carver and Robert Cushman:
Good Brethren,
We received several letters at the coming of Mr. Nash and our pilot, which was a great encouragement to us. Indeed, had you not sent him, many would have been ready to lose heart, and give up—partly because of the new conditions which have been accepted by you, which all are against; and partly for lack of our own ability to accomplish any of the important matters which you have commissioned us to do here. As to the former, of which Robert Cushman requests reasons for our dislike and promises to alter them accordingly, saying that otherwise we must

think he has no brains—we desire him to exercise them therein, referring him to our pastor's former reasons. But our desire is that you will not bind yourselves and us to any such unreasonable stipulation, viz., that the merchants shall have half the houses and lands at the dividend; and that the settlers shall be deprived of the two days a week for their own work, as agreed upon—otherwise we cannot conceive why any of us should take servants for our own help and comfort, since we could demand no service of them. This alteration we have gathered only by word from Mr. Nash, and not from any letters of yours; so we hope you have not proceeded far in so great a departure from the terms without our concurrence. However, requiring you not to exceed the bounds of your commission, which was to proceed upon the conditions agreed upon and expressed in writing, we leave it—not without wondering that you yourselves, as you write, knowing how small a thing disturbs our consultations, and how few understand the business aright, should trouble us with such matters as these.

Salute Mr. Weston from us, in whom we hope we are not deceived. Pray make known our present condition to him, and, if you think good, show him our letters. At least tell him that, under God, we rely much upon him and put our confidence in him; and that as you well know, if he had not joined with us, we should not have entered upon the enterprise, presuming that if he had not seen means to accomplish it, he would not have begun it. So we hope that he will so far help us that our expectations in him be not disappointed. Thus beseeching the Almighty, Who is all-sufficient, to raise us out of this depth of difficulties, and to assist us herein, and to supply means by His providence and fatherly care for us, His poor children and servants, that we may with comfort behold the hand of our God for good towards us in this our enter-

prise, which we undertake in His name and fear; we take leave and remain,
> Your perplexed, yet hopeful brethren,
> SAMUEL FULLER   WILLIAM BRADFORD
> EDWARD WINSLOW   ISAAC ALLERTON

June 10th, 1620.

Robert Cushman in England to the foregoing at Leyden:

Brethren,

I understand by letters that have come to me, that many of you greatly dislike my proceedings. Sorry I am to hear it, yet content to bear it, not doubting that partly by writing, and principally by word when we come together, I can satisfy any reasonable man. I have been persuaded by some, especially the bearer of this, to come and make things clear to you; but as things now stand I cannot be absent one day, without hazarding the whole voyage; nor do I conceive that any great good would come of it. Take then, brethren, this as a step to give you content. First, as to your dislike of the alteration of one clause in the conditions: if you see it aright, no blame can lie on me at all. The articles first brought over by John Carver were never seen by any of the adventurers here except Mr. Weston himself, when he had well considered it. £500 was withdrawn by Sir George Farrer and his brother because of it, and all the rest would have withdrawn (Mr. Weston excepted), if we had not altered the clause. Now when we at Leyden concluded upon certain points, as we did, we reckoned without our host, which was not my fault. Besides, I showed you by letter the equity of the new condition as against our inconveniences, which might be set against all the inconveniences cited by Mr. Robinson, and showed that without alteration of that clause, we could neither have means to get there, nor supplies for our subsistence when we arrived. Yet, notwithstanding all those reasons, which were not mine, but other men's wiser than myself, without answer to any one of them, many complaints are directed against me, of lording it over my brethren, and making conditions fitter for thieves and bondslaves than honest men. And at last came a paper of reasons against that clause in the conditions, which since they were delivered to me open, my answer shall be open to you all.

1. First, it is said that if there had been no division of houses and lands, it would have been better for the poor:

True—and that shows the inequality of the original conditions: we should more respect him that ventures both his money and his person, than him that ventures his person only.

2. Consider, further, that we are not giving alms, but furnishing a storehouse. No one will be poorer than his neighbor for seven years; and, from the nature of the enterprise, if any of us be rich, none of us can be poor. At any rate we must not in such an undertaking start out with the cry: Poor, poor! Mercy, mercy! Charity has its life in disasters, not in ventures.

3. This will hinder the building of good houses, which is contrary to sound politics:

So we would have it. Our purpose is, for the present, to build such houses as, if need be, we may with little grief set fire to and run away by the light. Our riches shall not be in pomp, but in strength. If God sends us riches, we will employ them to provide more men, ships, ammunition, etc. You will see it argued amongst the best politicians, that a commonwealth is readier to ebb than to flow when once fine houses and gay clothes appear.

4. The government can prevent excess in building:

But if it be generally resolved on beforehand to build modest houses, the Governor's labor is spared.

5. All men are not of one condition:

If by "condition" you mean "wealth," you are mistaken;

if you mean by "condition," "qualities," then I say that he who is not content that his neighbor shall have as good a house, fare, means, etc., as himself, is not of good quality. Such secluded persons as have an eye only to themselves, are fitter to come where catching is, than closing; and are fitter to live alone, than in any society, either civil or religious.

6. It will be of little value, scarcely worth £5:

True; it may not be worth half £5. If then so small a thing will content them, why strive we thus about it, and give them occasion to suspect us to be worldly and covetous? I will not say what I have heard since these complaints first reached us here.

7. Our friends that venture with us do not look to their own profit, as did the old adventurers:

Then they are better than we, who for a little matter of profit are ready to draw back. Look to it, brethren, you that make profit your main end; repent of this, or go not, lest you be like Jonas to Tarshis.[6] Though some of them have no eye for profit, others have; and why not they as much as we? Such ventures are undertaken by all sorts of men, and we must try to content them all if we can.

8. It will break up the community, as may be shown by many reasons:

That is only a statement; and I say again, it will best foster community, as may be shown by many reasons.

9. Great profit is likely to be made by trading, fishing, etc.:

As it is better for them, so for us; for half is ours, besides getting our living from it. And if profit comes largely in that way, we shall labor less on the land, and our houses and lands will be of less value.

10. Our risk is greater than theirs:

---

[6] Jonah, 1.

True, but do they force us to it? Do they urge or egg us? Has not the motion and resolution always been in ourselves? Do they, any more than in seeing us resolute if we had means, help us to means upon equal terms and conditions? If we do not wish to go, they are content to keep their money. Thus I have pointed out a way to loose those knots, which I hope you will consider seriously, and let me have no more stir about them.

Now, further, I hear a noise about slavish conditions being made; but surely this is all that I have altered and I have sent you the reasons. If you mean about the two days a week for personal occupations, you are misled. You can have three days a week, as far as I care, if you wish; and when speaking to the adventurers about times of working, they said they hoped we were men of discretion and conscience, and fit to be trusted with that. But indeed the grounds of our proceedings at Leyden were mistaken.

As for those of Amsterdam, I thought they would as soon have gone to Rome as with us; for our liberty is to them as rat's-bane, and their rigor as bad to us as the Spanish Inquisition. If any action of mine discourage them, let them withdraw. I will undertake they shall have their money back at once, paid here. Or if the congregation think me the Jonas, let them dismiss me before we go; I shall be content to stay with good will, having but the clothes on my back. Let us then have quietness, and no more of these clamors; little did I expect these things which are now come to pass.

Yours,
ROBERT CUSHMAN.

Whether this letter of his ever came to their hands at Leyden, I know not; I rather think it was intercepted by Mr. Carver and kept by him, for fear it should give offense. But the letter which follows was received.

Robert Cushman in England in reply to the joint letter from Leyden:

I received your letter yesterday through John Turner, with another the same day from Amsterdam through Mr. W., savoring of the place whence it came. And indeed, the many discouragements I find here, together with the demurs there, made me say I would give up my accounts to John Carver, and at his coming acquaint him fully with all, and so leave it entirely with only the poor clothes on my back. But gathering myself up, on further consideration I resolved to make one trial more, and to acquaint Mr. Weston with the unstable conditions of things. He has been very discontented with us of late, and has even said that but for his promise he would have nothing more to do with the business; but considering how far we have gone already and how it stood with our credit, he pulled himself together, and coming to me two hours after, he told me he would not yet abandon it. So we decided to hire a ship, and have taken the option of one till Monday. It is small, but except one that was too large for our purpose, we could not get a larger; but it is a fine ship. Since our friends over there are so close-fisted, we hope to secure her without troubling them any further; and if the ship is too small, it is only fitting that those who stumble at straws so early in the day, shall rest them there awhile, lest worse blocks come in the way ere seven years be ended. If you had faced this business so thoroughly a month ago, and had written as you do now, we could have concluded things with less difficulty. But it is as it is. I hope our friends there, if they are quit of the ship-hire, will be induced to venture the more. All that I now require is that salt and nets may be bought there—all the rest we will provide here; and if even that be impossible, let them give you credit for a month or two, and we will take steps to pay it all. Let Mr. Reynolds remain there, and bring the ship to Southampton. We have hired another pilot here, a Mr. Clark, who went last year to Virginia with a ship of cattle.

You shall hear more exactly by John Turner, who I think will leave here on Tuesday night. I had thought to come with him to answer the complaints; but if I had more mind to go and dispute with them than I have care of this important project, I should be like those who live by clamor and jangling. But neither my mind nor my body is at liberty to do much, for I am fettered with business, and had rather study to be quiet than to make answer to their exceptions. Meanwhile, entreat our friends not to be too busy in questioning my actions before they know them. If I do things that I cannot give reasons for, it seems you have sent a fool about your business; in that case you had best return the reproof to yourselves, and send another, and let me return to my combes. The Lord, Who judges justly without respect of persons, see into the equity of my cause and give us quiet, peaceable, and patient minds in all these turmoils, and sanctify us unto all crosses whatsoever. And so I take my leave of you all, in all love and affection.

I hope we shall get all ready here in fourteen days.

Your poor brother,
ROBERT CUSHMAN.

June 11th, 1620.

There arose, also, a difference between the three that received the money and made the provisions in England; for besides the two formerly mentioned, sent from Leyden —John Carver and Robert Cushman—there was one chosen in England to join them in making provisions for the voyage. His name was Mr. Martin; he came from Billirike in Essex, whence several others came to join them, as well as from London and other places. It was thought right by those in Holland that these strangers who were to go with them should appoint someone, not so much from any great need of their help, as to avoid all suspicion or jealousy. Indeed their care not to give offense, both in this and other things, afterwards greatly inconvenienced them, as will appear. However, it showed their equal and honest minds. The provisions were made for the most part at Southampton, contrary to Mr. Weston's and Robert Cushman's advice (which generally concurred in these things). Reference to these matters is made in the following letter from Robert Cushman to Mr. Carver, and more will appear afterwards.

Robert Cushman in London to John Carver at Southampton:

Loving Friend,

I have received some letters from you, full of affection and complaints; but what it is you want me to do I know not. You cry out, Negligence, negligence, negligence: I marvel why so negligent a man as myself was employed to undertake the business. Yet you know that as far as my power permits, nothing shall be one hour behind, I warrant you. You call upon Mr. Weston to help us with more money than his share in the adventure; while he protests that, but for his promise, he would not have done anything further. He says we take a heady course; and he is offended that our provisions are being made so far off, and that he was not made acquainted with our quantity of things. He says that working thus, in three places, so far distant, we shall, with going hither and thither, wrangling and expostulating, let the summer slip by before we start. And to tell the truth, there is already a flat schism among us. We are readier to dispute than to undertake a voyage. I have received from Leyden, since you went, three or four letters directed to you; though as they only concern me I will not trouble you with them.

I have always feared the event of the Amsterdamers striking in with us. I trow you must excommunicate me, or else go without their company, or we shall not lack quarreling; but let that pass. We have reckoned, it seems, without our host; and counting upon 150 persons, we cannot raise above £1200 odd, besides some cloth, stockings, and shoes, which are not counted: so we shall come short at least three or four hundred pounds. I would have reduced the beer and other provisions; and now we could get, both in Amsterdam and Kent, beer enough; but we cannot accept it without prejudice.

You fear we have begun to build and shall not be able to make an end. Our plans for provisioning not having been made in consultation, we may justly fear the results. There was contention amongst us three at the first. You wrote to Mr. Martin to prevent the making of the provisions in Kent; which he did nevertheless, and decided how much he would have of everything, irrespective of us. However, your money which you must have there, we will provide you with instantly. £500 you say will serve; as for the rest, which will be required here and in Holland, we may go scratch for it. As for Mr. Crabe, the minister, of whom you write, he has promised to go with us; but I shall not be sure till I see him shipped, for he is contentious on many points; still, I hope he will not fail. Think the best of all, and bear with patience what is wanting, and the Lord guide us all.

Your loving friend,
ROBERT CUSHMAN.

London, June 10th, 1620.

I have been more discursive on these subjects—and shall crave leave to be so concerning some similar occurrences which will follow; though in other things I shall try to be more concise. My object is that their children may see with what difficulties their fathers had to wrestle in accomplishing the first beginnings; and how God ultimately brought them through, notwithstanding all their weakness and infirmities; also that some use may be made of them later, by others, in similar important projects. Herewith I will end this chapter.

"Let your wisdom and godliness appeare, not only in chusing shuch persons as doe entirely love and will promote the common good, but also in yeelding unto them all due honour and obedience in their lawfull administrations."

CHAPTER VII

OF THEIR DEPARTURE FROM LEYDEN, AND THEIR ARRIVAL IN SOUTHAMPTON, WHERE THEY MET TOGETHER AND TOOK IN PROVISIONS.

At length after much discussion everything was got ready. A small ship [1] was bought and fitted out in Holland, intended to help transport them, and then to remain in the country for fishing and such other pursuits as might benefit the colony. Another ship [2] was hired at London, of about 180 tons. When they were ready to depart, they had a day of solemn humiliation, their pastor taking his text from Ezra VIII, 21: "And there at the river, by Ahava, I proclaimed a fast that we might humble ourselves before our God, and seek of Him a right way for us and for our children, and for all our substance." Upon this discourse he spent a good part of the day very profitably. The rest of the time was spent in pouring out prayers to the Lord with great fervency and abundance of tears.

---

[1] The *Speedwell*.
[2] This was the *Mayflower*. The name does not appear in Bradford's chronicle.

The time having come when they must depart, they were accompanied by most of their brethren out of the city to a town several miles off, called Delfthaven, where the ship lay ready to take them. So they left that good and pleasant city, which had been their resting place for nearly twelve years; but they knew they were pilgrims, and lifted up their eyes to the heavens, their dearest country, and quieted their spirits. When they came to the place, they found the ship and everything ready, and such of their friends as could not come with them followed them, and several came from Amsterdam to see them shipped and to take leave of them. That night there was little sleep for most of them, for it was spent in friendly entertainment and Christian discourse and other real expressions of true Christian love.

The next day the wind being fair they went aboard and their friends with them—and truly doleful was the sight of that sad and mournful parting. What sighs and sobs and prayers rose from amongst them! What tears gushed from every eye, and pithy speeches pierced each heart! Many of the Dutch strangers who stood on the quay as spectators, could not refrain from tears. Yet it was comfortable and sweet to see such lively and true expressions of dear and unfeigned love. But the tide which stays for no man called them away, though loth to part; and their reverent pastor, falling down on his knees, and all with him, with watery cheeks commended them with most fervent prayers to the Lord and His blessing. Then with mutual embraces and many tears, they took their leave of one another—which proved to be the last leave for many of them.

Thus, hoisting sail, with a prosperous wind they came in short time to Southampton, where they found the bigger ship from London lying ready with all the rest of the company. After a joyful welcome and mutual congratulations with other friendly entertainment, they came to the subject of their business, and how to conclude it most expeditiously, and discussed with their agents the alteration of the conditions. Mr. Carver pleaded that he was employed here at Southampton, and did not know what his colleague had done in London. Mr. Cushman answered that he had done nothing but what was essential, both in fairness and of necessity, otherwise all would have been sacrificed and many ruined. He stated that at the outset he had acquainted his fellow-agents with what he had done, and that they had consented, and left it to him to execute, to receive the money in London and send it down to them at Southampton, where they wished to buy provisions; which he accordingly did, though it was against his advice and some of the merchants'. As for giving them notice at Leyden about this change, he could not, because of the shortness of time; again, he knew it would trouble them and hinder the business, which had already been too long delayed, considering the time of the year, which he feared they would find to their cost.

But these explanations did not content his hearers. Mr. Weston also came up from London to see them embark, and to have the conditions confirmed; but they refused, and told him that he knew well that they were not according to the first agreement, nor could they endorse them without the consent of the rest in Holland. In fact they had special orders when they came away, from the chief men of the congregation, not to do it. At this he was much offended, and told them in that case they must stand on their own legs; so he returned to London in displeasure. They lacked about £100 to clear their obligations; but he would not disburse a penny, and left them to shift as they could. So they were forced to sell some of their provisions, including some three or four firkins of butter, which they were best able to spare, having provided too much. Then they wrote a letter to the merchants and adventurers about the changes in the conditions as follows:

The Pilgrims at Southampton to the Merchants and Adventurers:

Beloved Friends,

We are sorry that it should be necessary to write to you at all, because we hoped to see most of you here; but especially we regret that there should be these differences between us. Since we cannot confer together, we think it proper to show you briefly the just cause of our dissenting from the articles last made by Robert Cushman, without our commission or knowledge. For, though he might make good excuses to himself, it in no way justifies his having done it. Our main differences lie in the fifth and ninth articles, concerning the division of houses or lands, the possession of which, as some of you know, was one special motive amongst others which induced us to go. This was thought so reasonable, that when your chief partner in this venture (whom we have much cause to respect) proposed conditions to us of his own accord, he added this one. A copy of these conditions we have sent to you, including some proposed by us; which being approved on both sides, and a day set for the payment of the money, those of Holland paid in theirs. After that, Robert Cushman, Mr. Pierce, and Mr. Martin put them into better form, and wrote them in a book now extant; and upon Robert's showing Mr. Mullins [3] a copy he paid in his

---

[3] Williams Mullins, a member of the Leyden church, was the father of Priscilla, the heroine of Longfellow's "The Courtship of Miles Standish."

money. And we of Holland had never seen any other agreement before our coming to Southampton, except for a private copy of changed conditions which reached us, and at which we manifested utter dislike; but having sold our estates and being ready to come, it was too late to give up the voyage. We beseech you, therefore, to judge impartially of things, and if a fault has been committed, lay it where it should be, and not upon us.

We never gave Robert Cushman commission to draw up a single article for us, but only sent him to receive money upon the articles before agreed on, and to arrange for the provisions till John Carver came, and to assist him in it. However, since you conceive yourselves wronged as well as we, we have made an addition to our 9th article, such as will almost heal the wound of itself. But that it may appear to all that we are not lovers of ourselves only, but desire also the good of our friends who have ventured their money with our persons, we have added the last article to the rest, promising you again by letter, on behalf of the whole company, that if large profits should not arise during the seven years, we will remain longer with you if the Lord give a blessing. We are in such straits at present that we are forced to sell £60 worth of our provisions to clear the Haven, and put ourselves upon bare necessities, scarcely having any butter, no oil, not a soul to mend a shoe, nor every man a sword to his side, lacking many muskets, much armor, etc. And yet we are willing to expose ourselves to such imminent dangers as are likely to ensue, and trust to the good providence of God, rather than His name and truth should be evil spoken of through us. Thus saluting all of you in love, we take our leave and rest,

Yours, etc.

Aug. 3rd, 1620.

It was subscribed with the names of the chief members of the congregation.

At their parting Mr. Robinson wrote a letter to the whole party of the Pilgrims which, though it has already been printed,[4] I thought well to insert here; also a brief letter written at the same time to Mr. Carver, in which the tender love and godly care of a true pastor appears.

Mr. John Robinson in Holland to John Carver at Southampton:

My dear Brother,

I received enclosed in your last letter the note of information, which I shall certainly keep and make use of, when occasion arises. I have a true feeling of your perplexity of mind and toil of body; but I hope that you, who have always been able so plentifully to administer comfort to others in their trials, are so well furnished for yourself that even far greater difficulties than you have yet undergone (though I conceive them to have been great enough) cannot oppress you, though they press you, as the Apostle says. The spirit of a man, sustained by the spirit of God, will sustain his infirmity, and, I doubt not, so will yours; and much the better when you enjoy the presence and help of so many godly and wise brethren, in bearing part of your burden, who will not admit into their hearts the least thought or suspicion of the least negligence, still less presumption, to have been in you, whatever they may think of others. Now what shall I say and write to you and your good wife, my loving sister?[5] Even only this: I desire, and always shall, from the Lord unto you as unto my own soul; and assure yourself that my heart is with you, and that I will not delay my bodily coming at the first op-

---

[4] In *Mourt's Relation*, 1622.
[5] Catherine Carver was the sister of Robinson's wife, Bridget.

portunity. I have written a large letter to the whole company, and am sorry that I shall not be able to speak with them; the more so considering the want of a preacher, which will be an additional spur to my hastening after you. I do ever commend my best affection to you, which if I thought you doubted, I would express in more words. And the Lord in whom you trust, and whom you serve ever in this business and journey, guide you with His hand, protect you with His wing, and show you and us His salvation in the end, and bring us in the meanwhile together in the place desired, if such be His good will, for His Christ's sake. Amen.

Yours,

JOHN ROBINSON.

July 27th, 1620.

This was the last letter that Mr. Carver lived to see from him.

Mr. John Robinson in Holland to the Pilgrims departing from Southampton for New England:

Loving Christian Friends,

I salute you all heartily in the Lord, as being they with whom I am present in my best affections and most earnest longings, though I am constrained for a time to be bodily absent from you. I say constrained, God knowing how willingly, and much rather than otherwise, I would have borne my part with you in this first brunt, were I not by strong necessity held back for the present. Think of me in the meanwhile as of a man divided in himself with great pain, and (physical limitations set aside) as having his better part with you. Though I doubt not that in your godly wisdom, you foresee what is applicable to your present condition, I have thought it but my duty to add some further spur, even to those who run already—not because you need it, but because I owe it in love and duty.

First, as we ought daily to renew our repentance with our God, especially for our sins known, and generally for our unknown trespasses, so doth the Lord call us in a singular manner, upon such an occasion of difficulty and danger as lies before you, both to more narrow search and careful reformation of our ways in His sight, lest He, calling to remembrance of our sins forgotten by us or unrepented of, take advantage of us, and, as a judgment upon us, leave us to be swallowed up in one danger or another. Whereas, on the contrary, sin being taken away by earnest repentance, and the pardon thereof from the Lord sealed up into a man's conscience by His spirit, great shall be his security and peace in all dangers, sweet his comforts in all distresses, with happy deliverance from all evil, whether in life or in death.

Now next after this heavenly peace with God and our own conscience, we are carefully to provide for peace with all men so far as in us lieth especially with our associates; and for that we must be watchful that we ourselves neither give, nor easily take, offense. Woe be unto the world for offenses; for though it be necessary (considering the malice of Satan and man's corruption) that offenses come, yet woe unto the man or woman either, by whom the offenses come, saith Christ (Matt. XVIII, 7). And if offenses arising from unseasonable actions, innocent in themselves, are more to be feared than death itself, as the Apostle teacheth (I Cor. IX, 15), how much more when arising from things simply evil, in which neither honor of God nor love of man is thought worthy to be regarded. Nor is it sufficient that we keep ourselves by the grace of God from giving offense, except we be armed also against taking offense when it is given by others. For how imperfect is the work of grace in him who lacks the charity that covers a multitude of offense, as the Scripture says. Neither are you exhorted to this grace only upon the common grounds of Christianity. Persons ready to take offense, either lack the charity which should cover offenses; or the wisdom duly to weigh human frailty; or lastly, are gross though close hypocrites, as Christ our Lord teaches (Matt. VII, 1, 2, 3). In my own experience I have found few who are quicker to give offense than those who easily take it. They who have nourished this touchy humor have never proved sound and profitable members in societies.

But there are, besides, many reasons why you, above others, should use special care in this direction. You are, many of you, strangers to each other and to the infirmities of one another, and so stand in need of the more watchfulness, lest when unsuspected qualities appear in men and women, you be inordinately affected by them. This requires at your hands much wisdom and charity. Further, the plans for your intended civil community will furnish continual occasion of offense, and will be as fuel to the fire, unless you diligently quench it with brotherly forbearance. And if taking offense causelessly or easily at men's doings should be so carefully avoided, how much more is it to be heeded lest we take offense at God himself —which we do as often as we murmur at His providence in our crosses, or bear impatiently such afflictions as He pleases to visit upon us. Store up, therefore, patience against the evil day, with which we take offense at the Lord Himself in His holy and just works.

A fourth thing is carefully to be provided for, to wit, that with your employments, which will be common to all, you join affections truly bent upon the general good, avoiding, as a deadly plague of your comfort, all retiredness of mind for selfish advantage. Let everyone repress within himself, as so many rebels against the common good, all private partialities, not consistent with the general convenience and as one is careful not to have a new house shaken with any violence before it is well settled and the parts firmly knit, so be you, I beseech you brethren, much more careful, that the house of God, which you are and are to be, be not shaken with unnecessary novelties or other oppositions at the first settling thereof.

Lastly, whereas you are to become a body politic, administering among yourselves civil government, and are furnished with persons of no special eminence above the rest, from whom you will elect some to the office of government, let your wisdom and godliness appear, not only in choosing such persons as will entirely love and promote the common good, but also in yielding them all due honor and obedience in their lawful administrations; not beholding in them the ordinariness of their persons, but God's ordinance for your good; nor being like the foolish multitude, who honor a gay coat more than either the virtuous mind of the wearer or the glorious ordinance of the Lord. But you know better, and understand that the image of the Lord's power and authority which the magistrate bears, is honorable, in how humble persons soever. And this duty you can the more willingly perform, because you are at present to have only those for your governors as you yourselves shall choose.

Several other things of importance I could put you in mind of, but I will not so far wrong your godly minds as to think you heedless of these things, there being many among you well able both to admonish themselves and others. These few things, therefore, I do earnestly commend unto your care and conscience, joining therewith my daily incessant prayers unto the Lord, that He Who has made the heavens and the earth, the sea and all rivers of waters, and Whose providence is over all His works, especially over all His dear children for good, would so guide and guard you in your ways, as inwardly by His spirit, so outwardly by the hand of His power, that both you and we also may praise His name all the days of our lives. Fare you well in Him in Whom you trust, and in Whom I rest.

An unfeigned well-willer of your happy success in this hopeful voyage,

JOHN ROBINSON.

This letter, though long, being so suitable to the occasion I thought well to insert here.

Everything being now ready and all business completed, the company was called together, and this letter was read to them, and was well received by all, and afterwards bore fruit in many. Then they allotted the company to each ship as they thought best, and chose governors and two or three assistants, to take charge of the people on the way, and to see to the distribution of their provisions, and such affairs. Which done, they set sail from Southampton, about the 5th of August; but what befell them further upon the coast of England will appear in the next chapter.

"And thus like Gedion's armie, this small number was devided, as if the Lord by this worke of his providence thought these few to many for the great worke he had to doe."

CHAPTER VIII

Of the troubles that befell them on the coast; and at sea being forced to leave one of their ships and some of their company behind.

*H*aving thus put to sea, they had not gone far when Mr. Reynolds, the captain of the smaller ship, complained that he found her so leaky that he dare not go further till she was mended. So the captain of the bigger ship, Mr. Jones,[1] being consulted with, they both resolved to put into Dartmouth and have her mended, which accordingly was done, at great expense and loss of time and a fair wind. She was here thoroughly searched from stem to stern, some leaks were found and mended, and it was then believed that she might proceed without danger. So with good hope they put to sea again, thinking they would go comfortably on, not looking for any more hindrances of this kind. But after they had gone a hundred leagues beyond Land's End holding together all the while, the captain of the small ship again complained that she was so leaky that he must bear up or sink at sea, for they could scarcely keep her afloat by pumping. So they consulted

---
[1] The captain of the *Mayflower* was Christopher Jones.

again, and both ships resolved to bear up again and put into Plymouth, which accordingly was done. No special leak could be found, but it was judged to be the general weakness of the ship, and that she would not prove equal to the voyage. Upon which it was resolved to dismiss her and part of the company, and proceed with the other ship; which, though it caused great discouragement, was put into execution. So after they had taken out such provisions as the other ship could well stow, and decided what persons to send back, they made another sad parting, the one ship going back to London, and the other proceeding on her voyage. Those that went back were mostly such as were willing to do so, either from discontent or fear of the ill success of the voyage, seeing they had met with so many crosses and the year was so far spent. Others, owing to their weakness and having many young children, were thought least useful and most unfit to bear the brunt of this arduous adventure; to which work of God and the judgment of their brethren they were contented to submit. And thus, like Gideon's army,[2] this small number was divided, as if the Lord thought these few too many for the great work He had to do.

It was afterwards found that the leakiness of the ship was partly caused by being overmasted and too much pressed with sail; for after she was sold and put into trim she made many voyages, to the profit of her owners. But it was partly due to the cunning and deceit of the captain and his crew, who had been hired to stay a whole year at the settlement, and now, fearing want of victuals, they plotted this stratagem to free themselves, as was afterwards confessed by some of them. Yet in order to encourage the

---

[2] Judges, VII, 2-8.

captain, the majority of those who had come from Leyden had been put aboard this ship, to content him. But so strong was self-love that he forgot all duty and former kindnesses, and dealt thus falsely with them, though he pretended otherwise.

Among those who returned was Mr. Cushman and his family, whose heart and courage had failed them before. He was assistant to Mr. Martin, who was governor in the bigger ship. I insert here a passionate letter he wrote to a friend in London from Dartmouth, whilst the ship lay there mending, which, besides the expression of his own fears, shows how the providence of God was working for their good beyond man's expectations, and other things concerning their condition in these straits. And though it discloses some infirmities in him (as who under temptation is free), he afterwards continued to be a special instrument for their good, and performed the offices of a loving friend and faithful brother to them, and was a partaker of much comfort with them.

Robert Cushman at Dartmouth to Edward Southworth,[3] *at Heanage House, Duke's Place, London:*

Loving Friend,

My most kind remembrances to you and your wife, with loving E. M., etc., whom in this world I never look to see again. For beside the imminent dangers of this voyage, which are no less than deadly, an infirmity has seized me which will not in all likelihood leave me till death. What to call it I know not; but it is, as it were, a bundle of lead crushing my heart more and more these fourteen days,

---

[3] Southworth was a member of the Leyden congregation who did not go to New England. When he died, his widow, Alice, went to Plymouth to become Bradford's second wife.

so that though I perform the actions of a living man I am but as dead; but the will of God be done.

Our pinnace will not cease leaking, else I think we had been half way to Virginia. Our voyage hither has been as full of crosses as ourselves have been of crookedness. We put in here to trim her, and I think if we had stayed at sea but three or four hours more she would have sunk. And though she was twice trimmed at Southampton she is still as open and leaky as a sieve. We lay at Southampton seven days, in fair weather, waiting for her; and now we lie here waiting for her in as fair a wind as can blow, and so have done these four days, and are likely to lie four more, and by that time the wind may have turned as it did at Southampton. Our victuals will be half eaten up, I think, before we leave the coast of England, and if our voyage last long we shall not have a month's victuals when we arrive.

Nearly £700 has been spent in Southampton, upon what I know not. Mr. Martin says he neither can nor will give any account of it; and if he is called upon for accounts he cries out that we are ungrateful for his pains and care, and that we are suspicious of him. Also he insults our poor people, and treats them with scorn and contempt, as if they were not good enough to wipe his shoes. It would break your heart to hear the mourning of our poor people. They complain to me, and alas! I can do nothing for them. If I speak to him he flies in my face as mutinous, and says no complaints shall be heard or received but by himself, and they are forward, waspish, and discontented people. There are others who would gladly lose all they have put in, or make satisfaction for what they have had, if they might only depart; but he will not listen to them or allow them to go ashore lest they should run away. The sailors, too, are so annoyed at his ignorant boldness, in meddling with things he knows nothing of, that some threaten to do him mischief. He makes himself a laughing stock.

As for Mr. Weston, unless grace is with him he will hate us ten times more than ever he loved us, for not confirming the conditions. Now that they have met some reverses they begin to see the truth, and say Mr. Robinson was at fault to tell them never to consent to those conditions, or put me in office. But he and they will rue it too late. Four or five of the chief of them from Leyden came resolved never to go on those conditions. Mr. Martin said he never received any money on those conditions, and that he was not beholden to the merchants for a pin; that they were bloodsuckers, and I know not what. Simple man, he indeed never made any conditions with the merchants, nor ever spoke with them. But did all that money fly to Southampton, or was it his own? Who would go and lay out money so rashly and lavishly as he did, and never know how he comes by it or on what conditions? Secondly, I told him of the alterations long ago, and he was content; but now he domineers, and says I betrayed them into the hands of slave-drivers; he is not beholden to them; he can fit out two ships himself for a voyage—when he has only £50 worth of shares in the venture, and if he gave in his accounts he would not have a penny left, as I am persuaded.

Friend, if ever we establish a colony, God works a miracle; especially considering how scanty our provisions will be and most of all how disunited we are among ourselves, and devoid of good leaders. Violence will break all. Where is the meek and humble spirit of Moses and of Nehemiah, who re-edified the walls of Jerusalem and the state of Israel? Is not the sound of Rehoboam's bragging daily among us here? [4] Have not the philosophers and all wise men observed, that even in settled commonwealths violent governors bring either themselves or people or both to ruin? How much more in the building of commonwealths, when the mortar is scarcely hardened which

---

[4] I Kings, XII, 6-14.

is to bind the walls. If I were to write you everything that foreruns our ruin, I should overcharge my weak head and grieve your tender heart; only this—prepare for evil tidings of us every day. But pray for us instantly. It may be the Lord may yet be entreated.

I see not how in reason we can escape the gasping of hunger-starved persons; but God can do much, and His will be done. It is better for me to die now than to bear it. Poor William King and I strive who shall first be meat for the fishes; but we look for a glorious resurrection, knowing Christ Jesus after the flesh no more; but, looking unto the joy that is before us, we will endure all these things and account them light in comparison of the joy we hope for. Remember me in all love to our friends, as if I named them, whose prayers I desire earnestly, and wish again to see, but not till I can look them in the face with more comfort. The Lord give us that true comfort which none can take from us. I desired to send a brief account of our condition to some friend. I doubt not but you will know when to speak a word in season. What I have written is true, and much more which I have foreborne to mention. I write it as upon my life and my last confession in England. What you deem well to mention at once, you may speak of; and what is best to conceal, conceal. Excuse my weak manner, for my head is weak and my body is feeble. The Lord make me strong in Him, and keep both you and yours.

Your loving friend,
ROBERT CUSHMAN.

Dartmouth, Aug. 17th, 1620.

These being his fears at Dartmouth, they must needs be much stronger when he arrived at Plymouth.

"They had now no freinds to wellcome them, nor inns to entertaine or refresh their weatherbeaten bodies, no houses or much less townes to repaire too, to seek for succoure."

CHAPTER IX

OF THEIR VOYAGE AND SAFE ARRIVAL AT CAPE COD.

These troubles being over, and all being together in the one ship,[1] they put to sea again on September 6th with a prosperous wind, which continued for several days and was some encouragement to them, though, as usual, many were afflicted with seasickness. I must not omit to mention here a special example of God's providence. There was an insolent and very profane young man —one of the sailors, which made him the more overbearing—who was always harassing the poor people in their sickness, and cursing them daily with grievous execrations, and did not hesitate to tell them that he hoped to help throw half of them overboard before they came to their journey's end. If he were gently reproved by anyone, he would curse and swear most bitterly. But it pleased God, before they came half seas over, to smite the young man with a grievous disease, of which he died in a desperate manner, and so was himself the first to be thrown over-

---

[1] Of the 102 passengers on the *Mayflower*, only forty-one were from the Leyden congregation—seventeen men, ten women, and fourteen children. The remaining sixty-one were for the most part orthodox churchmen, although there were a few Puritans in this group. See Introduction, p. xxii.

board. Thus his curses fell upon his own head, which astonished all his mates for they saw it was the just hand of God upon him.

After they had enjoyed fair winds and weather for some time, they encountered cross winds and many fierce storms by which the ship was much shaken and her upper works made very leaky. One of the main beams amidships was bent and cracked, which made them afraid that she might not be able to complete the voyage. So some of the chief of the voyagers, seeing that the sailors doubted the efficiency of the ship, entered into serious consultation with the captain and officers, to weigh the danger betimes and rather to return than to cast themselves into desperate and inevitable peril. Indeed there was great difference of opinion among the crew themselves. They wished to do whatever could be done for the sake of their wages, being now half way over; on the other hand they were loth to risk their lives too desperately. But at length all opinions, the captain's and others' included, agreed that the ship was sound under the water-line, and as for the buckling of the main beam, there was a great iron screw the passengers brought out of Holland, by which the beam could be raised into its place; and the carpenter affirmed that with a post put under it, set firm in the lower deck, and otherwise fastened, he could make it hold. As for the decks and upper works, they said they would calk them as well as they could; and though with the working of the ship they would not long keep stanch, yet there would otherwise be no great danger, if they did not overpress her with sail.

So they committed themselves to the will of God, and resolved to proceed. In several of these storms the wind was so strong and the seas so high that they could not carry a knot of sail, but were forced to hull for many days. Once, as they thus lay at hull in a terrible storm, a strong young man, called John Howland, coming on deck was thrown into the sea; but it pleased God that he caught hold of the topsail halliards which hung overboard and ran out at length; but he kept his hold, though he was several fathoms under water, till he was hauled up by the rope, and then with a boathook helped into the ship and saved; and though he was somewhat ill from it he lived many years and became a profitable member both of the church and commonwealth. In all the voyage only one of the passengers died, and that was William Button, a youth, servant to Samuel Fuller, when they were nearing the coast. But to be brief, after long beating at sea, on November 11th they fell in with a part of the land called Cape Cod, at which they were not a little joyful. After some deliberation among themselves and with the captain, they tacked about and resolved to stand for the southward, the wind and weather being fair, to find some place near Hudson's River for their habitation. But after they had kept that course about half a day, they met with dangerous shoals and roaring breakers,[2] and as they conceived themselves in great danger—the wind falling—they resolved to bear up again for the Cape, and thought themselves happy to get out of danger before night overtook them, as by God's providence they did. Next day they got into the bay, where they rode in safety.

A word or two, by the way, of this Cape. It was first thus named by Captain Gosnold and his people in 1602, because they caught much of that fish there; and after-

---

[2] This was near the present town of Chatham.

wards was called Cape James by Captain Smith;[3] but it retains the former name among seamen. The point where they first met with those dangerous shoals they called Point Care, or Tucker's Terror; but the French and Dutch to this day call it Malabar.

Having found a good haven [4] and being brought safely in sight of land, they fell upon their knees and blessed the God of Heaven who had brought them over the vast and furious ocean, and delivered them from all the perils and miseries of it, again to set their feet upon the firm and stable earth, their proper element. And no marvel that they were thus joyful, when the wise Seneca was so affected with sailing a few miles on the coast of his own Italy that he affirmed he had rather taken twenty years to make his way by land, than to go by sea to any place in however short a time—so tedious and dreadful it was to him.

But here I cannot but make a pause, and stand half amazed at this poor people's present condition; and so I think will the reader, too, when he considers it well. Having thus passed the vast ocean, and that sea of troubles before while they were making their preparations, they now had no friends to welcome them, nor inns to entertain and refresh their weatherbeaten bodies, nor houses—much less towns—to repair to.

It is recorded in Scripture (Acts, XXVIII) as a mercy to the Apostle and his shipwrecked crew, that the barbarians showed them no small kindness in refreshing them; but these savage barbarians when they met with them (as will

---
[3] Captain John Smith, famous as founder of the first Virginia colony, had explored the coast from Maine southward in an open boat in 1614. The Pilgrims had a copy of the map he had made of this region, with the names then given to the natural features.
[4] This was Provincetown harbor.

appear) were readier to fill their sides full of arrows than otherwise! As for the season, it was winter, and those who have experienced the winters of the country know them to be sharp and severe, and subject to fierce storms, when it is dangerous to travel to known places—much more to search an unknown coast. Besides, what could they see but a desolate wilderness, full of wild beasts and wild men; and what multitude there might be of them they knew not! Neither could they, as it were, go up to the top of Pisgah, to view from this wilderness a more goodly country to feed their hopes; for which way soever they turned their eyes (save upward to the heavens!) they could gain little solace from any outward objects. Summer being done, all things turned upon them a weatherbeaten face; and the whole country, full of woods and thickets, presented a wild and savage view.

If they looked behind them, there was the mighty ocean which they had passed, and was now a gulf separating them from all civilized parts of the world. If it be said that they had their ship to turn to, it is true; but what did they hear daily from the captain and crew? That they should quickly look out for a place with their shallop, where they would be not far off; for the season was such that the captain would not approach nearer to the shore till a harbor had been discovered which he could enter safely; and that the food was being consumed apace, but he must and would keep sufficient for the return voyage. It was even muttered by some of the crew that if they did not find a place in time, they would turn them and their goods ashore and leave them.

Let it be remembered, too, what small hope of further assistance from England they had left behind them, to support their courage in this sad condition and the trials they were under; for how the case stood between the settlers and the merchants at their departure has already been described. It is true, indeed, that the affection and love of their brethren at Leyden towards them was cordial and unbroken; but they had little power to help them or themselves.

What, then, could now sustain them but the spirit of God, and His grace? Ought not the children of their fathers rightly to say: Our fathers were Englishmen who came over the great ocean, and were ready to perish in this wilderness; but they cried unto the Lord, and He heard their voice, and looked on their adversity. . . . Let [5] them therefore praise the Lord, because He is good, and His mercies endure forever. Yea, let them that have been redeemed of the Lord, show how He hath delivered them from the hand of the oppressor. When they wandered forth into the desert wilderness, out of the way, and found no city to dwell in, both hungry and thirsty, their soul was overwhelmed in them. Let them confess before the Lord His loving kindness, and His wonderful works before the sons of men!

---

[5] The following passage is a free paraphrase of parts of Psalm CVII, a song of thanksgiving.

"But aboute midnight they heard a hideous and great crie, and their sentinell caled, 'Arme, arme.'"

CHAPTER X

Showing how they sought out a place of habitation, and what befell them there.

They thus arrived at Cape Cod on the 11th of November, and necessity called on them to look out for a place of habitation. Having brought a large shallop with them from England, stowed in quarters in the ship, they now got her out, and set their carpenters to work to trim her up; but being much bruised and battered in the foul weather they saw she would be long mending. So a few of them volunteered to go by land and explore the neighboring parts, whilst the shallop was put in order; particularly since, as they entered the bay, there seemed to be an opening some two or three leagues off, which the captain thought was a river. It was conceived there might be some danger in the attempt; but seeing them resolute, sixteen of them, well-armed, were permitted to go, under charge of Captain Standish.[1]

---

[1] Myles Standish had fought with the English armies in Flanders. He became acquainted with the Pilgrims in Leyden and attached himself to the expedition, although he did not share their religious beliefs and never became a member of the church. His ability and experience led to his prompt selection as military leader, a post he filled with exceptional courage. Enemies called him "Captain Shrimp" because of his red face and short stature.

They set forth on the 15th of November, being landed by the ship's boat, and when they had marched about the space of a mile by the seaside, they espied five or six persons with a dog coming towards them. They were savages; but they fled back into the woods, followed by the English, who wished to see if they could speak with them, and to discover if there were more lying in ambush. But the Indians, seeing themselves followed, left the woods, and ran along the sands as hard as they could, so our men could not come up with them, but followed the track of their feet several miles. Night coming on, they made their rendezvous, and set sentinels, and rested in quiet.

Next morning they again pursued the Indians' tracks, till they came to a great creek, where they had left the sands and turned into the woods. But they continued to follow them by guess, hoping to find their dwellings; but soon they lost both the Indians and themselves, and fell into such thickets that their clothes and armor were injured severely; but they suffered most from want of water. At length they found some, and refreshed themselves with the first New England water they had drunk; and in their great thirst they found it as pleasant as wine or beer had been before. Afterwards they directed their course towards the other shore, for they knew it was only a neck of land they had to cross over. At length they got to the seaside, and marched to this supposed river, and by the way found a pond of fresh water, and shortly after a quantity of cleared ground where the Indians had formerly planted corn; and they found some of their graves.[2]

Proceeding further, they saw stubble where corn had been grown the same year, and also found a place where a

---

[2] Near Truro.

house had lately been, with some planks, and a great kettle and heaps of sand newly banked, under which they found several large baskets filled with corn, some in the ear of various colors, which was a very goodly sight, they having never seen any like it before. This was near the supposed river [3] that they had come to seek. When they reached it, they found that it opened into two arms, with a high cliff of sand at the entrance, but more likely to be creeks of salt water than fresh, they thought. There was good harborage for their shallop, so they left it to be further explored when she was ready. The time allowed them having expired, they returned to the ship, lest the others should be anxious about their safety. They took part of the corn and buried the rest; and so, like the men from Eschol, carried with them of the fruits of the land, and showed their brethren; at which the rest were very glad, and greatly encouraged.

After this, the shallop being ready, they set out again for the better reconnoitering of the place. The captain of the ship desired to go himself, so there were some thirty men. However, they found it to be no harbor for ships, but only for boats. They also found two of the Indians' houses covered with mats, and some of their implements in them; but the people had run away and could not be seen. They also found more corn, and beans of various colors. These they brought away, intending to give them full satisfaction when they should meet with any of them, —as about six months afterwards they did.

And it is to be noted as a special providence of God, and a great mercy to this poor people, that they thus got seed to plant corn the next year, or they might have

---

[3] Pamet River, nearby.

starved; for they had none, nor any likelihood of getting any, till too late for the planting season. Nor is it likely that they would have got it if this first voyage had not been made, for the ground was soon all covered with snow and frozen hard. But the Lord is never wanting unto His in their great need; let His holy name have all the praise.

The month of November being spent in these affairs, and foul weather coming on, on the sixth of December they sent out their shallop again with ten of their principal men and some sailors upon further discovery, intending to circumnavigate the deep bay of Cape Cod. The weather was very cold, and it froze so hard that the spray of the sea froze on their coats like glass. Early that night they got to the lower end of the bay, and as they drew near the shore they saw ten or twelve Indians very busy about something. They landed about a league or two from them; though they had much ado to put ashore anywhere, it was so full of flats. It was late when they landed, so they made themselves a barricade of logs and boughs as well as they could in the time, and set a sentinel and betook them to rest, and saw the smoke of the fire the savages made that night. When morning came they divided their party, some to coast along the shore in the boat, and the rest to march through the woods to see the land, and, if possible, to find a fit place for their settlement. They came to the place where they had seen the Indians the night before and found they had been cutting up a great fish like a grampus, covered with almost two inches of fat, like a hog. The shallop found two more of the same kind of fish dead on the sands, a usual thing after storms there, because of the great flats of sand.

They ranged up and down all that day, but found no people nor any place they liked. When the sun got low they hastened out of the woods to meet their shallop, making signs to it to come into a creek hard by, which it did at high water. They were very glad to meet, for they had not seen each other since the morning. They made a barricade, as they did every night with logs, stakes, and thick pine boughs, the height of a man, leaving it open to leeward; partly to shelter them from the cold wind, making their fire in the middle and lying around it; and, partly to defend them from any sudden assaults of the savages, if they should try to surround them. So being very weary, they betook them to rest. But about midnight they heard a hideous cry, and their sentinel called "Arm, arm!" So they bestirred themselves and took to their arms, and shot a couple of muskets and then the noise ceased. They concluded it was a pack of wolves, or some such wild beasts; for one of the sailors told them he had often heard such noises in Newfoundland. So they rested till about five o'clock in the morning.

After prayer they prepared for breakfast, and it being day dawning, it was thought best to be carrying things down to the boat. Some said it was not best to carry the guns down; others said they would be the readier, for they had wrapped them up in their coats to keep them from the dew. But some three or four would not carry their guns down to the boat till they went themselves. However, as the water was not high enough, the others laid theirs down on the bank of the creek, and came up to breakfast. But soon, all of a sudden, they heard a great and strange cry, which they knew to be the same as they had heard in the night, though with various notes. One of the company who was outside came running in and cried: "Men! Indians, Indians!" and at that their arrows came flying amongst them. The men ran down to the creek with all speed to recover their guns, which by the providence of God they succeeded in doing. In the meantime two of those who were still armed discharged their muskets at the Indians; and two more stood ready at the entrance of the rendezvous, but were commanded not to shoot till they could take fell aim at them; and the other two loaded again at full speed, there being only four guns there to defend the barricade when it was first assaulted.

The cry of the Indians was dreadful, especially when they saw the men run out of the rendezvous towards the shallop to recover their guns, the Indians wheeling about them. But some of the men, armed with coats of mail and with cutlasses in their hands, soon got their guns and let fly among them, which quickly stopped their violence. There was one big Indian, and no less valiant, who stood behind a tree, within half a musket-shot, and let his arrows fly at them. He was seen to shoot three arrows, which were all avoided. He stood three musket-shots, till one of them made the bark and splinters of the tree fly about his ears, at which he gave an extraordinary shriek, and away all of them went. The men left some of the party to guard the shallop, and followed the Indians about a quarter of a mile, shouting once or twice, and shooting off two or three guns, and then returned. They did this so that the natives might not think they were afraid of them.

Thus it pleased God to vanquish their enemies and give them deliverance; and by His special providence so to dispose that not one of them was hit, though the arrows came close to them, on every side, and some of their coats which were hung up in the barricade were shot through and through. Afterwards they gave God solemn thanks and praise for their deliverance, and gathered up a bundle of the arrows, and later sent them to England by the captain of the ship. They called the place "The First Encounter."

Then they left, and coasted all along, but discovered no likely place for a harbor. So they made all speed to a spot which their pilot—a Mr. Coppin, who had been in the country before—assured them was a good harbor, which he had been in, and which they might fetch before night. Of this they were glad, for the weather began to be foul.

After some hours' sailing, it began to snow and rain, and about the middle of the afternoon the wind increased, and the sea became very rough. They broke their rudder, and it was as much as two men could do to steer her with a couple of oars. But the pilot bade them be of good cheer, and said he saw the harbor; but the storm increasing and night drawing on, they carried all the sail they could to get in while they could see. Then their mast broke in three pieces, and the sail fell overboard in a very heavy sea, so that they were in danger of being wrecked; but by God's mercy they recovered themselves, and having the tide with them, struck in towards the harbor.

But when they came to, the pilot found he had mistaken the place, and said the Lord be merciful to them, for he had never seen the place before; and he and the mate were about to run her ashore, in a cove full of breakers, before the wind. But one of the seamen, who steered, bade the rowers, if they were men, about with her, or they would all be cast away; which they did with speed. So he bid them be of good cheer and row lustily for there was a fair sound before them, and he did not doubt but they would find a place where they could come to safely. Though it was very dark and rained hard, they ultimately got under the lee of a small island, and remained there safely all night; but they did not know it was an island till morning. They were divided in their mind; some wished to stay in the boat, for fear there would be more Indians; others were so weak and cold they could not endure it, but got ashore and with much ado made a fire—everything being wet—and then the rest were glad enough to join them; for after midnight the wind shifted to the northwest and it froze hard.

But though this had been a night of much hardship and danger, God gave them a morning of comfort and refreshment, as He usually doth to His children; for the next day was a fair sun-shining day, and they found they were on an island secure from the Indians, where they could dry their stuff, fix their arms, and rest themselves and give God thanks for his mercies in their manifold deliverances. This being the last day of the week they prepared to keep the Sabbath there. On Monday they sounded the harbor [4] and found it fit for shipping; and marching inland they found several cornfields and little running brooks—a place, as they supposed, fit for a settlement; at least it was the best they could find, and considering the season of the year and their present necessity they were thankful for it. So they returned with this news to the rest of their people aboard the ship, which cheered them greatly.

On the 15th day of December they weighed anchor to go to the place they had discovered, and came within two

---

[4] This was Plymouth. The historic landing on Plymouth Rock was that of this shallop party. It was unfortunate for the Pilgrims that they missed Boston harbor by such a short distance. No rivers emptied into Plymouth bay, whereas three rivers found an outlet in Boston harbor. Since fur trading was to be the chief support of the colony and rivers were the only means of transportation into the interior, the Boston settlement of ten years later rapidly took preeminence.

leagues of it, but had to bear up again. On the 16th day the wind came fair, and they arrived safe in the harbor. Afterwards they took a better view of the place, and resolved where to pitch their dwellings; and on the 25th day they began to erect the first house for common use, to receive them and their goods.

PART TWO

History of the Colony

at New Plymouth

1620-1646

> *sd by them done (this their condition considered) might be as firme as any patent; and in some respects more sure. The forme was as followeth.*
>
> *In y̆ name of god Amen. We whose names are underwriten, the loyall subjects of our dread soueraigne Lord King Iames by y̆ grace of god, of great Britaine, franc, & Ireland king, defendor of y̆ faith, &c*
>
> *Haueing undertaken, for y̆ glorie of god, and aduancemente of y̆ christian faith, and honour of our king & countrie, a voyage to plant y̆ first colonie in y̆ Northerne parts of Virginia. doe by these presents solemnly & mutualy in y̆ presence of god, and one of another, Couenant, & combine our selues togeather into a Ciuill body politick; for our better ordering, & preseruation & furtheranc̄e of y̆ ends aforesaid; and by vertue hearof to enacte, constitute, and frame such just & equall lawes, ordinances, Acts, constitutions, & offices, from time to time, as shall be thought most meete & conuenient for y̆ generall good of y̆ Colonie: Vnto which we promise all due submission and obedience. In witnes wherof we haue here vnder subscribed our names at Cap= Codd y̆ ·11· of Nouember in y̆ year of y̆ raigne of our soueraigne Lord king Iames of England, france, & Ireland y̆ eighteenth and of Scotland y̆ fiftie fourth. An: Dom. 1620.*

The Mayflower Compact, the covenant which bound the Mayflower passengers into a "civill body politick," signed shortly before they landed on Cape Cod.

"But that which was most lamentable was that in two or three months halfe of their company dyed."

CHAPTER I

[*1620*]

The rest of this work—if God give me life and opportunity—I shall, for brevity's sake, handle in the form of Annals, noting only the principal doings, chronologically.

First, I will turn back a little, and begin with a compact [1] or deed drawn up by them before they went ashore to settle, constituting the first foundation of their government. This was occasioned partly by the discontented and mutinous speeches that some of the strangers amongst them had let fall: that when they got ashore they would use their liberty, that none had power to command them, the patent procured being for Virginia, and not for New England, which belonged to another company, with which

---

[1] This is the famous Mayflower Compact. Although it was not the revolutionary charter which it has been called, it was a sound statement of the aim to establish an orderly civil government, with equal and just laws for all. The order of signing is an indication of the Pilgrims' respect for property and position; the gentry and aristocrats affixed their signatures first—Carver, Bradford, Winslow, Brewster, and Allerton; then came tradesmen and members of the middle class—Standish, Fuller, Martin, Mullins, White, Warren; next, the so-called "goodmen," yeomen and laborers; and, finally, a few of the servants.

the Virginia company had nothing to do. And, further, it was believed by the leading men among the settlers that such a deed, drawn up by themselves, considering their present condition, would be as effective as any patent, and in some respects more so.

The form of the deed was as follows:

In the name of God, Amen. We whose names are underwritten, the loyal subjects of our dread sovereign lord, King James, by the grace of God, of Great Britain, France and Ireland, King, Defender of the Faith, etc., having undertaken for the glory of God, and advancement of the Christian faith, and honor of our king and country, a voyage to plant the first colony in the northern parts of Virginia, do by these presents solemnly and mutually in the presence of God and of one another, covenant and combine ourselves into a civil body politic, for our better ordering and preservation, and the furtherance of the ends aforesaid and by virtue hereof to enact, constitute, and frame, such just and equal laws, ordinances, acts, constitutions, and offices, from time to time, as shall be thought most meet and convenient for the general use of the Colony, unto which we promise all due submission and obedience. In witness whereof we have here underscribed our names at Cape Cod, 11th of November, in the year of the reign of our sovereign lord, King James of England, France and Ireland the eighteenth, and of Scotland the fifty-fourth.
A.D. 1620.

They then chose, or rather confirmed, Mr. John Carver,[2] a godly man and highly approved among them, as their governor for that year. After they had provided a place for their goods and common stores, which they

---

[2] John Carver had been appointed governor of the *Mayflower* before the ship sailed; therefore his formal election here is called confirmation.

were long in unlading owing to want of boats, the severity of the winter weather and sickness, and had begun some small cottages for dwellings—as time would admit they met and consulted of law and order, both for civil and military government, as seemed suited to their conditions, adding to them from time to time as urgent need demanded. In these arduous and difficult beginnings, discontent and murmuring arose amongst some, and mutinous speech and bearing in others; but they were soon quelled and overcome by the wisdom, patience, and just and equal administration of things by the Governor and the better part, who held faithfully together in the main.

But soon a most lamentable blow fell upon them. In two or three months' time half of their company died, partly owing to the severity of the winter, especially during January and February, and the want of houses and other comforts; partly to scurvy and other diseases, which their long voyage and their incommodious quarters had brought upon them. Of all the hundred odd persons, scarcely fifty remained, and sometimes two or three persons died in a day.[3] In the time of worst distress, there were but six or seven sound persons, who, to their great commendation be it spoken, spared no pains night or day, but with great toil and at the risk of their own health,

---

[3] This sickness was probably typhus or ship fever; the bad food, the hardships of the voyage, and the strains and exposure suffered during the first weeks after landing were factors which lowered everybody's resistance. Whole families were wiped out, and when the epidemic had subsided only three married couples remained unbroken, and only one family—the disreputable Billingtons—was untouched. Bradford's wife Dorothy died on Dec. 7, by falling overboard as the ship rested at anchor; Rose, the wife of Myles Standish, died while her husband was away with the exploring party in mid-December.

fetched wood, made fires, prepared food for the sick, made their beds, washed their infected clothes, dressed and undressed them—in a word, did all the homely and necessary services for them which dainty and queasy stomachs cannot endure to hear mentioned; and all this they did willingly and cheerfully, without the least grudging, showing their love to the friends and brethren; a rare example, and worthy to be remembered.

Two of these seven were Mr. William Brewster, their reverend elder, and Myles Standish, their captain and military commander, to whom myself and many others were much beholden in our low and sick condition. And yet the Lord so upheld these men that in this general calamity they were not at all infected with sickness. And what I have said of these few, I should say of many others who died in this general visitation, and others yet living, that while they had health or strength, they forsook none that had need of them. I doubt not that their recompense is with the Lord.

But I must not pass by another remarkable and unforgettable occurrence. When this calamity fell among the passengers who were to be left here to settle, they were hurried ashore and made to drink water, so that the sailors might have the more beer, and when one sufferer in his sickness desired but a small can of beer, it was answered that if he were their own father he should have none. Then the disease began to seize the sailors also, so that almost half of the crew died before they went away, and many of their officers and strongest men, amongst them the boatswain, gunner, three quartermasters, the cook and others. At this the captain was somewhat struck, and sent to the sick ashore and told the Governor that he could send

THE PSALMES
in Metre.

PSALME 1.

Bless'd man, that doth not in the wickeds counsel walk: nor stand in synners way, nor sit in seat of scornful folk. But setteth in Iehovahs law, his pleasureful delight: and in his law dooth meditate, by day and eke by night.

3. And he shalbe, like-as a tree,
by water brooks planted;
which in his time, shal give his fruit;
his leaf eke shall not fade;
and whatsoever he shall doe,
it prosprously shall thrive.
4. Not so the wicked: but as chaff,
which wind away-doth-drive.
5. Therefore, the wicked shall not in
the judgement stand-upright:
and in th'assemblie of the just,
nor any synful-wight.
6. For, of the just, Iehovah he
acknowledgeth the way:
and way, of the ungracious
shall utterly-decay.

PSALME 2.
Sing this as the 18. Psalme.

WHy doe the heathens rage tumultuously:
and peoples, meditate on vanity?
2. Kings of the earth,
themselves presenting-sett;
and Princes for
to plot togither-get:
against Iehovah, 'gainst his Christ also.
3. Break we, their bands:
and their cords from us throw.
4. He laugheth, that
in heavens doeth reside:
the Lord, he them
doth mockingly-deride.
5. Then in his anger speak to them will hee:
and in his wrath,
them trouble-suddainlie.
6. And I, anoynted-have my King: upon
the mountayn of
my holynes, Sion.
7. Tel wil I the
decree: IAH sayd to mee,
thou art my son;
this day begat I thee.
8. Ask me, and I
wil-give thyne heritance,
hethens: and earths
ends, thy firm-retenance.
9. Thou shalt them roughly-rule with yron rod:
as Potters vessel scatter them abroad.
10. And now, ye Kings
be wise: be nurtured,
ye earths Iudges.
11. Iehovah serve with dread:
and joy, with trembling. Kyss the Son, lest he
be wroth, and pe-

A page of the Ainsworth Psalm Book, prepared for the fugitive congregation of Separatists in Holland by Henry Ainsworth, and first published in Amsterdam in 1612. This psalter was used at Plymouth until about 1692, when it was replaced by the Bay Psalm Book.

for beer for those that had need of it, even should he have to drink water on the homeward voyage.

But amongst the sailors there was quite a different bearing in their misery. Those who before, in the time of their health and welfare, had been boon companions in drinking and jollity, began now to desert one another, saying they would not risk their lives for the sick among them, lest they should be infected by coming to help them in their cabins; if they died, let them die! But the passengers who were still aboard showed them what pity they could, which made some of their hearts relent, such as the boatswain, who was an overbearing young man, and before would often curse and scoff at the passengers. But when he grew weak they had compassion on him and helped him. Then he confessed he did not deserve it at their hands, for he had abused them in word and deed. "Oh," said he, "I see now you show your love like Christians indeed to one another; but we let one another lie and die like dogs." Another lay cursing his wife, saying if it had not been for her he had never come on this unlucky voyage; and anon cursed his fellows, saying he had done this or that for some of them, he had spent so much and so much amongst them, and they were now weary of him, and did not help him in his need. Another made over to one of his mates all he had, when he should die, if he would but help him in his weakness. So his companion went and got a little spice and prepared some food once or twice; and when he did not die as soon as he expected, he went among his comrades and swore the rogue would cheat him of his inheritance; he would see him choke before he prepared him any more food; and so the poor fellow died before morning!

All this while the Indians came skulking about those

who were ashore and would sometimes show themselves aloof, at a distance, but when any approached them, they would run away. Once they stole away the men's tools, where they had been at work and were gone to dinner. About the 16th of March a certain Indian came boldly among them, and spoke to them in broken English, which they could well understand, but were astonished at it. At length they understood by speaking with him that he was not of these parts, but belonged to the eastern country where some English ships came to fish; and with some of these English he was acquainted, and could name several of them. From them he had got his knowledge of the language.

He became useful to them in acquainting them with many things concerning the state of the country in the east parts where he lived, as also of the people there, their names and number, their situation and distance from this place, and who was chief among them. His name was Samoset.[4] He told them also of another Indian whose name was Squanto, a native of this part, who had been in England and could speak English better than himself. After some time of entertainment, being dismissed with gifts, in a little while he returned with five more, and they brought back all the tools that had been stolen, and made way for the coming of their great sachem, called Massasoyt, who about four or five days after, came with the chief of his friends and other attendants, and with Squanto. With him, after friendly entertainment and some gifts, they made a peace which has now continued for twenty-four years.[5]

---

[4] Samoset was a sachem from Monhegan in Maine. Squanto, or Tisquantum, served the Pilgrims faithfully as guide and interpreter.
[5] It lasted for fifty years.

These were the terms:

1. That neither he nor any of his, should injure or harm any of their people.
2. That if any of his did any harm to any of theirs, he should send the offender, that they might punish him.
3. That if anything were taken away from any of theirs, he should cause it to be restored; and they should do the like to his.
4. If any made unjust war against him, they would aid him; if any made war against them, he should aid them.
5. He should send to his neighboring confederates to certify them of this, that they might not wrong them, but might be likewise comprised in the conditions of peace.
6. That when their men came to them, they should leave their bows and arrows behind them.

After this he returned to his place, called Sowams, some forty miles off, but Squanto stayed with them, and was their interpreter, and became a special instrument sent of God for their good, beyond their expectation. He showed them how to plant their corn, where to take fish and other commodities, and guided them to unknown places, and never left them till he died. He was a native of these parts, and had been one of the few survivors of the plague [6] hereabouts. He was carried away with others by one Hunt,[7] a captain of a ship, who intended to sell them for slaves in Spain; but he got away for England, and was received by a merchant in London, and employed in Newfoundland and other parts, and lastly brought into these parts by a Captain Dermer, a gentleman employed by Sir Ferdinand Gorges and others, for discovery and other proj-

---

[6] The fishing and exploring parties had probably infected the Indians with the plague.
[7] Thomas Hunt was a captain of one of John Smith's ships.

ects in these parts. Of Captain Dermer I will say something, because it is mentioned—in a book published A.D. 1622, by the President and Council of New England—that he made peace between the savages of these parts and the English, of which this plantation, as it is there intimated, had the benefit. But what kind of a peace it was appears by what befell him and his men.

Captain Dermer had been here the same year that our people arrived, as appears in an account written by him, and given to me by a friend, bearing date, June 30th, 1620; and as we came in the November following, there was but four months' difference. In this account to his honored friend, he makes the following references to this very place:

"I will first begin," says he, "with the place from which Squanto (or Tisquantem) was taken away, which in Captain Smith's map is called 'Plymouth'; and I would that Plymouth had the same commodities. I could wish that the first plantation might be situated here, if there came to the number of fifty persons or upward; otherwise at Charlton, because there the savages are less to be feared. The Pokanokets, who live to the west of Plymouth, bear an inveterate hatred to the English, and are of greater strength than all the savages from there to Penobscot. Their desire of revenge was occasioned by an Englishman, who having invited many of them on board slaughtered them with small shot, when, as the Indians say, they offered no injury on their part. Whether they were English or no, it may be doubted; but they believe they were, for the French have so assured them. For this reason Squanto cannot deny but they would have killed me when I was at Namasket, had he not interceded hard for me. The soil of the borders of this great bay may be compared to most of the plantations which I have seen in Virginia. The land is of various sorts.

Patuxet is a stubborn but strong soil; Nauset and Satucket are for the most part a blackish and deep mold, much like that where the best tobacco in Virginia grows. In the great bay itself is a quantity of cod and bass, or mullet."

But above all, he commends the Pokanokets' country for the richest soil, and much open ground fit for English grain, etc.

"Massachusetts, about nine leagues from Plymouth, and situated between both, is full of islands and peninsulas, for the most part very fertile."

He was taken prisoner by the Indians at Manamoick,[8] a place not far off, now well known. He gave them what they demanded for his liberty, but when they had got what they desired, they still kept him, and endeavored to kill his men; but he freed himself by seizing some of them, whom he kept bound till they gave him a canoe-load of corn (of which, see Purch: lib. ix, fol. 1778).[9] But this was A.D. 1619.

After the writing of the foregoing narrative, Dermer went with Squanto to the Island of Capawack,[10] which lies south of this place on the way to Virginia. There he went ashore amongst the Indians to trade, as he used to do, but was betrayed and assaulted by them, and all his men were killed except one who kept the boat. He himself got aboard very sorely wounded, and they would have cut off his head as he climbed into his boat, had not the man rescued him. They got away, and made shift to reach Virginia, where he died. This shows how far the natives were from peace, and under what dangerous conditions this

---

[8] Now Chatham.
[9] The reference is to *Pilgrimes*, by Samuel Purchas, London, 1625.
[10] Nantucket.

plantation was begun, but for the powerful hand of the Lord, which protected them. This was partly the reason why they kept aloof, and were so long before they came to the English.

Another reason, as afterwards they themselves stated, was that about three years before, a French ship was wrecked at Cape Cod, but the men got ashore and saved their lives and a large part of their provisions. When the Indians heard of it, they surrounded them and never left watching and dogging them till they got the advantage and killed them, all but three or four, whom they kept, and sent from one Sachem to another, making sport with them and using them worse than slaves. Of these, Captain Dermer released two. So the Indians thought that this ship had now come to revenge these outrages. It was also later disclosed, that before they came to the English to make friends, they got all the powwows of the country together for three days to curse and execrate them in a horrid and devilish manner with conjurations, holding their assembly in a dark and dismal swamp.

But to return. The spring now approaching, it pleased God the mortality began to diminish among them, and the sick recovered apace, which put new life into them all; though they had borne their sad afflictions with as much patience and contentedness as I think any people could do. But it was the Lord who upheld them, and had beforehand prepared them, many having long borne the yoke, yea, even from their youth. Many other minor matters I will omit, several of them having been published already in a journal written by one of the company,[11] and

---

[11] *Mourt's Relation*, published in London in 1622 This first book about New England was written largely by Bradford, supple-

some other narratives and descriptions of journeys, already published, to which I refer those who wish to acquaint themselves more closely. Having now come to the 25th of March, I will begin the year 1621.

---

mented by contributions from others, including Winslow. Since its aim was to attract colonists, it minimized the difficulties and troubles, and painted a glowing picture of life in the New World, even going so far as to compare the climate favorably to that of England.

A page of one of Bradford's notebooks showing his exercises in Hebrew, the study of which he began at an advanced age. Bradford wrote: "Though grown aged, yet I have had a longing desire, to see with mine own eyes, something of that most ancient language, and holy tongue, in which the law and oracles of God were write; and in which God and angels, spake to the holy patriarchs, of old time; and what names were given to things, from the creation. And though I cannot attaine to much herein, yet I am refreshed, to have seen some glimpse hereof; (as Moses saw the land of Canan afarr of) my aime and desire is, to see how the words and phrases lye in the holy texte; and to discerne somewhat of the same, for my owne contente."

Though I am growne aged, yet I have had a longing
desire, to see with my owne eyes, somthing of that most
ancient Language, and holy tongue, in which tho Law
and oracles of God were write; and in which God,
and angels spake to the holy patriarks, of old
time; and what names were given to things,
from the creation And though I cannot
attaine to much herein, yet I am refresh
ed, to have seen some glimpse hereof;
(as moyses saw the land of ca=
nan afarr of) my aime and
desire is to see how the words,
and phrases lye in the
holy texte; and to
discerne somewhat
of the same,
for my owne
Contente

וְחֶסֶד יְהוָה מָלְאָה הָאָרֶץ The earth is full of ye mercie of Jehovah.	שָׁם פָּחֲדוּ פָחַד לֹא הָיָה פָחַד Ther they feared a fear, wher no fear was
וַיַּרְא אֱלֹהִים כִּי טוֹב And God saw that it was good	הוֹן יוֹסִיף רֵעִים רַבִּים Riches gather many friends
לֹא טוֹב הֱיוֹת הָאָדָם לְבַדּוֹ It is not good that man should be alone	רַע רַע יֹאמַר הַקּוֹנֶה It is naught, it is naught, saith the buyer
כַּבֵּד אֶת אָבִיךָ וְאֶת אִמֶּךָ honour thy father, and thy mother	מָצָא אִשָּׁה מָצָא טוֹב he that findeth a wife findeth good
וּשְׂמַח מֵאֵשֶׁת נְעוּרֶיךָ And rejoyce with the wife of thy youth	וַאֲנִי בְּרֹב חַסְדְּךָ אָבוֹא בֵיתֶךָ But I in multitude of thy mercies, will come into thy house
זְנוּת וְיַיִן וְתִירוֹשׁ יִקַּח לֵב whordome, and wine, a new wine take away the harte	וְהָיָה כְּעֵץ שָׁתוּל עַל פַּלְגֵי מָיִם And he shall be as a tree planted by the brooks of waters
קוֹל דְּמֵי אָחִיךָ צוֹעֲקִים אֵלַי The voyce of thy brothers bloud crieth unto me	חַכְמוֹת נָשִׁים בָּנְתָה בֵיתָהּ A wise woman buildeth her house
דָּן דִּין עָנִי Judge the	נְקִי כַפַּיִם וּבַר לֵבָב Innocente in hands, & pure in hart

III

BY F. & R.M.L.
A MAP SHOWING the PILGRIM & PURITAN SETTLEMENTS & Location of Indian Tribes
Kennebec (Augusta)
Cobisconte (Gardiner)
Kennebec River
Damariscode Islands
Merrimac R.
Piscataqua (Portsmouth)
CAPE ANN
Naumkeag (Salem)
Newtown (Cambridge)
Charles River
Boston
Merry Mount (Quincy)
Wessagusset (Weymouth)
MASSACHUSETTS BAY
Provincetown
Pamet Harbor (Truro)
Connecticut River
MONHIGGS
MASSASOYT'S COUNTRY
Plymouth
CAPE COD BAY
POKANOKETS
Manomet (Sandwich)
PEQUOTS
NARRAGANSETTS
Saybrook
Isle of Capawack (Martha's Vineyard)
Nantucket Island
Munisses (Block Island)

"Afterwards they (as many as were able) began to plant their corn, in which service Squanto stood them in great stead. . . ."

CHAPTER II

[*1621*]

They now decided to send back the ship which had brought them over, and which had remained till about this time or the beginning of April. The reason, on their part, why she had stayed so long, was the necessity and danger they were under. It was well towards the end of December before she could land anything, or they were in a condition to receive anything ashore. And after that on the 14th of January, the house they had built for a general rendezvous accidentally caught fire, and some of them had to go aboard the ship for shelter.[1] Then the sickness began to fall among them sorely, and the weather was so bad that they could not hasten their preparations. Again the Governor and the chief members, seeing so many fall sick and die daily, thought it was unwise to send the ship away, considering their condition and the danger they were in from the Indians, till they could procure some shelter; and therefore thought it better to incur further expense for themselves and their friends, than to

---

[1] This fire which burned the roof of their first structure was a disaster; Bradford, Carver, and others were lying ill inside, and had to be carried to safety.

risk everything. And though before, the captain and sailors had hurried the passengers ashore, so that they could be gone; now many of the crew being dead—and some of the ablest of them—and of the rest many lay sick and weak, the captain did not dare put to sea till he saw them begin to recover, and the heart of winter over.

The settlers, as many as were able, then began to plant their corn, in which service Squanto stood them in good stead, showing them how to plant it and cultivate it. He also told them that unless they got fish to manure this exhausted old soil, it would come to nothing, and he showed them that in the middle of April plenty of fish would come up the brook by which they had begun to build, and taught them how to catch it, and where to get other necessary provisions; all of which they found true by experience. They sowed some English seed, such as wheat and pease, but it came to no good, either because of the badness of the seed or the lateness of the season or some other defect.

This April, while they were busy sowing their seed, their Governor, Mr. John Carver, one hot day came out of the field very sick. He complained greatly of his head and lay down, and within a few hours his senses failed. He never spoke again, and died a few days after. His death was much lamented and depressed them deeply, with good cause. He was buried in the best manner possible, with some volleys of shot by all that bore arms; and his wife, a weak woman, died five or six weeks after him.

Shortly after, William Bradford [2] was chosen governor in his stead, and having not yet recovered from his illness,

---

[2] Bradford was now thirty-two; with only brief periods of respite, he was to keep the affairs of the colony in order for thirty-six years, until his death in 1657.

in which he had been near the point of death, Isaac Allerton was appointed assistant to him. These two, by renewed election each year, continued several years together. This I here note, once for all.

On May 12th the first marriage here took place,[3] which, according to the laudable custom of the Low Countries [4] in which they had lived, it was thought proper for the magistrate to perform, as a civil institution upon which many questions about inheritances depend, and other things requiring their cognizance, as well as being consonant with the Scriptures (Ruth IV), and nowhere mentioned in the Gospels as a part of the minister's duty.

Having now made some progress with their affairs at home, it was thought advisable to send a deputation to their new friend Massasoyt, and to bestow upon him some gratuity to bind him faster to them; also at the same time to view the country, and see in what manner he lived, what strength he had about him, and what was the way to his place, if at any time they should have need. So on July 2nd they sent Mr. Edward Winslow and Mr. Hopkins, with the aforesaid Squanto for their guide. They gave Massasoyt a suit of clothes, and a horseman's coat, with some other small things, which were kindly accepted, though they

---

[3] The marriage was that of Susanna White and Edward Winslow. Because of the high mortality, marriages were many and frequent among the Pilgrims.

[4] This decree, or law, about marriage, was published by the States of the Low Countries, A. D. 1590: "That those of any religion, after lawful and open publication, coming before the magistrates, in the Town or State-House, were to be orderly by them married, one to another." (Petet's Hist., fol. 1029). And this practice was continued by the Colony, and has been followed by all the famous churches of Christ in these parts to this time,—A. D. 1646. (B.)

found but short commons, and came home both weary and hungry. The Indians in those times did not have nearly so much corn as they have had since the English supplied them with hoes, and set them an example by their industry in preparing new ground therewith. Massasoyt's place was found to be forty miles off and the soil good. But his people had died in great numbers during the recent plague throughout these parts, about three years before the coming of the English. Thousands of them died, until the living were not able to bury the dead, and their skulls and bones were found in many places lying still above ground, where their houses and dwelling places had been—a very sad spectacle. But they brought word that the Narragansetts lived just on the other side of the great bay, and were a strong populous tribe living close together, and had not been attacked by this wasting plague.

About the latter end of this month, one John Billington lost himself in the woods, and wandered up and down for about five days, living on berries and what he could find. At length he came across an Indian plantation, twenty miles to the south, called Manomet.[5] They conveyed him further off to Nauset, among the Indians who had set upon the landing party when they were coasting and whilst their ship lay at the Cape, as before noted. But the Governor caused him to be inquired for among the Indians, and at length Massasoyt sent word where he was, and the Governor sent a shallop for him, and had him delivered. The Indians there also came and made their peace and full satisfaction was given by the settlers to those whose corn they had found and taken when they were at Cape Cod.

---

[5] Near the present site of Bourne.

Thus their peace and acquaintance was pretty well established with the natives about them. Another Indian, called Hobbamok [6] came to live with them, a fine strong man, of some account amongst the Indians for his valor and qualities. He remained very faithful to the English till he died. He and Squanto having gone upon business among the Indians, a sachem called Corbitant, allied to Massasoyt, but never a good friend to the English to this day, met with them at an Indian town called Namasket, fourteen miles west of this, and whether out of envy of them or malice to the English began to quarrel with them, and threatened to stab Hobbamok; but he, being a strong man, cleared himself of him, and came running away, all sweating, and told the Governor what had befallen him, and that he feared they had killed Squanto, for they threatened them both, for no other reason than that they were friends to the English and serviceable to them.

The Governor taking counsel, it was decided not to pass it over, for if they allowed their friends and messengers to be harmed, none would associate with them or give them intelligence or do them service afterwards; and next thing the Indians would fall upon them, too. So it was resolved to send the Captain and fourteen men, well armed, and to go and fall upon them in the night; and if they found that Squanto was killed, to cut off Corbitant's

---

[6] Hobbamok, one of Massasoyt's trusted councilors, shared with Squanto the tasks which devolved on them as interpreters, guides, and liaison men. They played the English and the several tribes of Indians skillfully against each other, conscious of the power which their position gave them, and not losing sight of their own interests. There was considerable rivalry between them to do favors for one group or another, with a view to appropriate reward. Hobbamok lived in the Standish household, as the Captain's special aide, while Squanto was the Governor's "man."

head, but not to hurt any but those who had a hand in it. Hobbamok was asked if he would go and be their guide, and bring them there before day. He said he would, and could show them the house where Corbitant lived, and which he was.

They set forth on the 14th of August, and surrounded the house; and the Captain, giving orders to let none escape, entered to search for him. But he had gone away that day; so they missed him, but learned that Squanto was alive, and that Corbitant had only threatened to kill him, and made as if to stab him, but did not. So they withheld their punishment, and did no more harm; and the people came trembling and brought them the best provisions they had, when they had been acquainted by Hobbamok with their purpose. Three Indians, badly wounded, broke out of the house, and tried to pass through the guard. These they brought back with them, and had their wounds dressed and cured, and then sent them home. After this they had many greetings from various sachems and much firmer peace. Even the Indians of the Island of Capawack sent to declare friendship; and Corbitant himself used the mediation of Massasoyt to make his peace, but was shy to come near them for a long time after.

After this, on the 18th September, they sent out their shallop with ten men and Squanto as guide and interpreter to Massachusetts, to explore the bay and trade with the natives, which they accomplished, and were kindly received. The Indians were much afraid of the Tarantines,[7] a tribe to the eastward, who used to come at harvest time and take away their corn, and often kill some of them. They returned in safety, and brought home a good quan-

---

[7] This was a fierce tribe living along the Maine coast.

tity of beaver, and reported on the place, wishing they could have settled there. But it seems that the Lord, Who assigns to all men the bounds of their habitations, had appointed it for another use. And thus they found the Lord to be with them in all their ways, and to bless their outgoings and incomings, for which let His holy name have the praise forever, to all posterity.

They began now to gather in the small harvest they had, and to prepare their houses for the winter, being well recovered in health and strength, and plentifully provisioned; for while some had been thus employed in affairs away from home, others were occupied in fishing for cod, bass, and other fish, of which they caught a good quantity, every family having their portion. All the summer there was no want. And now, as winter approached, wild fowl began to arrive, of which there were plenty when they came here first, though afterwards they became more scarce. As well as wild fowl, they got abundance of wild turkeys, besides venison, etc. Each person had about a peck of meal a week, or now, since harvest, Indian corn in that proportion; and afterwards many wrote at length about their plenty to their friends in England—not feigned but true reports.[8]

In November, about twelve months after their arrival, there came a small ship unexpectedly, bringing Mr. Cushman (so much spoken of before), and with him thirty-five persons to remain and live in the plantation; at which they

---

[8] Although not mentioned by Bradford, it was at this time that the first harvest festival, later to become Thanksgiving Day, was celebrated, with Massasoyt and his braves participating. There was plentiful and varied food, but none of the items subsequently associated with Thanksgiving—turkey, cranberry sauce, and pumpkin pie—graced the tables this year.

rejoiced not a little. And the new arrivals, when they came ashore and found all well, and saw plenty of victuals in every house, were no less glad. Most of them were healthy young men, many of them wild enough, who had little considered what they were undertaking—till they reached the harbor of Cape Cod, and there saw nothing but a naked and barren place. They then began to wonder what would become of them, should the people be dead or cut off by the Indians. So, hearing what some of the sailors were saying, they began to plot to seize the sails, lest the ship should go and leave them there. But the captain, hearing of it, gave them good words, and told them that if any misfortune should have befallen the people here, he thought he had food enough to take them to Virginia, and whilst he had a bit, they should have their share, which satisfied them. So they were all landed; but they brought not so much as biscuitcake, or any other victuals with them, nor any bedding, except some poor things they had in their cabins; nor pot nor pan to cook any food in; nor many clothes, for many of them had sold their coats and cloaks at Plymouth on their way out. But some burching-lane [9] suits were sent over in the ship, out of which they were supplied. The plantation was glad of this addition of strength, but could have wished that many of them had been of better class, and all of them better furnished with provisions; but that could not now be helped.

In this ship Mr. Weston sent a long letter to Mr. Carver, the late Governor, now deceased, full of complaints and expostulations about the former troubles at Southampton,

---

[9] The word is derived from Birchover Lane, a center of the clothing business in London.

and keeping the ship so long in the country, and returning her without lading, etc.—most of which for brevity I omit. The rest is as follows.

Mr. Weston in England to Mr. John Carver at New Plymouth:

I never dared acquaint the adventurers with the alterations in the conditions first agreed on between us, which I have since been very glad of, for I am well assured that had they known as much as I do, they would not have ventured a halfpenny of what was necessary for this ship. That you sent no lading back with the ship is strange, and very properly resented. I know your weakness was the cause of it; and I believe more weakness of judgment than weakness of hands. A quarter of the time you spent in discoursing, arguing, and consulting, would have done much more; but that is past. . . . If you mean, bona fide, to perform the conditions agreed upon, do us the favor to copy them out fair, and subscribe them with the names of your principal members and likewise give us account, as particularly as you can, how our money was laid out. Then I shall be able to give them some satisfaction, while I am now forced to put them off with good words. And consider that the life of this business depends on the lading of this ship. If you do so satisfactorily, so that I may recoup the great sums I disbursed for the former voyage, and must do for this one, I promise you I will never forsake this enterprise, though all the other adventurers should do so.

We have procured you a charter,[10] the best we could, which is better than the former, and with less limitations. As for anything else that is worth writing, Mr. Cushman

---

[10] This was the patent to replace the one the Pilgrims brought over with them, which specified settlement in Virginia.

can inform you. I pray write instantly for Mr. Robinson to come to you. And so, praying God to bless you with all graces necessary both for this life and that to come, I rest,

> Your very loving friend,
> THOS. WESTON.

London, July 6th, 1621.

This ship, called the *Fortune,* was speedily despatched back, laden with good clapboard, as full as she could stow, and two hogsheads of beaver and otter skins,[11] which they had traded in exchange for a few trifling commodities brought with them at first, being otherwise altogether unprovided for trading; nor was there a man among them who had ever seen a beaver skin till they came here, and were instructed by Squanto. The freight was estimated to be worth nearly £500. Mr. Cushman returned with the ship, as Mr. Weston and the rest had commissioned him, for their better information. And neither he nor the settlers doubted that they would receive speedy supplies, considering that, owing to Mr. Cushman's persuasion, and to letters which they had received from the congregation at Leyden, urging them to do so, they agreed to the aforesaid conditions, and signed them. But it proved otherwise, for Mr. Weston, who had made that large promise in his letter, that if all the rest should drop out, he would never quit the business, but would stick to them if they signed the conditions and sent some lading on the ship—and of this Mr. Cushman was equally confident, confirming it by Mr. Weston's own words and serious protestations to himself before he left—all this, I say, proved but wind, for

---

[11] In addition, bear, marten, deer, and black wolf were skins in demand for the fur trade.

he was the first and only man that forsook them, and that before he had so much as heard of the return of the ship, or knew what had been done. So vain is confidence in man! But of this, more in its place.

A letter in answer to that written by Mr. Weston to Mr. Carver was sent from the Governor, of which so much as is pertinent to the thing in hand I will insert here:

Governor Bradford at New Plymouth to Mr. Weston in England:

Sir,

Your long letter written to Mr. Carver, and dated July 6th, 1621, I received on November 10th, wherein, after the apology made for yourself, you lay many imputations upon him and us all. Touching him, he is now departed this life, and is at rest in the Lord from all these troubles and encumbrances with which we yet strive. He needs not my apology; for his care and pains were so great for the common good, both ours and yours, that as it is thought, he thereby oppressed himself and shortened his days; of whose loss we cannot sufficiently complain. At great expense in this adventure I confess you have been, and many losses may sustain; but the loss of his and many other industrious men's lives cannot be valued at any price. Of the one there may be hope of recovery, but the other no recompense can make good. However, I will not confine myself to general statements, but will deal with your particular charges.

You greatly blame us for keeping the ship so long in the country, and then sending her away empty. She lay five weeks at Cape Cod, whilst with many a weary step, after a long journey and the endurance of many a hard brunt we sought out in the depth of winter a place of habitation. Then we set about, as well as we could, to provide shelter for ourselves and our goods upon which task many of our arms and legs can tell us to this day that we were not negligent! But it pleased God to visit us then with death daily, and with a disease so disastrous that the living were scarcely able to bury the dead, and the healthy not in any measure to tend the sick. And now to be so greatly blamed for not freighting the ship touches us near and discourages us much. But you say you know we shall plead weakness; and do you think we had not cause? Yes, you tell us you believe it—but that it was more weakness of judgment than of hands! Our weakness herein is great, we confess; therefore we will bear this rebuke patiently, with the rest, till God send us wiser men. But those who told you we spent so much time in discoursing and consulting, etc., their hearts can tell their tongues they lie. They care not, so that they salve their own sores, how they wound others. Indeed it is our calamity that we are, beyond expectation, yoked with some ill-disposed people, who, while they do no good themselves, corrupt and abuse others.

The rest of the letter stated that they had subscribed to the conditions according to his desire, and sent him the previous accounts very exactly; also how the ship was laden, and in what condition their affairs stood; that the arrival of the new people would bring famine upon them unavoidably, if they did not receive supplies in time— as Mr. Cushman could more fully inform him and the rest of the adventurers. Also that, seeing he was not satisfied in all his demands, he hoped offenses would be forgotten, and he would remember his promise, etc.

After the departure of this ship, which did not stay above fourteen days, the Governor and his assistant having disposed the new arrivals among several families as best they could, took an exact account of all their provisions in store, and proportioned the same to the number of persons, and found that it would not hold out above six months at half allowance, and hardly that. They could not well give less this winter, till fish came in again. So they were presently put on half allowance, one as well as another. It became irksome, but they bore it patiently, hoping to receive fresh supplies.

Soon after this ship's departure, the great Narragansett tribe, in a braving manner, sent a messenger to them with a bundle of arrows tied about with a great snake skin, which their interpreters told them was a threatening challenge. Upon which the Governor, with the advice of the others, sent them a round answer, that if they would rather have war than peace, they might begin when they would; they had done them no wrong, neither did they fear them, nor would they find them unprepared. They sent the snake skin back by another messenger with bullets in it; but they would not receive it, and returned it again. These things I need merely mention, because they are fully dealt with in print [12] by Mr. Winslow, at the request of some friends. The reason was probably their own ambition, thinking, since the death of so many of the Indians, to domineer and lord it over the rest, and that the English would be a bar in their way, Massasoyt having taken shelter already under their wings.

But this made the settlers more careful to look to themselves. They agreed to enclose their dwellings in a good strong stockade and make flankers in convenient places, with gates to shut. These they locked every night and a watch was kept, and when need required there were also

---

[12] In *Good News from New England*, London, 1624. This was another rosy account of life at Plymouth.

outposts in the daytime. The colonists, at the Captain's and Governor's advice, were divided into four squadrons, and everyone had his quarter appointed, to which to repair at any sudden alarm; and in case of fire, a company with muskets was appointed as a guard, to prevent Indian treachery, whilst the others quenched it. This was accomplished very cheerfully, and the town was enclosed by the beginning of March, every family having a pretty garden plot.

Herewith I shall end this year—except to recall one more incident, rather amusing than serious. On Christmas Day,[13] the Governor called the people out to work as usual; but most of the new company excused themselves, and said it went against their consciences to work on that day. So the Governor told them, if they made it a matter of conscience, he would spare them till they were better informed. So he went with the rest, and left them; but on returning from work at noon he found them at play in the street, some pitching the bar, some at stool-ball, and such like sports. So he went to them and took away their games, and told them that it was against his conscience that they should play and others work. If they made the keeping of the day a matter of devotion, let them remain in their houses; but there should be no gaming and reveling in the streets. Since then, nothing has been attempted in that way, at least openly.

---

[13] The Pilgrims did not observe either Christmas Day or Easter, since, as they said, they could find no authorization in Scripture for such observance. They branded the celebration of these days as "Roman corruption" and declared that no one who participated in the customary rites could be called a true Christian.

"Now the wellcome time of harvest aproached, in which all had their hungrie bellies filled."

CHAPTER III

[*1622*]

They had arranged with the Massachusetts to go again and trade with them in the spring, and began to prepare for the voyage about the latter end of March. But Hobbamok, their Indian, told them that, from some rumors he had heard, he feared they had joined the Narragansetts and might betray them if they were not careful. He also intimated some suspicion of Squanto, from what he had observed of some private whisperings between him and other Indians. But they resolved to proceed, and sent out their shallop with ten of their chief men about the beginning of April, both Squanto and Habbamok with them, considering the jealousy between them. But they had not been gone long from the settlement, before an Indian belonging to Squanto's family came running in, apparently in great fear, and told them that many of the Narragansetts with Corbitant, and he thought also Massasoyt, were coming to attack them; and he got away to tell them, not without danger. And being examined by the Governor, he made as if the enemy were at hand, and kept looking back as if they were at his heels. At which the Governor ordered the settlers to take arms and stand on their guard; and believing the boat would be still within hearing, since it was calm, he caused a warning piece or two to be shot off, which they heard and returned. But no Indians appeared, and though watch was kept all night, nothing was seen. Hobbamok was confident of Massasoyt's good faith and thought it was all false. But the Governor had him send his wife privately to see what she could observe, on pretense of other purposes, but nothing was found and all was quiet. So they proceeded on their voyage to the Massachusetts and had good trade, and returned in safety, blessed be God!

But by what had passed they began to see that Squanto sought his own ends and played his own game, by frightening the Indians and getting gifts from them for himself, making them believe he could stir up war against them if he would, and make peace for whom he would. He even made them believe that the English kept the plague buried in the ground, and could send it among them whenever they wished, which terrified the Indians and made them more dependent on him than on Massasoyt. This made him envied, and was likely to have cost him his life; for after discovering this, Massasoyt sought it both privately and openly. This caused Squanto to stick close to the English, and he never dared leave them till he died. The colony also made good use of the emulation between Hobbamok and him, which made them behave more squarely, the Governor seeming to countenance the one and the Captain the other, by which they procured better intelligence and made them both more zealous in their service.

Now their provisions were practically all exhausted and they looked anxiously for supplies, but none came. About the latter end of May, however, they spied a boat at sea, which at first they thought was some Frenchman; but it proved to be a shallop which came from a ship which

Mr. Weston and another man had sent out fishing at a place called Damariscove,[1] 40 leagues to the eastward of them, where that year many ships had come to fish. This boat brought seven passengers and some letters, but no provisions and no hope of any. Part of this letter I will give.

Mr. Weston in England to Mr. John Carver at New Plymouth:

The *Fortune*, in which Mr. Cushman went—who I hope is with you, for we daily expect the ship back again—left England at the beginning of July with 35 persons, though not over well provided with necessaries owing to the parsimony of the adventurers. I have begged them to send you a supply of men and provisions before she returns. They all answer they will do great things when they hear good news—nothing before, so faithful, constant, and careful of your good are your old and honest friends, that if they hear not from you, they are not likely to send you supplies. . . . I will now explain the sending of this ship, hoping if you give me credit, you will have a more favorable opinion of the project than some here, whereof Pickering is one. . . . Mr. Beauchamp [2] and I have bought this little ship, and have fitted her out, partly, it may be, to benefit the plantation, and partly to recoup ourselves for former losses; though we are censured. . . . This is the reason we have sent this ship and these passengers, on our own account; and we desire you to entertain them and supply them with such necessaries as you can spare. . . . And among other things, pray lend or sell them some seed corn, or if you have some of the salt remaining from last year, let them have it for their present use, and we will

---

[1] Now Damariscove Island on the Maine coast.
[2] Pickering and Beauchamp were two of the merchant adventurers.

either pay you for it, or give you more when our salt pan is at work, which we want to have set up in one of the little islands in your bay. . . . We intend, if God please, and the others will not join us, to send within a month another ship, which, having discharged her passengers, will go to Virginia. . . . And perhaps we shall send a small ship to remain with you on the coast, which should be a great help to the plantation. In order that we may accomplish our endeavors, which will be also for your good, pray give them entertainment in your houses while they are with you, so that they may lose no time, but may at once proceed to fell trees and cleave them, so that lading may be ready, and the ship be not delayed.

Some of the adventurers have sent you herewith some directions for your furtherance in the common enterprise —like those whom St. James speaks of, that bid their brother eat, and warm himself, but give him nothing;[3] so they bid you make salt, and uphold the plantation, but send you no means wherewith to do it. . . . By the next ship we intend to send more people on our own account, and to take a patent; lest your people should be as inhuman as are some of the adventurers, and should not permit us to dwell with them, which would be such extreme barbarism that I will not let myself think you have any such Pickerings among you. Yet to satisfy our passengers I must perforce do it, and for some other reasons which I need not write. . . . I find the rest so backward, and your friends at Leyden so cold, that I fear you must stand on your own legs, and trust (as they say) to God and yourselves.

Subscribed,
Your loving friend,
THOS. WESTON.

---

[3] Epistle of James, II, 15, 16.

Several other things I pass over, being tedious and impertinent.

All this was but cold comfort with which to fill their hungry bellies and a slender performance of his recent promise, and as little did it either fill or warm them as those the Apostle James speaks of, to which he refers. And well might it make them remember what the psalmist says: "It is better to trust in the Lord than to have confidence in man." [4]

There came by the same ship other letters, but of later date, one from Mr. Weston and another from some of the other adventurers, as follows.

Mr. Weston in England to Mr. John Carver at New Plymouth:

Mr. Carver,

Since my last, in order that we might more readily help the company, at a meeting of some of the principal adventurers a proposition was made and agreed to by all present, except Pickering, that each man should further adventure the third part of what he had formerly done. Some others followed Pickering's example and would adventure no more. Therefore, the greater part of the adventurers being willing to support the enterprise, seeing no reason why those who were willing should carry on the business of those who were unwilling, and whose backwardness discouraged those who would go forward, and hindered other new adventurers from joining, we, having well considered the matter, have resolved according to the article in our agreement (that, by general consent, the adventurers and settlers for just cause may break off their joint stock), to break it off; and beg you to ratify and confirm the same

---

[4] Psalm CXVIII, 8.

on your parts. This being done we shall the more willingly proceed to provide you with necessary supplies. But in any case you must agree to the articles and send them back under your hands and seals by the first ship. So I end,

Your loving friend,
THOS. WESTON.

Jan. 17th, 1621.[5]

Another letter was written by part of the company of the adventurers to the same purpose, and subscribed with nine of their names, of which Mr. Weston's and Mr. Beauchamp's were two. This inconstancy and shuffling seemed strange, and it appeared there was some mystery in the matter. So the Governor concealed these letters from the public and only imparted them to some trusted friends for advice, who agreed with him that to inform them would tend to disband and scatter them in their present necessity; and if Mr. Weston and others like-minded should come over with shipping, provisioned as his letters suggested, most of the advantage would fall to him, to the prejudice of themselves and their friends and the rest of the adventurers, from whom as yet they had heard nothing. Indeed it was doubted whether he had not sent over the people in the former ship with this idea. However, they took compassion on the seven whom this ship, fishing to the eastward, had kept till planting time was over, so that it was too late for them to set their corn, and who brought no food, for they turned them ashore without any. Nor had the salt-pan come; so they could not accomplish any of the things which Mr. Weston had men-

---

[5] Modern style, 1622.

tioned, and might have starved if the plantation had not succored them. Their wants were supplied exactly as the rest of the settlers'. The ship went down to Virginia, where they sold both ship and fish, of the proceeds of which Mr. Weston received a very slender share, it is understood.

After this came another of his ships, bringing letters dated the 10th April, from Mr. Weston, as follows.

Mr. Weston in England to Governor Bradford at New Plymouth:

Mr. Bradford, these, etc.

The *Fortune* has arrived, whose good news concerning you I am very glad to hear. And though she was robbed on the way by the French, yet I hope your loss will not be great, for the prospect of so great a return much encourages the adventurers, so that I hope some matter of importance will be done by them. . . . As for myself, I have sold my adventure and debts to them, so I am quit of you, and you of me, for that matter. . . . And now, though I have no position as an adventurer amongst you, I will advise you a little for your good, if you like to avail yourselves of it. I know as well as any the disposition of your adventurers, whom the hope of gain has drawn on to what they have done; but I fear that hope will not draw them much further. Besides, most of them are against sending your friends at Leyden, in whose interests this business was first begun; and some of the most religious (for instance a Mr. Greene) takes exception to them. So that my advice is (you may follow it if you please) that you forthwith break off your joint stock, which you have the right to do both in law and conscience, since the majority of the adventurers have sanctioned it in a former letter. The resources you have there, which I hope will be to some purpose by means of this spring's trade, may, with the help of some friends here, meet the expense of transporting the Leyden contingent, and when they are with you I do not question but by God's help you will be able to subsist of yourselves. But I leave you to your own discretion.

I requested several of the adventurers, Mr. Pierce, Mr. Greene, and others, if they had anything to send you—such as food or letters—to send them by these ships; and wondering that they sent not so much as a letter, I asked our passengers what letters they had, and after some hesitation one of them told me he had one, which was delivered him with a great show of secrecy; and for its greater security he was told to buy a pair of new shoes, and sew it between the soles for fear of its being intercepted. I, taking the letter, wondering what mystery might be in it, broke it open and found this treacherous letter subscribed by the hands of Mr. Pickering and Mr. Greene. Had it come to your hands without comment, it might have injured, if not ruined, us all. For assuredly if you had followed their instructions, and had treated us as unkindly as they advise you to, distrusting us as enemies, etc., it might have set us together by the ears to our destruction. For I believe that in such a case, knowing the nature of past business between us, not only my brother, but others also, would have been violent and heady against you. . . . I meant to have settled the people I before and now send you, with or near you, for mutual security and defense and help on all occasions. But I find the adventurers so jealous and suspicious that I have altered my resolution, and have given orders to my brother and those with him to do as he and they shall find fit.

Your loving friend,
THOS. WESTON.

April 10th, 1621.

Part of Mr. Pickering's and Mr. Greene's letter to the Settlers at New Plymouth:

To Mr. Bradford and Mr. Brewster, etc.

    My dear love remembered to you all, etc.

The company has bought out Mr. Weston, and are very glad they are freed of a man who thought himself superior to the rest, and not expressing so much fear of God as was meet. I need say no more: a few words to the wise.

Mr. Weston will not permit letters to be sent in his ships, nor anything for your good or ours, since it would be contrary to his interests. His brother Andrew, whom he sends as principal in one of these ships, is a violent, heady young man, and set against you there and the company here. He and Mr. Weston plot their own ends, which tend to your and our undoing in respect of our estates there. We are informed by credible testimony that his purpose is to come out to your colony, pretending he comes for and from the adventurers, and will try to get whatever you have in readiness aboard his ships, as if they came from the company; and all will then be so much profit to himself. Further, they intend to inform themselves what special places or sources of profit you have discovered, so that they may suppress and deprive you. . . .

The Lord, who is the watchman of Israel and sleepeth not, preserve you and deliver you from unreasonable men. I am sorry that there is cause to admonish you of these things concerning this man; so I leave you to God, Who bless and multiply you into thousands, to the advancement of the glorious gospel of Our Lord Jesus. Amen. Farewell.

                    Your loving friends,
                        EDWARD PICKERING.
                        WILLIAM GREENE.

I pray conceal both the writing and delivery of this letter, but make the best use of it. *We hope to fit out a ship ourselves within this month.*

The following are of the chief points of Mr. Weston's comments on the foregoing letter:

Mr. Bradford, this is the letter I wrote you of, which to answer in every particular were needless and tedious. My own conscience and all our people can, and I think will, testify that my end in sending the ship *Sparrow* was your good. . . . Now I will not deny that there are many of our people rude fellows, as these men term them; yet I presume they will be governed by such as I set over them, and I hope not only to be able to reclaim them from their profaneness, but, by degrees, draw them to God. . . . I am so far from sending you rude fellows to deprive you either by fraud or violence of what is yours, that I have ordered the captain of the *Sparrow* to leave with you 2000 of bread, and a good quantity of fish.[6] . . . But I will leave it to you to consider what evil this letter might have done, had it come to your hands and taken the effect its writers desired.

Now if you be of the same mind as these men, deal plainly with us, and we will seek our residence elsewhere. If you are as friendly as we have thought you to be, give us the entertainment of friends and we will take nothing from you, neither meat, drink, nor lodging, without in some way or other paying you for it. . . I shall leave in the country a little ship, if God send her safe thither, with sailors and fishermen, to stay there to coast and trade with the savages and the old plantation. It may be we shall be as helpful to you as you will be to us. I think I shall see you next spring; so I commend you to the protection of God, Who ever keep you.

Your loving friend,
THOS. WESTON.

---

[6] But he did not leave his own men a bite of bread! (B.)

Thus all their hopes in regard to Mr. Weston were laid in the dust, and all his promised help turned into empty advice, which they saw it was neither lawful nor profitable for them to follow. And they were thus not only left destitute of help in their extreme want, having neither food nor anything to trade with, but others were preparing to glean up what the country might have afforded for their relief. As for the harsh censures and suspicions intimated in the former and following letters, they desired to judge them as charitably and wisely as they could, weighing them in the balance of love and reason; and though they came in part from godly and loving friends, they recognized that much might arise from overdeep jealousy and fear, or from provocation—though they saw clearly that Mr. Weston pursued his own ends and was embittered in spirit. After the receipt of the former letters the Governor received one from Mr. Cushman, who went home in the ship and was always intimate with Mr. Weston, as former passages prove. It had seemed strange that nothing was heard from him all this while; but it seems it was the difficulty of sending, for this letter was directed as if from a wife in England to her husband who was here, and was brought by him to the Governor. It was as follows.

Robert Cushman in England to Governor Bradford at New Plymouth:

Beloved Sir,
I heartily salute you, trusting you are well, and with many thanks for your love. By God's providence we got home safely on the 17th Feb., being robbed by the French on the way and taken by them into France, where we were kept fifteen days and lost all that we had that was worth taking. But thanks be to God we escaped with our lives and our ship. It does not seem to have discouraged

any here. I purpose by God's grace to see you shortly, I hope in June next or before. In the meantime consider well the following. Mr. Weston has quite broken off from our company, through some disagreement that arose between him and some of the other adventurers, and has sold all his adventurers and has now sent three small ships for his particular colony. Of the biggest of these, which is 100 tons, Mr. Reynolds is captain; Mr. Weston intends to come himself with the others—why I know not.

The people they take are no men for us, so I beg you not to entertain them nor to exchange men with them, except perhaps some of your worst. He has taken out a patent for himself. If they offer to buy anything of you let it be such as you can spare and let them give full value for it. If they borrow anything of you let them leave a good pawn. . . . It is probable he will settle southward of the Cape, for William Trevor [7] has lavishly told what he knew (or imagined) of Capawack, Monhegan and the Narragansetts. I fear these people will hardly deal as well with the savages as they should. I advise you therefore to signify to Squanto that they are a distinct body from us, and we have nothing to do with them; that we must not be blamed for their faults—much less can we warrant their fidelity. We are about to recover our losses in France. Our friends at Leyden are well, and as many as can will come this time. I hope all will turn out for the best, so I pray you not to be discouraged, but to meet these difficulties cheerfully and with courage, in that place wherein God has set you until the day of refreshing come. And the Lord God of sea and land bring us comfortably together again, if it may stand with His glory.

Yours,
Robert Cushman.

---

[7] Trevor, who came in the *Mayflower*, returned to England after a year.

On the other side of the leaf in the same letter, came these few lines from Mr. John Pierce, in whose name the patent here was taken, and of whom more will follow in its place.

John Pierce in England to Governor Bradford at New Plymouth:

Worthy Sir,
I desire you to take into consideration what is written on the other side, and in no way to let your own colony be contaminated, whose strength is but weakness and may therefore be more enfeebled. As for the Letters of Association, by the next ship we send I hope you will receive satisfaction; in the meantime, whom you admit I will approve. As for Mr. Weston's company, I think them so inferior for the most part that they do not seem fit for honest men's company. I hope they may prove otherwise. It is not my purpose to write at length, but cease in these few lines, and so rest,
Your loving friend,
JOHN PIERCE.

All this they considered carefully; but they decided to give the men friendly entertainment, partly out of regard for Mr. Weston himself, considering what he had done for them, and partly out of compassion for the people, who had come into a wilderness (as they themselves had before) and were presently to be put ashore altogether ignorant of what to do.[8] The ship was then to carry other passengers to Virginia. So, as they had received Mr.

---

[8] Sharing their reduced stores with these strangers, who had come without provisions, meant that the Pilgrims had to decrease their own rations to a near-starvation level. How this generosity was repaid will be seen later.

Weston's former company of seven men, and victualed them as their own hitherto, they received these—about sixty strong men—and gave them housing for themselves and their goods; and many of them who were sick had the best the place could afford them. They stayed most of the summer, till the ship came back again from Virginia; then by the direction of those set over them, they moved to Massachusetts Bay,[9] where Mr. Weston had obtained a patent for some land on the strength of reports which he had got in some of the letters previously sent home. They left all their sick folk here till they were settled and housed. But of the provisions of this contingent the New Plymouth Colony accepted none—though they were in great want—nor anything else in return for any courtesy rendered by them; nor did they desire it, for they were an unruly company, without proper government, and would inevitably soon fall into want, if Mr. Weston did not come out to them. So, to prevent all chance of subsequent trouble, they would accept nothing from them.

In these straits, deserted by those from whom they had hoped for supplies, and famine beginning to pinch them severely, the Lord, Who never fails His, provided assistance beyond all expectation. A boat which came from the eastward brought them a letter from a stranger whose name they had never heard before, the captain of a fishing ship. This letter was as follows.

Captain John Huddleston to the Colony at New Plymouth:
To all good friends at New Plymouth, these, etc.,
    Friends, Countrymen, and Neighbors,
I salute you and wish you all health and happiness in the Lord. I make bold to trouble you with these lines, because

---
[9] The Weston colony was at Wessagusset, now Weymouth.

unless I were inhuman I could do no less. Bad news spreads itself too far; but still, I may inform you that I and many good friends in the south colony of Virginia, have sustained such a loss as the lives of 400 persons would not suffice to make good. Therefore I hope, although not knowing you, that the old rule which I learnt at school may be sufficient: that is—Happy is he whom other men's ills doth make to beware! And now again and again wishing all those that willingly would serve the Lord all health and happiness in the world, and everlasting peace in the world to come, I rest,

      Yours,
       JOHN HUDDLESTON.

By this boat the Governor returned a grateful answer, and also sent a boat of their own with Mr. Winslow, to procure what he could from the ships. He was kindly received by the captain, who not only spared what provisions he could but wrote to others to do the same. By this means he got a good quantity and returned in safety. Thus the plantation had a double benefit: first, they were refreshed at the time by the food obtained; secondly, they knew the way to those parts to their advantage thereafter. What this small boat brought, divided among so many, came to but little; still, by God's blessing it sustained them until harvest. It amounted to a quarter of a pound of bread a day for each person; and the Governor had it given out daily, otherwise, had it been in their own custody, they would have eaten it up and then starved. In this way with what else they could get they made fair shift till their corn was ripe.

This summer they built a fort with good timber—a handsome building and a good defense made with a flat roof and battlement, on which their ordnance was mounted, and where they kept constant watch, especially in time of danger. It served them also as a meeting house and was fitted accordingly for that use. It was a big undertaking for them at this period of weakness and want; but the dangerous times necessitated it; and the continual rumors about the Indians here, especially the Narragansetts, and also the news of the great massacre in Virginia, made all hands willing to complete it.

Now the welcome time of harvest approached, in which all had their hungry bellies filled. But it amounted to but little compared with a full year's supply, partly because they were not yet used to the culture of Indian corn (they had no other), partly owing to their many other employments; but chiefly their weakness for want of food prevented them from cultivating it as they should have done. Again, much was stolen even before it became eatable, and much more afterwards—and though many were well whipped when they were caught stealing a few ears of corn, hunger drove others to it, whom conscience did not restrain. It was quite clear that famine would prevail again next year if not prevented, or if their supplies, to which they dare not trust, should fail. Markets there were none to go to, except the Indians; and even then they had no trading commodities.

Behold now another providence of God. A ship comes into the harbor in charge of a Captain Jones, fitted out by some merchants to discover all the harbors between here and Virginia and the shoals of Cape Cod, and to trade along the coast where they could. This ship had supplies of English beads, which were then good trade, and some knives—though the Captain would sell none except at high prices and in large quantities. But they were so glad of the chance that they were willing to buy at any rate—even at a premium of 100 percent, if not more, and even then to sell coat-beaver at three shillings per pound, which a few years after fetched twenty shillings. By this means they were able again to trade for beaver and other things, and intended to buy what corn they could.

But I will here take the liberty of making a little digression. There was aboard this ship a gentleman, by name Mr. John Pory,[10] who had been secretary in Virginia, and was now going home as a passenger. After his departure he wrote a letter to the Governor, in the postscript of which were these lines:

To yourself and Mr. Brewster I must acknowledge myself much indebted, and would have you feel that his books are well bestowed on one who esteems them such jewels. My haste would not suffer me to remember, much less to ask for, Mr. Ainsworth's elaborate work upon the five Books of Moses. Both his and Mr. Robinson's highly commend the authors, as conversant with the Scriptures above all others. And who knows what good it may please God to work by them, through my unworthy hands, who finds such high content in them. God have you all in His keeping.

Your unfeigned and firm friend,
JOHN PORY.

Aug. 28th, 1622.

This I insert here in honor of the author's memory, which this gentleman thus ingenuously acknowledges; and he, upon his return, did the plantation much credit amongst men of no mean rank. But to return.

Shortly after harvest, Mr. Weston's people, who were

---

[10] Pory, a member of Parliament, had traveled to Virginia, and became speaker of the first elected assembly in the New World, that which met in Jamestown in 1619.

now settled in Massachusetts, and had, by disorder as it seems, made havoc of their provisions, began now to realize that want would press them. Finding that the people here had bought trading commodities, and intended to trade for corn, they wrote to the Governor and asked that they might join them in trading, employing their small ship for the purpose; and further requested them either to lend or to sell them some of their trading commodities in return, and they would undertake to make payment when Mr. Weston or their supplies should come. The Governor agreed to do so upon equal terms, intending to go round the Cape southwards with the ship, where corn might be got. Captain Standish was appointed to go with them, and Squanto as a guide and interpreter, about the latter end of September; but the winds drove them in; and putting out again, Captain Standish fell ill with fever, so the Governor went himself. But they could not get round the shoals of Cape Cod, for flats and breakers, and Squanto could not direct them better. The captain of the boat dare not venture any further, so they put into Manamoick Bay, and got what they could there.

Here Squanto fell ill of Indian fever, bleeding much at the nose—which the Indians take for a symptom of death—and within a few days he died. He begged the Governor to pray for him, that he might go to the Englishmen's God in heaven, and bequeathed several of his things to some of his English friends, as remembrances. His death was a great loss.

On this voyage they got in one place or another about twenty-six or twenty-eight hogsheads of corn and beans, which was more than the Indians could well spare hereabouts, for they sowed but little till they got English hoes. So they had to return, disappointed that they could not get round the Cape and were not better laden. Afterwards the Governor took a few men and went to inland places to get what he could, to be fetched home in the spring, which was some help.

In February a messenger came from John Sanders, who was left in charge of Mr. Weston's men at the Bay of Massachusetts, bringing a letter telling of the great want they had fallen into. He wished to borrow a hogshead of corn from the Indians, but they would lend him none. He asked whether he might not take it from them by force to supply his men till he returned from the east, where he was going. The Governor and the rest dissuaded him strongly, for it might exasperate the Indians and endanger their safety, and all might smart for it. Already it had been rumored how they had wronged the Indians by stealing their corn, etc., and that they were much incensed against them. But so depraved were some of Mr. Weston's people, that they went and told the Indians that the Governor intended to come and take their corn by force. This and other things made them enter into a conspiracy against the English, of which more in the next chapter. Herewith I end this year.

"—the vanitie of that conceite of Platos and other ancients —that ye taking away of propertie, and bringing in comunitie into a comone wealth, would make them happy and flourishing; as if they were wiser then God."

CHAPTER IV

[*1623*]

It may be thought strange that the Weston colony should have fallen into such extremity in so short a time, being fully provided when the ship left them, in addition to their share of the corn which was got by trade, besides much that they got by one means or another from the Indians where they lived. It must needs have been their lack of order, spending excessively whilst they had it, and may be wasting part among the Indians—for the chief man amongst them was said to keep Indian women, how truly I know not. Then, when they began to want, many sold their clothes and bed-coverings; others—so depraved were they—became servants to the Indians, cutting them wood and fetching them water for a capful of corn; others fell to plain stealing from the Indians of which they complained grievously. In the end some starved and died with cold and hunger; one in gathering shellfish was so weak he stuck fast in the mud, and was found dead in the place; at last most of them left their dwellings, and scattered up and down in the woods and by the water-side, a few here and a few there, wherever they could find groundnuts and clams.

The Indians scorned them for such conduct, and began to insult them in a most insolent manner. Often, while they were cooking a pot of groundnuts or shellfish, when it was ready, the Indians would come and eat it up; and at night they would come and steal the blankets from such few as had them, and let them lie in the cold. Their condition was very lamentable, and in the end, in order to satisfy the Indians, they were obliged to hang one of their men whom they could not keep from stealing.

While things went on thus, the Governor and the people here had notice that their friend Massasoyt was sick, and near to death. They visited him, and took whatever they could to relieve him; and he recovered. He then discovered a conspiracy amongst the Indians of Massachusetts, and other neighboring tribes with whom they had conspired, to wipe out Mr. Weston's people, in revenge for the continual injuries they did them, taking opportunity of their weakness to do it. And believing that the people at New Plymouth would avenge their death, they decided to do the same by them, and had solicited Massasoyt to join them. He advised them to prevent it, by speedily capturing some of the chief of the conspirators before it was too late, for he assured them of the truth of it.

This troubled them much, and they took it into serious deliberation, and upon examination found other evidence too long to relate. In the meantime one of Mr. Weston's people came from Massachusetts, with a small pack on his back; and though he did not know a foot of the way, he got here safe. He lost his way, which was well for him, for, though pursued, he was missed. He told them here how everything stood among them, and that he dared stay no longer. He believed, by what he observed, they would all be knocked on the head shortly.

So the people at New Plymouth made the more haste, and they despatched a boat with Captain Standish and some men, who found them in a miserable condition out of which he rescued them, and killed some few of the chief conspirators among the Indians, and according to his order, offered to bring the remnant of the Weston settlement here if they thought well, in which case they should fare no worse than the colonists themselves, till Mr. Weston or some supplies came to them. Or, if they preferred any other course, he was to give them any assistance he could. They thanked him, but most of them begged he would give them some corn so that they could go with their small ship to the eastward, where they might hear of Mr. Weston or get some supplies from him, since it was the time of the year for the fishing ships to be in that region. If not, they would work among the fishermen for their living, and get their passage back to England, if they heard nothing from Mr. Weston in the meantime. So he put aboard what they had, and he got them all the corn he could, scarcely leaving enough to bring himself home, and saw them well out of the bay, under sail at sea. Then he came back, not accepting a penny worth of anything from them. I have but touched these things briefly because they have been published in print more completely already.

This was the end of those who at one time boasted of their strength—all able, lusty men—and what they would do in comparison with the people here, who had many women and children and weak ones among them, and who had said, on their first arrival, when they saw the want here, that they would take a very different course and not to fall into any such condition as these simple people had come to. But a man's way is not in his own hands. God can make the weak to stand: let him also that standeth take heed lest he fall!

Shortly after, when he heard of the ruin and destitution of his colony, Mr. Weston came over with some of the fishermen, under another name, and disguised as a blacksmith. He got a boat, and with a man or two came to see how things were there. But on the way ashore he was caught in a storm, and his shallop was sunk in the bay between Merrimac river and Piscataqua,[1] and he barely escaped with his life. Afterwards he fell into the hands of the Indians, who robbed him of all that he had saved from the wreck, and stripped him of all his clothes to his shirt. At last he got to Piscataqua and borrowed a suit of clothes, and so came to New Plymouth. A strange alteration there was in him, to such as had seen him in his former flourishing condition; so uncertain are the mutable things of this unstable world! And yet men set their hearts upon them, though they daily see their vanity.

After many arguments and much discourse—former troubles boiling in his mind and rankling there, as was discerned—he asked to borrow some beaver from them, and told them he had hopes that a ship with good supplies was on its way to him, and that then they should have anything they stood in need of. They gave little credit to his report of supplies, but pitied his condition and remembered former courtesies. They pointed out to him their own wants, and said they did not know when they might get any supplies. He well knew, also, how the case stood between them and the adventurers in England. They had

---

[1] Near the present site of Portsmouth.

not much beaver, and if they should let him have it, it would be enough to cause a mutiny among their people, since there were no other means of procuring them the food and clothes which they so much wanted. Nevertheless, they told him they would help him, considering his necessity; but that it must be done secretly for the above reasons. So they let him have 100 beaver skins, which weighed 170 lbs. odd. Thus they helped him when all the world failed him; and with this he went again to the ships, and supplied his small ship and some of his men, and bought provisions and fitted himself out; and it was this supply alone which enabled him to pursue his course thereafter. But he requited them ill, proving himself a bitter enemy upon every opportunity, and never repaying them to this day—except in reproaches and calumnies.

All this while no supplies were heard of, nor did they know when they might expect any. So they began to consider how to raise more corn, and obtain a better crop than they had done, so that they might not continue to endure the misery of want. At length after much debate, the Governor, with the advice of the chief among them, allowed each man to plant corn for his own household, and to trust to themselves for that; in all other things to go on in the general way as before. So every family was assigned a parcel of land, according to the proportion of their number with that in view—for present purposes only, and making no division for inheritance—all boys and children being included under some family. This was very successful. It made all hands very industrious, so that much more corn was planted than otherwise would have been by any means the Governor or any other could devise, and saved him a great deal of trouble, and gave far better satisfaction. The women now went willingly into the field, and took their little ones with them to plant corn, while before they would allege weakness and inability; and to have compelled them would have been thought great tyranny and oppression.

The failure of this experiment of communal living, which was tried for several years, and by good and honest men proves the emptiness of the theory of Plato and other ancients, applauded by some of later times—that the taking away of private property, and the possession of it in community, by a commonwealth, would make a state happy and flourishing; as if they were wiser than God. For in this instance, community of property (so far as it went) was found to breed much confusion and discontent, and retard much employment which would have been to the general benefit and comfort. For the young men who were most able and fit for service objected to being forced to spend their time and strength in working for other men's wives and children, without any recompense. The strong man or the resourceful man had no more share of food, clothes, etc., than the weak man who was not able to do a quarter the other could. This was thought injustice. The aged and graver men, who were ranked and equalized in labor, food, clothes, etc., with the humbler and younger ones, thought it some indignity and disrespect to them. As for men's wives who were obliged to do service for other men, such as cooking, washing their clothes, etc., they considered it a kind of slavery, and many husbands would not brook it. This feature of it would have been worse still, if they had been men of an inferior class.

If (it was thought) all were to share alike, and all were to do alike, then all were on an equality throughout, and one was as good as another; and so, if it did not actually abolish those very relations which God himself has set among men, it did at least greatly diminish the mutual respect that is so important should be preserved amongst them. Let none argue that this is due to human failing, rather than to this communistic plan of life in itself. I answer, seeing that all men have this failing in them, that God in His wisdom saw that another course was fitter for them.

But to return. After this had been settled, and their corn was planted in this way, all their food supplies were consumed, and they had to rely upon God's providence, often at night not knowing where to get a bit of anything next day; and so, as one well observed, they had need above all people in the world to pray to God that He would give them their daily bread. Yet they bore their want with great patience and cheerfulness of spirit, and that for upwards of two years; which reminds me of what Peter Martyr writes in praise of the Spaniards, in his *Fifth Decade*, page 208.[2] "They," says he, "led a miserable life five days together, with the parched grain of maize only," and concludes, "that such pains, such labor, and such hunger, he thought none living, who was not a Spaniard could have endured." But alas! these colonists, when they had maize —that is Indian corn—thought it as good as a feast; and not only lacked bread for days at a time, but sometimes for two or three months continuously were without bread or any kind of corn. Indeed, in another place—his *Second Decade*, page 94, the same writer mentions how some others were even worse put to it, and ate dogs, toads, and dead men—and so died almost all. From these extremities

---

[2] Peter Martyr, an Italian courtier and scholar, who held high offices in Spain until his death in 1526, was the author of a Latin account of the New World, that covered the first thirty years of discovery and exploration in America.

the Lord in His goodness kept these His people, and in their great need preserved both their lives and their health; let His name have the praise. Yet let me here make use of the same writer's conclusion, which in a manner may be applied to the people of this colony: "That with their miseries they opened a way to these new lands; and after these hardships, with what ease other men came to inhabit them, owing it to the calamities which these forerunners had suffered; so that they who followed seemed to go, as it were, to a bride feast, where all things are provided for them."

As for fishing, having but one boat left, and she not very well fitted, they were divided into several crews, six or seven to a crew, who went out with a net they had bought, to catch bass and other fish, each party taking its turn. No sooner was the boat emptied of what she had brought, than the next crew took her and went out with her, not returning till they had caught something, even though it were five or six days, for they knew there was nothing at home, and to go home empty would be a great disappointment to the rest. They tried who could do best. If she stayed long or got little, then all went to seeking shellfish, which at low water they dug out of the sands. This was what they lived on in the summer time, till God sent them better; and in winter there were groundnuts and fowl to help them out. In the summer now and then they got a deer, one or two of the fittest being told off to hunt in the woods. What was got in that way was divided among them.

At length they received a letter from the adventurers, too long and tedious to record here in full, which told of their further crosses and frustrations, beginning in this manner.

The Adventurers in England to the Settlers at New Plymouth:

Loving Friends,

As your sorrows and afflictions have been great, so our crosses and interruptions in our proceedings here have not been small. After we had, with much trouble and expense, sent the *Parragon* away to sea, and thought all the trouble was at an end, about fourteen days after, she returned leaking dangerously and battered with storms, so that she had to be put into dock and have £100 spent on her. All the passengers lay upon our hands for six or seven weeks, and much discontent was occasioned. But we trust all will be well, and result to our mutual advantage, if you can wait with patience and have but strength to hold on to life. While these things were happening, Mr. Weston's ship came, and brought various letters from you. . . We rejoice to hear the good reports that many have brought home about you. . . .

This letter was dated December 21st, 1622.

This ship was brought out by Mr. John Pierce, and fitted out at his own expense, in hope of doing great things. The passengers and goods which the company had sent in her he took aboard as freight, arranging to land them here. This was the man in whose name the colony's first patent was taken out, because of the acquaintance of their friends with him, though his name was only used in trust. But when he saw that they were settled here thus hopefully, and by the success God gave them had obtained the favor of the Council of New England, he goes to the Council, as if on behalf of the settlers—asks them for another patent, much more extensive, which he thus easily obtained. But he meant to keep it to himself, and allow the colonists what he pleased to grant them as his tenants, and sue to the courts as chief lord, as will appear by what follows. But the Lord prevented him; for after the first return of the ship, and the expenses above mentioned, when she was fitted again, he takes in more passengers, and those not very good, to try and meet his losses, and sets out a second time. But what the result was will appear in another letter from one of the chief members of the company, dated 9th of April, 1623, written to the Governor here, as follows:

Loving Friend,

When I sent my last letter, I hoped to have received one from you by this time; though when I wrote in December, I little thought I should see Mr. John Pierce till he brought tidings of you. But it pleased God that he brought us only the woeful tidings of his return, driven back by violent storms when he was half way over, wherein the goodness and mercy of God appeared in sparing their lives—in all 109 souls! The loss is great to Mr. Pierce, and the company is put to great expense. . . .

At last, with great trouble and loss, we have got Mr. John Pierce to assign to the Company the grand patent which he had taken in his own name, the former grant being made void. I am sorry to write that many here think that the hand of God was justly against him, both the first and second time of his return; for it appears that he, whom you and we so confidently trusted only to use his name for the company, should actually aspire to be supreme over us all, and to make you and us tenants at his will and pleasure, our patent having been annulled by his means. I desire to judge charitably of him; but his unwillingness to part with his royal lordship, and the high rate he put it at, which was £500—it cost him 50—makes many speak hardly of him. The company are out for goods in his ship, with expense of passengers, £640. . . .

We have hired from two merchants a ship of 140 tons, called the *Anne*, which is to be ready the last of this month, to bring sixty passengers and 60 tons of goods. . . .

This is their own judgment of the man's proceedings. I thought it better to describe them in their words than my own. Yet, though no other compensation was got from him than the reversion of this patent and the shares he had in the adventure, he was never quiet, but sued them in the chief courts of England, and when he was still frustrated, brought it before Parliament. But he is now dead, and I will leave him to the Lord.

His ship was in greater extremity at sea, during her second attempted passage, than one could often hear of—without being wrecked—as I have been informed by Mr. William Pierce who was then captain of her, and by many others who were passengers on her. It was about the middle of February. The storm lasted for fourteen days altogether; but for two or three days and nights continuously it was of fearful violence. After they had cut down their mast, their round house and all their upper works were swept away; three men had all they could do to keep the helm, and the man who held the ship before the wind was obliged to be bound fast to prevent him from washing away. The seas so over-raked them, that many times those on the deck did not know whether they were within board or without; and once she was so foundered in the sea that they all thought she would never rise again. But yet the Lord preserved them, and brought them at last safe to Portsmouth, to the wonder of all who saw what a state she was in, and heard what they had endured.

About the latter end of June there arrived a ship, with Captain Francis West,[3] commissioned to be Admiral of New England, to restrain interlopers and such fishing ships

---

[3] A brother of Lord De la Warr, who had explored the coast south of the mouth of the Hudson in 1610, and from whom Delaware derived its name.

as came to fish and trade without a license from the Council of New England, for which rights they were to be made to pay a substantial sum of money. But he could do no good with them; they were too strong for him, and he found the fishermen stubborn fellows; and their owners, upon complaint made to Parliament, procured an order that fishing should be free.[4] He told the Governor they spoke with a ship at sea and were aboard her, which was coming to this settlement, in which there were several passengers; he wondered she had not arrived and feared some mischance, for they parted company in a storm shortly after they had been aboard. This report filled them with fear, though they still had hopes. The captain of this ship had some two hogshead of peas to sell, but seeing their need he held them at £9 sterling a hogshead, and would not take under £8, and yet he wanted to buy their beaver at less than the market rate. So they told him they had lived so long without, they would do so still, rather than give such an unreasonable price. So he went on to Virginia.

About fourteen days after, the ship called the *Anne* arrived, of which Mr. William Pierce was captain; and about a week or ten days later came the pinnace [5] which they had lost in foul weather at sea—a fine new vessel, of about forty-four tons, which the company had built to stay in the country. They brought about sixty settlers for the colony, some of them very useful persons, who became good members to the body, and some were the wives and children of those who were here already. Some of the new settlers were so unruly, that they were obliged to go to the expense of sending them home again the next year.

---

[4] This was part of the general movement in England against the royal granting of monopolies or exclusive rights and privileges.
[5] This was the *James*.

Besides these there were a number who did not belong to the general body, but came on their own resources, and were to have lands assigned to them, to work for themselves, but subject to the general government. This caused some differences, as will appear. I shall here again take the liberty to insert a few things out of letters which came in this ship, desiring to give account of things in their own words as much as may be.

Robert Cushman in England to the Settlers at New Plymouth:

Beloved Friends,

I kindly salute you all, with trust of your healths and welfare. I am sorry that no supplies have been sent to you all this time, and in explanation I must refer you to our general letters. Nor have we now sent you all that we would, for want of money. But there are people more than enough—though not all are fit to go—for people come flying in upon us, but money comes creeping in. Some few of your old friends have come. . . . So they come dropping to you, and by degrees, I hope ere long, you will enjoy them all. As people are pressing so hard upon us to go, and often they are none of the fittest, I pray you write earnestly to the treasurer, and direct what persons should be sent. It grieves me to see so weak a company sent you, and yet had I not been here, they would have been weaker. You must still call upon the company here to see that honest men are sent you, and threaten to send back others. . . . In no way are we in such danger as from corrupt and disorderly persons. Such and such came without consent; but the importunity of their friends got our treasurer's word in my absence. There is no need why we should take lewd men for we have honest men enough. . . .

Your assured friend,
R. C.

Thirteen of the Adventurers in England to the Settlers at New Plymouth:

Loving Friends,

We most heartily salute you in all love and hearty affection, hoping that the same God Who has hitherto preserved you in such a marvelous manner continues your lives and health, to His own praise and all our comforts. We are very sorry that you have not been sent to all this time. . . . We have in this ship sent such women as were willing and ready to go to their husbands and friends, with their children. . . . We would not have you discontented because we have not sent you more of your old friends, and especially him on whom you most depend, John Robinson. Far be it from us to neglect you or slight him. But as the original intent was, so the results shall show that we will deal fairly, and squarely answer your expectations to the full. There also come to you some honest men to settle near you, on their own account, which, if we had not allowed, would have been to wrong both them and you—them, by inconveniencing them, and you, because, being honest, they will be a support to the place and good neighbors to you. In regard to these private planters we have made two stipulations:

First, the trade in skins is to be confined to the colonists till the dividends; secondly, while they may settle near you, it shall be at such distance as is neither inconvenient to the apportionment of your lands, nor to your easily assembling together in case of need.

We have sent you several fishermen, with salt. . . We have sent you various other provisions, as will appear in your bill of lading, and though we have not sent all we would, because our cash is small, it is what we could.

Although as it seems, you have discovered many more rivers and fertile grounds than where you are, since by God's providence the place fell to your lot, let it be accepted as your portion; and rather fix your eyes upon what may be done there, than languish in hope after things elsewhere. If your site is not the best, it is the better because you will be envied or encroached upon less, and such as are earthly minded will not settle too near your border. If the land afford you bread, and the sea yield you fish, rest you awhile contented. God will one day grant you better fare; and all men shall know that you are neither fugitives nor discontents, but can, if God so order it, take the worst to yourselves with content, and leave the best to your neighbors with cheerfulness.

Let it not grieve you that you have been instruments to break the ice for others, who come after with less difficulty; the honor shall be yours to the world's end. . . .

We bear you always in our breasts, and our hearty affection is towards you all, as are the hearts of hundreds more who have never seen your faces, but who doubtless pray for your safety as their own, as we do and ever shall— that the same God which has so marvelously preserved you from seas, fogs, and famine, will still preserve you from all future dangers, and make you honorable among men, and glorious in bliss at the last day. And so the Lord be with you all, and send us joyful news of you, and enable us with one shoulder so to accomplish and perfect this work, that much glory may come to Him that confoundeth the mighty by the weak, and maketh small things great. To Whose greatness be all glory, for ever and ever.

This letter was subscribed with thirteen of their names.

The passengers, when they saw the poor conditions of those ashore, were much daunted and dismayed, and according to their different characters, were differently affected. Some wished themselves in England again; others began weeping, fancying what their own misery would be from what they saw before them; others pitied the distress they saw their friends had been in so long, and still were under; in a word, all were full of sadness. Some few of their old friends rejoiced to see them again, and to know that it was no worse with them, for they could not expect it to be better; and hoped that now they would enjoy better days together. And it was certainly not unnatural that the new arrivals should be thus affected; for the settlers were in very poor case—many were ragged in apparel, and some little better than half naked; though some few, who were well stocked before, were well enough clothed. But as for food, they were all alike, except some who had got a few peas from the ship that was last here. The best dish they could present to their friends was a lobster, or a piece of fish, without any bread, or anything else but a cup of fair spring water. The long continuance of this diet and their labors had somewhat abated the freshness of their complexions. But God gave them health and strength and showed them by experience the truth of that word (Deut. VIII, 3): "Man liveth not by bread alone, but by every word that proceedeth out of the mouth of the Lord doth a man live."

When I think how sadly the Scripture speaks of the famine in Jacob's time, when he said to his sons, "Go buy us food, that we may live and not die" (Gen. XLII, 2, and XLIII, 1); and that the famine was great in the land and yet they had such great herds of cattle of various kinds, which besides meat produces other foods, such as milk, butter and cheese, etc., and yet it was counted as a sore affliction; when we think of this, then we see that the affliction of these settlers must have been very great, who not only lacked the staff of life but all these things, and had no Egypt to go to. But God fed them out of the sea for the most part, so wonderful is His providence over His in all ages; for His mercy endureth forever.

Now the original settlers were afraid that their corn, when it was ripe, would have to be shared with the newcomers, and that the provisions which the latter had brought with them would give out before the year was over—as indeed they did. So they went to the Governor and begged him that as it had been agreed that they should sow their corn for their own use, and accordingly they had taken extraordinary pains about it, they might be left to enjoy it. They would rather do that than have a bit of the food just come in the ship. They would wait till harvest for their own and let the newcomers enjoy what they had brought; they would have none of it, except what they could purchase by bargain or exchange. Their request was granted them and it satisfied both sides; for the newcomers were much afraid the hungry settlers would eat up the provisions they had brought, and then that they would fall into like conditions of want.

The ship was laden in a short time with clapboard, by the help of many hands. They also sent in her all the beaver and other furs they had, and Mr. Winslow was sent over with her, to give information and to procure such things as were required. Harvest time had now come, and then instead of famine, God gave them plenty, and the face of things was changed, to the rejoicing of the hearts of many for which they blessed God. And the effect of their particular planting was well seen, for all had, one way or another, pretty well to bring the year about, and some of the abler sort and more industrious had to spare, and sell to others—in fact, no general want or famine has been amongst them since, to this day.

Those that came on their own venture looked for greater things than they found, or could attain to, such as building great houses in pleasant situations, as they had fancied—as if they could be great men and rich, all of a sudden; but they proved castles in the air.

The following were the conditions agreed on between the colony and them:

1. That the Governor in the name and with the consent of the company embraces and receives them in all love and friendship; and is to allot them competent places for habitations within the town; and promises to show them all such other courtesies as shall be reasonable for them to desire, or us to perform.

2. That they on their parts be subject to all such laws and orders as are already made, or hereafter shall be made, for the public good.

3. That they be free and exempt from the general employments of the said company (which their present condition of community requires), except common defense, and such other employments as tend to the perpetual good of the colony.

4. Towards the maintenance of government and public officers of the said colony, every male above the age of 16 years shall pay a bushel of Indian wheat, or the worth of it, into the common store.

5. That according to the agreement the merchants made with them before they came, they are to be debarred from all trade with the Indians for all sorts of furs and such like commodities, till the time of community be ended.

About the middle of September Captain Robert Gorges [6] arrived in the Bay of Massachusetts, with sundry passen-

---

[6] The Pilgrims were undoubtedly disturbed by the arrival of Captain Gorges and his party, a well-selected and adequately subsidized group of gentlemen, farmers, traders, mechanics, and servants. The establishment of this colony, representing the Crown and the Established Church, meant that their freedom of worship might be endangered.

gers and families, intending to begin a plantation there; and pitched upon the place that Mr. Weston's people had forsaken. He had a Commission from the Council of New England to be Governor-General of the country, and they appointed for his counsel and assistance Captain Francis West, the admiral aforementioned. Christopher Levett,[7] Esquire, and the Governor of New Plymouth for the time being, etc. They also gave him authority to choose such other as he should see fit. Also, they gave (by their commission) full power to him and his assistants, or any three of them, whereof himself was always to be one, to do and execute what should seem to them good, in all cases capital, criminal, and civil, etc. with various other instructions. Of these and also his commission, it pleased him to let the Governor here take a copy.

He gave them notice of his arrival by letter, but before they could visit him, he went eastward with the ship he came in; but a storm got up, and as they lacked a good pilot to harbor them there, they bore up for this harbor. He and his men were kindly entertained here, and stayed fourteen days.

In the meantime Mr. Weston arrived with his small ship, which he had now recovered. Captain Gorges, who informed the Governor here that one purpose of his going east was to meet with Mr. Weston, took this opportunity to call him to account for some abuses he had to lay to his charge. Whereupon he called Weston before him and some other of his assistants, with the Governor of this place; and charged him first with the ill carriage of his men in Massachusetts, by which means the peace of the

---

[7] Christopher Levett explored the coast, and wrote an account of his voyage after his return to England.

country had been disturbed, and he himself and the people he had brought over to settle there were much prejudiced. To this Mr. Weston easily answered that what had been done was in his absence, and might have befallen anyone; he left them sufficiently provided, and supposed they would be well governed; for any error committed he had sufficiently smarted. This particular charge was passed by.

The second charge was of a wrong done towards his father, Sir Ferdinand Gorges, and to the State. The offense was this: Mr. Weston had used him and others of the Council of New England, to procure him a license for the purchase and transportation to New England of many pieces of great ordnance, on the plea of great fortifications in this country, etc. Having obtained them, he went and sold them beyond the seas for his private profit; at which, he said, the State had been much offended, and his father had been sharply rebuked, and he had orders to apprehend him for it. Mr. Weston excused it as well as he could, but could not deny it, it being the main reason why he had left England. But after much argument, by the mediation of the Governor and some other friends here, Captain Gorges was inclined to be lenient, though he foresaw the vexation of his father. When Mr. Weston saw this he grew more presumptuous and made such provoking and cutting speeches that the Governor-General rose up in great indignation and distemper, and vowed that he would either curb him or send him home to England. At which Mr. Weston was somewhat daunted, and came privately to the Governor here, to know whether he would allow him to be apprehended. He was told they could not prevent it, and blamed him much that, after having pacified things, he should again break out and by his own folly and rashness bring trouble upon himself and them too. He confessed it was his temper, and prayed the Governor to intercede for him, and smooth things if he could. At last he did so with much ado; so he was summoned again, and the Governor-General consented to accept his own bond, to be ready to make further answer, when either he or the Lords should send for him. Finally, he took only his word, and there was a friendly parting on all hands.

But after he had gone, Mr. Weston, in lieu of thanks to the Governor-General and his friends here, gave them this quip behind their backs, for all their pains: That though they were but young justices, they were good beggars. Thus they parted for the time, and shortly after the Governor took his leave and went to Massachusetts by land, very grateful for his kind entertainment.

The ship stayed here and fitted herself to go to Virginia, having some passengers to deliver there, and with her there returned several of those who had come over privately, some from discontent and dislike of the country, others because of a fire that broke out, burning the houses they lived in and all their provisions. The fire was caused by some of the seamen who were roistering in a house where it first began. It being very cold weather, they had made a great fire, which broke out of the chimney and set alight the thatch, and burnt down three or four houses, and all the goods and provisions in them. The house in which it began was right against the common storehouse, in which were all their provisions; and they had much difficulty in saving it. If it had been lost the plantation would have been ruined. But through God's mercy it was saved by the great efforts of the people, and the care of the Governor and some about him. Some advised that the goods be thrown out; but then there would have been much stolen by the rough crews of the two ships, who were almost all ashore. But a reliable company was placed within, so that if necessity required they could have got them all out with speed, and others with wet cloths and other means kept off the fire outside.

For they suspected some malicious dealing, if not plain treachery; though whether it was only suspicion or no, God knows. But this is certain, that when the tumult was greatest, a voice was heard—from whom it was not known—that bid them look well about them, for all were not friends near them. And shortly after, when the worst of the fire was over, smoke was seen to rise from a shed adjoining the end of the storehouse, which was wattled up with boughs, the withered leaves of which had caught fire. Those who ran to put it out found a large firebrand, about a yard long, lying under the wall on the inside, which could not possibly have come there by accident, but must have been put there intentionally, as all thought who saw it. But God kept them from this danger, whatever was intended.

Shortly after Captain Gorges, the Governor-General, had got home to Massachusetts, he sent a warrant to arrest Mr. Weston and his ship, and sent a seaman to sail her thither, and one Captain Hanson, of his suite, to be in charge of him. The Governor and others were very sorry to see him take this course, and took exceptions to the warrant, as not legal or sufficient, and wrote to him to dissuade him from this course, showing him that he would but entangle and burden himself by doing this, and that he could not do Mr. Weston a better turn, as things now stood with him, for he had a great many men in his service in the ship, to whom he was deeply in debt for wages, and that he was practically out of provisions, and winter was at hand: for all of which Captain Gorges would be responsible if he arrested his ship. In the meantime Mr. Weston had notice to shift for himself; but it was supposed that he did not know where to go or how to better himself, but was rather glad of the issue, and so did not move.

But the Governor-General would not be dissuaded, and sent a very formal warrant under his hand and seal, with strict orders, as they would answer for it to the State; he also wrote that he had better considered things since he was here, and he could not answer for it to let him go, besides other things that had come to his knowledge since, which Mr. Weston must account for. So he was allowed to proceed; but he found in the end that what had been told him was true; for when an inventory was taken of what was in the ship, food was found sufficient for only fourteen days, at a bare allowance, and not much else of any worth, and the men clamored so for wages and rations in the meantime that he was soon weary. So in conclusion it turned to his loss, and the expense of his provisions; and towards the spring they came to an agreement, after they had been east, and the Governor-General restored him his vessel again, and made satisfaction in biscuit and meal and such like provisions for what he had used of his, or what had been wanted or consumed. So Mr. Weston came here again, and afterwards shaped his course for Virginia, and so for the present I shall leave him. He died afterwards at Bristol, at the time of the war, of the sickness there.

The Governor-General and some of his suite soon returned to England, having scarcely saluted the country put under his government, as he did not find the state of things here was suited to his station and way of life. The people dispersed; some went to England, others to Virginia, some few remained and were helped with supplies from here. The Governor-General had brought over a minister of religion with him, one Mr. Morrell,[8] who, about a year after his return, took shipping from here. He had I know not what power and authority of superintendence over other churches granted him, and sundry instructions to that end; but he never showed it or made use of it. It seems he saw it was in vain, and he only spoke of it to some here at his departure. This was the end of the second settlement there.[9] This year there were also some scattered beginnings made in other places, as at Piscataqua by Mr. David Thomson, at Monhegan and some other places by several others.

It remains now for me to speak a word about the pinnace mentioned before, sent by the adventurers to be employed in the country. She was a fine vessel and bravely fitted out; but I fear the adventurers were over-proud of her, for she had ill success. However, they made a great mistake about two things in her. First, though she had a competent master, she was badly manned, and all the crew were upon shares, and none were to receive any wages but the captain. Secondly, though mainly busied with trade, they had sent nothing of any value to trade with. When they came over, they received bad advice from Mr. Weston and others of the same stamp, until neither the captain nor the Governor could control them, for they declared that they were abused and deceived; that they were

---

[8] William Morrell, an Anglican minister, was commissioned to make the colonists conform to the Church of England. When he saw how futile this mission was, he quickly abandoned it, and spent the winter composing a Latin poem on New England, which he published (with English translation) after his return to England. Of the Indians he wrote:
  "They're wondrous cruell, strangely base and vile,
  Quickly displeased and hardly reconciled."
[9] That is, at Weymouth.

told they would sail as a man of war, and take I know not whom—French, Spaniards, etc. They would neither trade nor fish without wages; in fine, they would obey no orders of the captain, and it was feared they would either make away with the vessel, or get off on the other ships and abandon her. So Mr. Pierce and other friends persuaded the Governor to change their conditions, and give them wages; which was accordingly done. Then the vessel was sent about the Cape to the Narragansetts to trade, but they made a poor voyage of it. They got some corn and beaver, but the Dutch had been used to trade with cloth and better commodities, and these had only a few beads and knives, which were not valued by the Indians. On her return home, at the very entrance into her own harbor, she was almost wrecked in a storm, and was forced to cut her main mast by the board, to save herself from driving onto the flats that lie outside, called Brown Islands, the force of the gale being so great that her anchors gave way, and she was being driven right upon them; but when her mast and tackling were gone, they were able to hold her till the wind shifted.

"They are too delicate and unfitte to begine new plantations and collonies that cannot enduer the biting of a muskeeto; we would wish such to keepe at home till at least they be muskeeto proofe."

CHAPTER V

[1624]

The time for the election of the officers for the year having come, the number of people having increased and the business of government accordingly, the Governor desired them to change the officials and renew the election and give the Governor more assistants for his help and advice, pointing out that if it was an honor or advantage, it was only fit that others should share it; if it was a burden—as doubtless it was—it was but fair that others should help to bear it, and that this, in fact, was the purpose of the annual elections. The outcome was that whereas before there had been only one assistant, they now chose five, giving the Governor a double voice; and afterwards they increased them to seven. This plan has been continued to this day.

Having at some trouble and expense new-masted and rigged their pinnace, at the beginning of March they sent her well-victualed to the eastward, fishing. She arrived safely at a place called Damariscove, and was well harbored where ships were accustomed to anchor, with some other ships from England already there. But shortly after there arose such a violent and extraordinary storm that the seas broke into the harbor in a way that had never been known before, and drove her against great rocks, which beat such a hole in her bulk that a horse and cart might have been driven through, and then she drifted into deep water, where she lay sunk. The captain was drowned; the rest of the men, except one, with difficulty saved their lives; all her provisions, salt, etc., were lost. And here I must leave her to lie till afterwards.

Some of those who still remained here on private venture, began secretly to plot, in league with a strong faction of the adventurers in England, on whom several of them depended. By their whisperings they drew some of the weaker members of the colony itself to their side, and made them so discontented that at last nothing would satisfy them but that they might be allowed to be on their own resources also, and even made large offers to be freed from the community. The Governor consulted with the ablest members of the colony, and it was decided to permit them to separate on the same terms as the other private settlers, with the additional stipulation that they should be bound to remain here till the general partnership was concluded; and that they should pay into the common store one half of all goods and commodities they might accumulate beyond their food, in consideration of expenses already incurred for them; and some other similar details. When this liberty was granted the defection soon stopped, for but few took this course when they came to consider it, and the rest soon wearied of it. It turned out that they had been told by the other private settlers and Mr. Weston that no more supplies would be sent to the general body, but that the private settlers had friends at home, who would do I know not what for them.

Shortly after, Mr. Winslow returned from England and brought a pretty good supply of provisions, with a ship sent for fishing—an enterprise never successful with the colony. He brought three heifers and a bull—the first cattle in the country—some clothing and other necessaries. He reported a strong faction amongst the adventurers against the colonists, and especially against sending the rest from Leyden. He related with what difficulty the present supply was procured, and that by their strong and long opposition his departure had been so delayed that not only had they now arrived too late for the fishing season here, but the best fishermen had gone to the west country and he was forced to take the best captain and crew he could procure. Some letters from the adventurers will make these things clearer.

James Sherley [1] *in England to the Settlers at New Plymouth:*

Most worthy and loving Friends,

Your kind and loving letters I have received with thanks. . . . It has pleased God to stir up the hearts of the adventurers to raise new stock for fitting out this ship, called the *Charity*, with men and necessaries both for the settlement and fishing—though with very great difficulty, since we have amongst us some who undoubtedly serve their private ends, and thwart the others here and worthy instruments of God's glory elsewhere,[2] rather than aiming at the general good and furtherance of this

---

[1] James Sherley was a goldsmith of London, now treasurer of the merchant adventurers.
[2] He means Mr. John Robinson. (B.)

noble enterprise. Still we have many others—I hope the majority—very honest Christian men, whose intent I am convinced is wholly for the glory of Our Lord Jesus Christ, the propagation of His gospel, and the hope of gaining these poor savages to the knowledge of God. But as the proverb says: One scabbed sheep may mar a whole flock—so these malcontented and turbulent spirits do what they can to draw men's hearts from you and your friends, and from the general business—even with a show of godliness and zeal for the plantation. Whereas the aim is quite contrary, as some of the honester hearted men (though lately of their faction) made clear at our last meeting. But why should I trouble either you or myself with these restless opposers of all goodness, who, I doubt not, will be continual disturbers of our friendly meetings and love. On Thursday, Jan. 8th, we had a meeting about the articles between you and us, at which they moved to reject what we had pressed you to grant [3] in our recent letters—an addition to the period of our joint stock. Their reason, as they stated, was that it troubled their conscience to exact longer time from you than had been agreed upon at first. That evening, however, they were so confused and wearied by their own perverse contentions that they even offered to sell their adventures—and some were willing to buy. But I, thinking it would only raise scandal and false reports, and so do us more harm, would not permit it. So on Jan. 12th we had another meeting. But in the interim several of us had talked with most of them privately, and had great combats and reasoning, pro and con. But that night, when we met to read the general letter, we had the friendliest meeting I ever knew, and our greatest enemies

---

[3] The period of joint stock partnership and common ownership of land, equipment, and produce of the colony by the merchants in England and the settlers in New Plymouth had been originally set for seven years.

offered to put up £50. So I sent for a bottle of wine—I would you could do the like—which we drank friendly together. Thus God can turn the hearts of men when it pleases Him. . . . Thus loving friends, I heartily salute you in the Lord, hoping ever to rest,

Yours to my power,
JAMES SHERLEY.

Jan. 25th, 1623.[4]

Robert Cushman in England to the Settlers at New Plymouth:

Beloved Sir,

We have now sent you, we hope, men and means to accomplish three things, viz., fishing, salt-making, and boat-making; if you can master them your wants will be supplied. I pray you exert yourselves to do so. Let the ship be loaded as soon as you can, and sent to Bilbao. You must send some competent representative, whom, once more, you must authorize to confirm the conditions. If Mr. Winslow could be spared, I wish he could come again. The boat-builder is believed to be one of the best in his trade, and will no doubt be of much service. Let him have absolute command over his assistants, and whomever you put under him. Let him build you two catches, a lighter, and some six or seven shallops, as soon as you can. The salt-maker is a skillful and industrious man. Put some assistants under him who will quickly learn the secret of it. The preacher we have sent is, we hope, an honest plain man, though none of the most eminent and rare. About his appointment, use your own liberty and discretion; he knows he has no authority among you, though perhaps custom and habit may make him forget himself. Mr.

---

[4] This and the following letter by modern reckoning would be dated 1624.

Winslow and myself gave way to his going, to satisfy some here, and we see no reason against it except his large family of children.

We have taken a patent[5] for Cape Ann. . . .

I am sorry more discretion is not used by some in their letters home.[6] Some say you are starved in body and soul; others that you eat pigs and dogs that have died; others that the reports of the fertility of the country are gross and palpable lies, that there is scarcely a fowl to be seen, or a fish to be caught, and so on. I wish such discontented men were back again, rather than the whole plantation shall be thus exposed to their passionate humors. Hereafter I shall prevent some from going who are not better disposed; in the meantime it is our cross, and we must bear it.

I am sorry we have not sent you more provisions, but we have run into so much expense to victual the ship, provide salt, fishing implements, etc., that we could not afford other comforts, such as butter, sugar, etc. I hope the return of this ship, and the *James*, will put us in cash again. The Lord make you full of courage in this troublesome business, which must now be stuck to, till God give us rest from our labors. Farewell, in all hearty affection.

Your assured friend,

R. C

Jan. 24th, 1623.

With the former letter from Mr. Sherley were sent various charges against the colony, of which he writes thus: "These are the chief objections which those just returned raise against you and the country. I pray you consider them, and answer them at your first convenience."

These objections were made by some of those who came

---

[5] The Council for New England tried to divide its coast among themselves. This patent was given to Winslow and Cushman.
[6] This was John Oldham, and his like. (B.)

over on private enterprise and had returned home, as before mentioned; they were of the same kind as those the last letter mentions. I shall record them here with the answers made to them and sent over at the return of this ship. The faultfinders were so confounded that some confessed, and others denied what they had said and ate their words; some have since come over again, and have lived here to convince themselves sufficiently.

Obj. 1. Diversity of religious beliefs.

Ans: We know of no such diversity, for there has never been any controversy, either public or private, to our knowledge, since we came.

Obj. 2. Neglect of family duties on the Lord's day.

Ans: We allow no such thing. They who report it, would have showed their Christian love more if they had told the offenders of it kindly, rather than thus to reproach them behind their backs. But, to say no more, we wish they themselves had given a better example.

Obj. 3. Want of both the sacraments.

Ans: The more is our grief that our pastor [7] is kept from us, at whose hands we might enjoy them. In Holland we used to have the Lord's Supper every Sabbath, and baptism as often as there were children to baptize.

Obj. 4. Children are not catechized, or taught to read.

Ans: Neither is true—several take pains with their own, as well as they can. We have no common school, for want of a fit person hitherto, or means to obtain one; though we hope now to begin.

Obj. 5. Many of the private members of the colony will not work for the community.

Ans: This also is not wholly true; for though some do it unwillingly, and others not honestly, still all do it. The worst of them gets his own food, and something besides.

---

[7] Mr. John Robinson, who was still in Leyden.

We do not excuse them, but try to reform them the best we can—or else quit the settlement of them.

Obj. 6. The water is not wholesome.

Ans: If they mean not so wholesome as the good wine and beer in London, which they so dearly love, we will not dispute them; but for water, it is as good as any in the world, so far as we know, and it is wholesome enough for us who can be content with it.

Obj. 7. The ground is barren, and grows no grass.

Ans: Here, as everywhere, some ground is better, some worse. The cattle find grass for they are as fat as need be; We wish we had but one beast for every hundred that there is grass to keep. This objection, like some others, is ridiculous to all here who see and know the country.

Obj. 8. The fish cannot be salted, to keep them sweet.

Ans: This is as true as writing that there is scarcely a fowl to be seen, or a fish to be caught; things likely to be true in a country where so many ships come fishing yearly! They might as well say that no ale or beer in London can be kept from going sour.

Obj. 9. Many of them steal from one another.

Ans: If London had been free from that crime, we should not have been troubled with it here. It is well known that several have smarted well for it—and so are the rest likely to do whenever they are caught.

Obj. 10. The country is overrun with foxes and wolves.

Ans: So are many other good countries, too; but poison, traps, and other such means will help to destroy them.

Obj. 11. The Dutch are settled near Hudson's Bay [8] and are likely to overthrow the trade.

Ans: They would come and settle here as well, if we and others did not, or if we went home and left it to them. We rather commend them than condemn them for it.

---

[8] Hudson River is meant. The Dutch had established a permanent settlement at the mouth of the Hudson in 1623.

Obj. 12. The people are much pestered with mosquitoes.

Ans: They are too delicate and unfit to begin new plantations and colonies who cannot endure the biting of a mosquito. We would wish such to keep at home—at least till they be mosquito proof. But this is as free as any, and experience teaches that the more the land is tilled and the woods cut down, the fewer there will be—and in the end scarcely any at all.

Having dispatched those objections, I will here insert two letters from Mr. Robinson, their pastor; the one to the Governor, the other to Mr. Brewster, their elder, which will throw much light on what has gone before, and show the tender love and care of a true pastor towards them.

John Robinson at Leyden to Governor Bradford at New Plymouth:

My loving and much beloved friend, whom God has hitherto preserved, preserve and keep you still to His glory and the good of many, that His blessing may make your godly and wise endeavors equal to the occasion. Of your love, too, and care for us here we have never doubted, and are glad to take full knowledge of it. Our love and care to and for you is mutual, though our hopes of coming to you are small, and weaker than ever. But of this at large in Mr. Brewster's letter, with whom you mutually communicate your letters, I know, as I desire you may do these, etc.

Concerning the killing of those poor Indians, of which we heard at first by rumor, and since by more definite report, oh! how happy a thing had it been if you had converted some, before you had killed any. Besides, where blood once begins to be shed, it is seldom staunched for a long time after. You will say they deserved it. I grant it; but upon what provocation from those heathenish Christians?[9] Besides, you, not being magistrates over them, had to consider not what punishment they deserved, but what you were by necessity constrained to inflict. Necessity of killing so many I cannot see. Methinks one or two principals should have been enough, according to the approved rule—the punishment to a few, and the fear to many. Upon this occasion let me be bold to exhort you seriously to consider the disposition of your Captain, whom I love, and am persuaded the Lord in great mercy and for much good has sent to you, if you use him right. He is a man humble and meek among you and towards all, under ordinary circumstances, but if this merely come from a humane spirit, there is cause to fear that on occasions of special provocation there may be wanting that tenderness of the life of man, made after God's image, which is meet. It is also apt to be more glorious in men's eyes than pleasing in God's, or fit for Christians, to be a terror to poor barbarous peoples; and indeed I am afraid lest, by this example, others should be drawn to adopt a kind of ruffling course in the world. I doubt not that you will take in good part these things that I write, and if there is cause make use of them. We wish we were present, to communicate our mutual help; but seeing that cannot be done, we shall always long after you, and love you, and wait God's appointed time. The adventurers, it seems, have neither money to send us, nor any great mind for us, for the most part. They deny it to be any part of the agreement between us that they should transport us, nor do I look for any further help from them till means come from you. My wife with me, re-salutes you and yours. Unto Him Who is the same to His in all

---

[9] Mr. Weston's men. (B.) The reference is to the killing of some Indian conspirators against the Weston settlement by Captain Standish the previous year. See above, pp. 147–148.

places, and near to them which are far from one another, I commend you, and all with you, resting,

>   Yours truly loving,
>   JOHN ROBINSON.

Leyden, Dec. 19th, 1623.

John Robinson at Leyden to William Brewster at New Plymouth:

Loving and dear friend and brother,

What I most desired of God for you, namely, the continuance of your life and health, and the safe coming of those sent to you, I most gladly hear of and praise God for it; and I hope Mrs. Brewster's weak state of health will be somewhat repaired by the coming of her daughters and the provisions sent in this and former ships, which makes us here bear more patiently the deferring of our desired transportation. I call it desired, rather than hoped for: for first, there is no hope at all that I know or can conceive of, of any new stock being raised for that purpose; so that everything must depend upon returns from you, which are surrounded by so many uncertainties. Besides, though for the present the adventurers allege nothing but want of money, which is an invincible obstacle, still if that be removed by you, other difficulties will be raised to take its place. In order to understand this better, we must divide the adventurers into three heads. Of these some five or six (as I believe) are absolutely in favor of us, before all; another five or six are openly our bitter adversaries; the rest —the main body—are I believe, honest minded, and friendly towards us; but they have other friends (namely, the forward preachers) nearer to them than we are, whose interests, in so far as they conflict with ours, they would rather advance than ours. Now what a pull these men have with the professors, you know; and I am convinced that they, of all others, are unwilling I should be transported; especially such of them as have an eye that way themselves, fearing that if I go there, their market will be marred in many respects. As for these adversaries, if they have but half as much wit as malice, they will stop my going as soon as they see it is intended; and as one restive jade can hinder, by hanging back, more than two or three can draw forward, so it will be in this case. A clear proof of this they gave in your messenger's presence, binding the company to promise that none of the money now subscribed should be expended to help any of us over to you.

Now as to the question propounded by you: I judge it not lawful for you—a ruling elder (Rom. XII, 7, 8; and I Tim. V, 17), as distinct from the elders that teach and exhort and labor in the word and doctrine, in whose duties the sacraments are included, to administer them—nor fitting, if it were lawful. Whether any learned man will come out to you, I do not know; if so, you must *Consilium capere in arena*.[10] Be you most heartily saluted, and your wife with you, both from me and mine. Your God and ours, and the God of all His, bring us together if it be His will, and keep us in the meanwhile and always to His glory, and make us serviceable to His majesty and faithful to the end. Amen.

Your very loving brother,
JOHN ROBINSON.

Leyden, Dec. 20th, 1623.

These matters premised, I will now proceed with my account of affairs here. But before I come to other things, I must say a word about their planting this year. They felt the benefit of their last year's harvest; for by planting corn

---

[10] Take counsel on the spot.

on their own account they managed, with a great deal of patience, to overcome famine. This reminds me of a saying of Seneca's (Epistle 123): that an important part of liberty is a well-governed belly, and patience in want. The settlers now began to consider corn more precious than silver; and those that had some to spare began to trade with the others for small things, by the quart, pottle, and peck, etc.; for they had no money, and if they had, corn was preferred to it. In order that they might raise their crops to better advantage, they made suit to the Governor to have some land apportioned for permanent holdings, and not by yearly lot, whereby the plots which the more industrious had brought under good culture one year, would change hands the next, and others would reap the advantage; with the result that the manuring and culture of the land were neglected. It was well considered, and their request was granted. Every person was given one acre of land, for them and theirs, and they were to have no more till the seven years had expired; it was all as near the town as possible, so that they might be kept close together, for greater safety and better attention to general employments. This often makes me think of what Pliny [11] (lib. 18, cap. 2) says of the Romans' first beginnings in the time of Romulus—how everyone contented himself with two acres of land, and had no more assigned to them; and (cap. 3) how it was thought a great public reward to receive a pint of corn from the people of Rome. And long after, the most generous present given to a captain who had won a victory over their enemies, was as much ground as he could till in one day; in fact a man was not considered a good but a dangerous citizen,

---

[11] The reference is to Pliny's *Natural History*.

who was not content with seven acres of land; also how they used to pound their corn in mortars, as the settlers were forced to do for many years, until they got a mill.

The ship which brought these supplies was speedily unloaded, and, with her captain and crew was sent out fishing to Cape Ann, where they had got a patent, as mentioned above. As the season was so far advanced, some of the planters were sent to help to build the landing stage, to their own hindrance. Partly owing to the lateness of the year, and more especially to the bad character of the captain, one Baker, they made a poor voyage of it. He proved a very drunken beast, and did little but drink and guzzle and consume time and victuals, most of the crew following his example; and though Mr. William Pierce was superintending the business and was to captain the ship home, he could do no good amongst them. The loss was great, and would have been more, but that they did some trade for skins, which was a help to them.

The shipbuilder who had been sent out to the colony was an honest and very industrious man. He and his assistants quickly built two good strong shallops, which afterwards did them great service, and a strong lighter; and he had hewn timber for two catches, when he fell sick with fever in the hot season of the year, and though he had the best attention the place could afford, he died. He was a very great loss, and they were very sorry for his death.

But the man sent out to make salt was an ignorant, foolish, self-willed fellow. He boasted that he could do great things in making salt-works; so he was sent to seek out fit ground for the purpose; and after some search he told the Governor that he had found a suitable place, with a good bottom to hold water, and otherwise very convenient, which, he doubted not, in a short time could be brought to perfection and yield them great profit; but he must have eight or ten men constantly employed. He was requested to make sure the ground was good and otherwise suitable, and that he could bring it to perfection; otherwise he would incur great expense by employing himself and so many men. But he was, after some trial, so confident, that he caused them to send carpenters to rear a great frame for a large house to receive the salt, and for other uses. But in the end it all proved useless. So he found fault with the ground, in which he said he had been mistaken; but if he might have the lighter to carry clay, he was sure he could do it. Now, though the Governor and some others saw that this would come to little good, they had so many malignant spirits amongst them, who, in their letters to the adventurers would have blamed them for not letting him bring his work to perfection; and the man himself, who by his bold confidence and large promises had deceived the adventurers in England, had so wound himself into the high esteem of some here, that they decided to let him go on till everyone saw his vanity. In the end all he could do was to boil salt in pans, and yet tried to make those who worked with him believe there was a great mystery in it, and used to make them do unnecessary things as a blind, until they saw through his deception. The next year he was sent to Cape Ann, and the pans were set up where the fishing was; but before the summer was out he had burnt the house, and the fire was so fierce that it spoiled the pans—at least some of them; and this was the end of that expensive business.

The third person of importance mentioned in the letters was the minister whom they sent over, by name of

Mr. John Lyford,[12] of whom and whose doings I must be more lengthy, though I will abridge as much as I can. When this man first came ashore, he saluted them with such reverence and humility as is seldom to be seen; indeed he made them ashamed, he so bowed and cringed to them, and would have kissed their hands, if they had allowed him. He wept and shed many tears, blessing God Who had brought him to see their faces, admiring what they had done in their need, as if he had been made all of love and was the humblest person in the world. And all the while (if we may judge by his after-behavior) he was only like him mentioned in Psalm x, 10, who croucheth and boweth, that heaps of poor may fall by his might. Or like that dissembling Ishmael (Jeremiah XLI, 6), who, when he had slain Gedelia, went out weeping, and met them who were coming to offer incense in the house of the Lord, saying: Come to Gedelia,—when he meant to slay them.

They gave him the best entertainment they could in all simplicity, and a larger allowance of food out of the store than any other had; and as the Governor in all weighty affairs had consulted their elder, Mr. Brewster, and his assistants, so now he called Mr. Lyford, too, to the council with them on the most important matters. After a short time he desired to become a member of the church here, and was accordingly received. He made a large confession of his faith, and an acknowledgment of his former disorderly walking, and his being entangled with many corruptions, which had been a burden to his conscience, and

---

[12] The Pilgrims had been without a qualified minister since their arrival. The Elder Brewster had fulfilled most of the pastor's functions, but was without authority to administer the sacraments, as Robinson, in the foregoing letter, states.

blessed God for this opportunity of freedom and liberty to enjoy the ordinances of God in purity among His people, with many similar expressions.

I must speak here a word, too, of Mr. John Oldham, who joined him in his after courses. He had been a chief stickler in the former faction among the private settlers, and an intelligencer to those in England. But now, since the coming of the ship with supplies he opened his mind to some of the chief members here, and confessed that he had done them wrong both by word and deed in writing thus to England; that he now saw the eminent hand of God was with them, which made his heart smite him; and he assured them that his friends in England should never use him against them again. He begged them that former things might be forgotten, and that they would look upon him as one who desired to support them in every way—and such like expressions. Whether this was hypocrisy or some sudden pang of conviction (which I rather think), God only knows. However, they at once showed themselves ready to embrace him in all friendliness, and called him to the council with them on all the chief affairs, without any distrust at all.

Thus everything seemed to go very comfortably and smoothly among them, at which they rejoiced. But it did not last long, for both Oldham and Lyford grew perverse, and showed a spirit of great malignancy, drawing as many into faction as they could. No matter how vile or profane, they backed the delinquents in all they did, so long as they would but uphold them and speak against the church here; so that there was nothing but private meetings and whisperings amongst them. Thus they fed themselves and others with what they would accomplish in England through their friends there, bringing others as well as themselves into a fool's paradise. However, they could not be so secret but that much of their doings and sayings was discovered; though outwardly they still showed a fair face.

At length, when the ship was ready to go, it was discovered that Lyford was long in writing, and sent many letters and could not forbear to communicate with his intimates such things therefrom as made them laugh in their sleeves, thinking he had done their errands satisfactorily. The Governor and some of his friends, knowing how matters stood in England, and what harm this might do, took a shallop and went out with the ship a league or two to sea, and called for Lyford's and Oldham's letters. Mr. William Pierce being captain of the ship, and knowing well the mischief they made both here and in England, afforded them all the assistance he could. He found about twenty of Lyford's letters, many of them long and full of slanders and false accusations, tending not only to their prejudice but even aiming at their ruin. Most of the letters they let pass, but took copies of them; of some they sent true copies and kept the originals, lest he should deny that he had written them. Amongst them they found copies of two, which he sent enclosed in a letter of his to Mr. John Pemberton, a minister and a great opponent of theirs. Of these two letters of which he had taken the copies, one of them was written by a gentleman in England to Mr. Brewster, the other by Mr. Winslow to Mr. John Robinson in Holland, at his coming away, as the ship lay at Gravesend. They were lying sealed in the main cabin; and whilst Mr. Winslow was busy about the affairs of the ship, this sly mischief-maker opens them, makes copies, and seals them up again; and not only sends the copies to his friend and their adversary, but adds in the margin many scurrilous and flouting annotations!

The ship went out towards evening, and in the night the Governor returned. They were somewhat blank at it, but after some weeks, as they heard nothing, they were as brisk as ever, thinking nothing was known and all had gone well for them, and that the Governor had only gone to despatch his own letters. The reason why the Governor and the rest took no steps at once was in order to let things ripen, so that they might the better discover their intention and see who were their adherents; for, amongst others they had found a letter from one of their confederates, stating that Mr. Oldham and Mr. Lyford intended a reformation in church and commonwealth, and that as soon as the ship was gone, they intended to join together and have the sacraments, etc.

As for Oldham, few of his letters were found, for he was so bad a scribe that his hand was scarcely legible; but he was as deeply involved as the other. So, thinking they were now strong enough, they began to pick quarrels at everything. Oldham being told off to stand watch according to order, refused to come, calling the captain a beggarly rascal, resisting him, and drawing his knife on him, though he had done him no wrong nor spoken to him improperly, but had merely required him with all fairness to do his duty. The Governor, hearing the tumult, sent to quiet it; but Oldham ramped more like a furious beast than a man, and called them all traitors, and rebels, and other such foul language as I am ashamed to remember; but after he had been clapped up awhile, he came to himself, and with some slight punishment was let go upon his behavior, pending further censure.

But, to cut things short, at length it came to this, that Lyford with his accomplices, without speaking one word to either the Governor, the church, or the elder, withdrew themselves, and held a separate public meeting on the Lord's day; and with many such insolent doings, too long to relate here, began to act publicly what they had been plotting privately. It was thought high time to prevent further mischief by calling them to account; so the Governor called a court, and summoned the whole company to appear, and charged Lyford and Oldham with their guilt. But they were stubborn, and resolutely denied the charges, and required proof. The court first alleged that from what had been written to them from England and from their practices here, it was evident they were plotting against them, and disturbing the peace, both in respect of their civil and church estate, which was most injurious to the colony; for both they and all the world knew that they had come here to enjoy liberty of conscience and the free use of God's ordinances, and for that end had ventured their lives and had already passed through so much hardship; and they and their friends had borne the expense of these beginnings, which was not small. They pointed out that Lyford for his part was sent over at their expense, and that both he and his large family were maintained by them; and that he had joined the church and was a member of it; and for him to plot against them and seek their ruin was most unjust and perfidious. As for Oldham, or anyone who came over at his own expense and were on their own resources, they had been received in courtesy by the plantation, coming to seek shelter and protection under its wings, being unable to stand alone; but as the hedgehog in the fable, whom the coney on a stormy day invited in pity into her burrow, would not be content to share it with her, but in the end with her sharp pricks forced the poor coney out, so these men, with similar injustice, endeavored to do the like by those who entertained them.

Lyford denied that he had anything to do with the people in England, or knew their plans, and pretended similar ignorance of the other charges. Then his letters were produced and some of them read, at which he was struck dumb. But Oldham began to rage furiously that they had intercepted and opened the letters. Threatening them in very high language, he stood up and in a most audacious and mutinous manner called upon the people, saying, "My masters, where are your hearts? Now show your courage; you have often complained to me so and so; now is the time; if you will do anything, I will stand by you," etc. Thinking that everyone who, knowing his humor, had soothed and flattered him, or otherwise in a moment of discontent uttered anything to him, would now side with him in open rebellion. But he was disappointed; not a man opened his mouth, for all were struck silent by the injustice of the thing.

Then the Governor turned to Mr. Lyford, and asked him if he thought he had done wrong to open his letters; but he was silent and dare not say a word, knowing well what they might reply. Then the Governor explained to the people that he had done it as a magistrate, and was bound to do it to prevent the mischief and ruin that this conspiracy and plot of theirs might otherwise have brought to the colony. But Lyford, besides his misbehavior here, had dealt treacherously with his friends that trusted him, and stole their letters and opened them, and sent copies of them with disgraceful annotations to his friends in England. Then the Governor produced them and his other letters under his own hand, which he could not deny, and had them read before all the people: at which all his friends were blank, and had not a word to say.

It would be too long and tedious to insert his letters here—they would almost fill a volume—though I have them by me. I shall only note a few of the chief things from them, with the answers to them as they were then given, as instances.

1. He said that the church desired that no one should live here except its members; nor would anyone willingly do so, if they had but company with which to live elsewhere.

Ans: Their answer was that this was false, in both its parts; for they were willing and desirous that any honest men should live with them, who would behave peaceably, and seek the common good—or at least do them no harm; and that there were many who would not live elsewhere, so long as they were permitted to live with them.

2. That if any honest men come over who were not dissenters, they soon disliked them, etc.

Ans: Their answer was as before, that it was a calumny, for they had many amongst them whom they liked well, and were glad of their company; and should be of any such who came to them.

3. That they took exception to him for these two doctrines from II Samuel XII, 7. First, that ministers must sometimes apply their teaching in particular to special persons; secondly, that great men may be reproved as well as humble.

Ans: Their answer was that both these charges were without truth or color of truth—as was proved to his face —and that they had taught and believed this long before they knew Mr. Lyford.

4. That they tried to ruin the private settlers, as was proved by this: they would not allow any of the colony either to buy or sell with them, or to exchange one commodity for another.

Ans: This was a most audacious slander, and void of all truth as was proved to him before all, for any of them bought, sold or exchanged with them as often as they pleased—and also both lent and gave to them, when they wanted; and this the private settlers themselves could not deny, but freely confessed in open court. But the ground whence this slander arose made it much worse; for he was at the council with them when a man was called before them, and was questioned for receiving powder and biscuit out of the company's supplies from the gunner of the small ship, which he had arranged should be put in at his window in the night; and also for buying salt of one who had no right to it. Lyford not only backed this defaulter —who was one of these private settlers—by excusing and extenuating him; but upon this ground he built this mischievous and false slander; that because they would not suffer a private settler to buy stolen goods, ergo, they sought their utter ruin. Bad logic for a divine!

5. Next he accused them of forcing men to become private settlers on their own resources, and then seeking to starve them, and deprive them of all means of subsistence.

Ans: To this it was answered, he did them manifest wrong, for they had turned none upon their own resources who had not of their own importunity and earnest desire urged and constrained them to do it. They appealed to the persons themselves for the truth of it, and they testified against him before all present, and that they had no cause to complain of any hard or unkind usage.

6. He accused them with unjust distribution, and wrote that it seemed strange that some should be allowed 16 lbs. of meal per week, and others only 4 lbs. And then adds floutingly: it seems that some men's bellies and mouths are very little and slender compared with others!

Ans: This might seem incomprehensible to those to whom he wrote his letters in England, and who did not know the reason for it; but to him and others it was well understood. The first comers had no allowance at all, but lived on their own corn. Those who came in the *Anne* the August before, and had to live thirteen months on the provisions they brought, had as good an allowance of meal and peas as would go round. A little while before harvest, when fish and fruits were to be got, they had only 4 lbs., being at liberty to make their own provisions in addition. But some of those who came last, such as the shipbuilder, the salt men, and others who were to follow constant employment and had not an hour's time from their labor to provide food besides their allowance—such workers had at first 16 lbs. allowed them, and afterwards, when fish and other food could be got, they had 14 lbs., 12 lbs., or some of them 8 lbs., as occasion required. But those who had time to plant corn for themselves, even though they received but 4 lbs. of meal a week from the store, lived better than the others, as was well known. And it must be remembered that Lyford and his family had always the highest allowance.

He accused them of many other things in his letters such as of great waste of tools and utensils—though he knew that an honest man was appointed to look after these very things; and of this, when it came to be examined, all the instances he could give was that he had seen an old hogshead or two fall to pieces, and a broken hoe or two left carelessly in the fields. But he had written such things as these to cast disgrace and prejudice upon them, thinking that what came from a minister would pass for true. He told them that Winslow had said that there were not above seven of the adventurers who sought the good of the colony; and he ended by saying that the faction here matched the Jesuits for cunning.

Finally he gave his friends advice and directions:

1. First, that the Leyden company (Mr. Robinson and the rest) must still be kept back, or all would be spoiled. Lest any of them should be taken in privately somewhere on the coast of England, as was to be feared, they must change the captain of the ship (Mr. William Pierce), and put someone else in Winslow's place as agent, or it could not be prevented.

2. He would have such further settlers shipped over as would outnumber those here; the private settlers should have votes in all courts and elections, and be free to bear any office; and every private settler should come over as an adventurer, even if he be only a servant, someone else investing the necessary £10, the bill being taken out in the servant's name, and then assigned to the party whose money it was, proper agreements being drawn between them for the purpose. These things said he, would be the means of strengthening the private settlers.

3. He told them that if that Captain they spoke of came over to take command, he was sure he would be elected, for "this Captain Standish looks like a silly boy, and is in utter contempt."

4. Then he argued that if by the aforementioned means they could not get control, it would be better to settle elsewhere by themselves, choosing the place they liked best within three or four miles, and showing that there were far better places for a settlement than this.

5. Lastly, he concluded that if neither of these things were accomplished, they must join the main body here, perforce. Then he added: "Since I began to write, some letters have come from your company, giving sole authority in various things to the Governor here; which, if it take place, then, *Vae nobis*.[13] But I hope you will be more vigilant hereafter, that nothing may pass in such a manner. I suppose Mr. Oldham will write to you further about

---

[13] Woe to us!

these things. I pray you conceal me as the source of these disclosures, etc."

I have thus briefly touched some things in his letters and shall now return to their proceedings with him. After reading his letters before the whole company, he was demanded what he could say in defense. But all the answer he made was that Billington and some others had informed him of many things, and had made sundry complaints—which they now denied. He was asked if that was sufficient ground for him thus to accuse them and traduce them by letter, never saying a word to his colleagues of the council. And so they went on from point to point, and demanded that neither he nor his confederates should spare them, if they had any proof or witness of wrong doing on their part. He said he had been misinformed, and so had wronged them. And this was all the answer they could get; for none would take his part, and Billington and others whom he named denied his statements and protested he wronged them, and that, on the other hand, he would have drawn them to such and such things, which they had declined to do, though they had sometimes attended his meetings.

Then they taxed him with dissembling about the church, professing to concur with them in everything; and with the large confession he made at his admittance, not considering himself a minister till he had a new calling, etc. Yet now he separated himself from them, and drew a number away and would administer the sacraments by his episcopal calling, without ever speaking a word to them, either as magistrates or as colleagues. In conclusion, he was fully convicted, and, bursting into tears, confessed: he feared he was a reprobate; his sins were so great he doubted if God would pardon them; he was unsavory salt, etc.; he had so wronged them that he could never make amends, confessing all that he wrote against them was false and empty, both in matter and manner—and all this as completely as words and tears could express.

After their trial and conviction the court censured them to be expelled the place; Oldham at once, though his wife and family had leave to stay all winter, or longer, till he could make provision to remove them comfortably. Lyford had leave to stay six months—with some eye to remission of the sentence, if he behaved himself well in the meantime and his repentance proved sound. Lyford acknowledged his censure was far less than he deserved.

Afterwards he confessed his sin publicly, with tears, in the church, more fully than before. I shall here record it, taken down in his own words. He acknowledged that he had done very evil and had slanderously abused them. He had thought that most of the people would take part with him, and he would carry all with a strong hand against them; that God might justly lay innocent blood to his charge, for he knew what harm might have come of his writings and blessed God they were intercepted. He had listened to any evil that was spoken, but shut his eyes and ears against all good; and if God should make him a vagabond on the earth, as was Cain, it was but just; for he had sinned in envy and malice against his brethren. He confessed three things to be the cause of his doings: pride, vainglory, and self-love—amplifying these generalities with many other sad expressions in particular.

They began to conceive well of him again after his repentance, and admitted him to preach amongst them as before; and Samuel Fuller, a deacon, and some other tender-hearted men amongst them were so taken in by his signs of sorrow and repentance, that they said they would fall upon their knees to have his sentence repealed.

But what amazed them all in the end, and will amaze all others who come to hear of it—for a rarer precedent can hardly be shown—was that after a month or two, notwithstanding all his former convictions, confessions, and public acknowledgments, both in the face of the church and the whole company, with so many sad tears and censures of himself before God and man, he should try again to justify what he had done.

For he secretly wrote a second letter to the adventurers in England, in which he justified all his former writings—except as regards some things in which he had disparaged them—which, as it is briefer than the former, I will here insert:

John Lyford at New Plymouth to the Adventurers in England:

Worthy Sirs,

Though the filth of my own doings may justly be cast in my face, and with blushing cause my perpetual silence, yet that the truth may not hereby be injured, yourselves any longer deluded, nor injurious dealings be continued with bold out-facings, I have ventured once more to write to you. First, I freely confess I dealt very indiscreetly in some of my particular letters which I wrote to private friends, concerning the motives in coming here and the like, which I do not seek to justify, though I was stirred up to it by seeing the indiscreet courses of others, both here and with you there, for effecting their designs. But I am heartily sorry for it, and do to the glory of God and my own shame acknowledge it. The said letters having been intercepted by the Governor, I am under sentence of banishment; and but for the respect I have for you, and some private matters, I should have returned by the pinnace to England, for here I do not intend to remain, unless I receive better encouragement from you than from the church (as they call themselves) here. I expected to undergo some hardships before I came, so I shall try cheerfully to bear with the conditions of the place, though they are very poor; and they have changed my wages ten times already. I suppose my letters—or at least copies of them—came into your hands, as they here report. If so, pray take notice of this: that I have written nothing but what is certainly true, and could prove it to any indifferent man. My object was not to make myself important, but to help several poor souls here, the care of whom in part belongs to you, and who are destitute of the means of salvation. The church itself is well provided for, the members forming the minority of the colony and monopolizing the ministry, believing that the Lord has not appointed any ministry for the conversion of those outside the church, so that some of the poor souls have with tears complained of this to me, and I was censured for preaching to all in general; though, in reality, they have had no ministry here since they came, but such as might be performed by any of you, whatever pretenses they make; but they equivocate about this, as about many other things. But I exceed the bounds I set myself; therefore, awaiting further from you, if it come within the time limited me, I rest, etc.

Remaining yours ever,
JOHN LYFORD, Exile.

Aug. 22nd, 1624.

They made brief answer to some things in this letter, but referred chiefly to their former one to this effect: That if God in His providence had not brought all this to their notice, they might have been traduced, abused, calumniated, overthrown, and undone; and never have known by whom or for what. They desired but this just favor; that the adventurers would be pleased to hear their defense, as well as his accusations, and weigh them in the balance of justice and reason, and then censure as they pleased.

I have been longer on this subject than I desired, but not longer than was necessary. But I will revert to other things.

To return to the pinnace left sunk near Damariscove. Some of the fishing boats' captains said it was a pity that so fine a vessel should be lost, and sent them word that if they would bear the expense, they would show them how to float her, and let them have their carpenters to mend her. They thanked them and sent men for the purpose and beaver to defray the cost. So they got coopers to trim I know not how many tons of casks, and having made them tight and fastened them to her at low water, they buoyed her up and hauled her ashore with many hands in a convenient place where she could be worked at; and then set several carpenters to work at her, and others to saw planks, and at last fitted her and got her home. But it cost a great deal of money to recover her, and to buy rigging and sails for her, both now and when she lost her mast before; so she proved an expensive vessel to the poor plantation. So they sent her home, and with her Lyford sent his last letter in great secrecy; but the party entrusted with it gave it to the Governor.

The winter passed in their ordinary pursuits, without any special matter worth noting—except that many who before stood somewhat aloof from the church, now seeing Lyford's unjust dealing and malignity, came forward and were made members, stating that it was not out of dislike of anything that they had stood off so long, but a desire to fit themselves better for such a state; and that they now saw that the Lord called for their help.

And so these troubles produced an effect on several here quite contrary to what their adversaries had hoped; and it was recognized as a great work of God, to draw men to him by unlikely means, and such as, in reason, might have been calculated to alienate them. And thus I shall end this year.

"In the meantime it pleased the Lord to give the plantation peace and health and contented minds, and so to blese ther labours . . ."

CHAPTER VI

[*1625*]

At the spring of the year, about the time of their elections,[1] Oldham came back again, and, though his sentence forbade his return without obtaining leave, his effrontery and the ill counsel of others led him to ignore it, and at the same time to give rein to his unruly passion beyond all reason and decency, so that some strangers who came with him were ashamed of his outrage and rebuked him, but all reproofs were but as oil to the fire, and enflamed his anger the more. He called them all good-for-nothings, and a hundred rebels and traitors, and I know not what. So they locked him up till he was tamer, and then he was made to pass down a line of guards, each of whom was ordered to give him a thump on the breech with the butt-end of his musket. Then he was conveyed to the waterside, where a boat was ready to take him away, and they bid him go and mend his manners.

Whilst this was going on Mr. William Pierce and Mr. Winslow came up from the shore, having arrived from England; but the others were so busy with Oldham that

---

[1] Annual meeting for the election of officers.

they never saw them until they thus came upon them. They told them not to spare either him or Lyford, for both had behaved villainously. But to make an end of Oldham I will here briefly relate what befell him in the future. After the removal of his family, he encountered difficulties and about a year afterwards, towards winter, he sailed for Virginia; but it pleased God that the ship was in great danger, and he and the other passengers despaired of life, many resorting to prayer and the examination of their consciences and confession of such sins as burdened them. Mr. Oldham then made a free and ample confession of the wrongs he had done to the people and the church here, saying that, as he had sought their ruin, so God had now met with him and might destroy him; aye, and he feared they all fared worse on account of his presence. He prayed God to forgive him, and made vows that if the Lord spared his life, he would repent. This I learned by reliable report of some who are still living at the Bay, and themselves shared the dangers of the shoals of Cape Cod and heard his very words. It pleased God to spare their lives, though they lost their voyage; and ever after Oldham behaved decently to them, acknowledging the hand of God to be with them. He seemed to respect them honestly, and so far made his peace with them that after a time he had liberty to come and go at his pleasure. He went afterwards to Virginia and there fell very ill; but he recovered and came back again to his family at the Bay, and lived there till many people had come over. At length, going trading in a small vessel among the Indians, and being weakly manned, upon some quarrel they knocked him on the head with a hatchet, so that he fell down dead and never spoke again. Two little boys that were related to him were saved, though injured, and the vessel was recovered from the Indians by another inhabitant of the Bay of Massachusetts. Oldham's death was in fact one cause of the subsequent Pequot war.

Now as to Mr. Lyford. His time having expired, his sentence was to be carried out. He was so far from fulfilling their hopes of amendment that he had doubled his offense, as shown. But behold the hand of God upon him, wherein the Psalmist is verified (Psalm VII, 15): He hath made a pit and digged it, and is fallen into the pit he made. He thought to bring disgrace upon them but instead he discloses his own shame to all the world. When he was confronted with his second letter, his wife was so stirred by his doings that she could no longer conceal her grief, and opened her mind to one of the deacons and some of her friends, and later to Mr. Pierce, on his arrival. She said that she feared some great judgment of God would fall upon the family, because of her husband; and now that they were about to remove she feared she would fall into the Indians' hands and be defiled by them as he had defiled other women, recalling God's threatened judgment upon David (II Samuel, XII, 11): I will raise up evil against thee out of thine own house, and will take thy wives before thine eyes, and give them unto thy neighbor.

Then she disclosed how he had wronged her, and that he had a bastard by another woman before they were married. She had had some inkling of it when he was courting her, and told him what she had heard rumored; but he not only stiffly denied it, but to satisfy her took a solemn oath; so she consented to marry him. Afterwards she found it was true, and the bastard was brought home to them. She reminded him of his oath, but he prayed her to pardon him, and pleaded that otherwise he would not have won her. And yet even after this she could keep no maidservant but he would be meddling with them, and sometimes she had taken him in the act. The woman was a respectable matron, of good behavior all the while she was here, and spoke out of the sorrow of her heart, sparingly, but circumstantially. What seemed to affect her most was his easy repentances, followed by a speedy return to the old paths.

This was all borne out by the reports of Mr. Winslow and Mr. Pierce on their return. Mr. Winslow informed them that they had had the same trouble with Lyford's friends in England as with himself and his friends here—his adherents crying out that to deal thus with a minister and a godly man was a great scandal, and threatening to prosecute them for it. So it was all referred to a further meeting of most of the adventurers there, who agreed to choose two eminent men as arbitrators. Lyford's faction chose Mr. White, a counselor at law; the others chose the Rev. Mr. Hooker, the minister. In the meantime God in His providence had disclosed Lyford's evil career in Ireland to some friends of the Company, who made it known to Mr. Winslow, and mentioned two godly witnesses who would testify upon their oath.

The fact was that when Lyford was in Ireland he had wound himself into the esteem of several worthy reformers, who, burdened with the ceremonies in England, found greater liberty of conscience there. Amongst them were the two men who gave evidence; and amongst others there was an honest young man who intended to marry, and had set his affection on a certain girl who lived there. But preferring the fear of God to all other things, before he suffered his affection to run too far, he resolved to take Mr. Lyford's advice and judgment about the girl—since he was the minister of the place—and so spoke of it to him.

He promised to inform him faithfully, but wished to get to know her better first, and have some private talk with her. In conclusion he recommended her highly to the young man as a very fit wife for him. So they were married.

But some time afterwards the woman was much troubled in mind and afflicted in conscience, and did nothing but weep and mourn; and it was long before her husband could find out the cause. But at length she told him—praying him to forgive her—that Lyford had overcome her and defiled her before marriage. The circumstances I forbear; suffice it, that though he satisfied his lust upon her, he endeavored to hinder conception. The young husband then took some godly friends with him to confront Lyford with this charge. At length he confessed it with a great deal of seeming repentance and sorrow, but he was forced to leave Ireland, partly for shame and partly for fear of further punishment; and so, coming to England, unhappily he was hit upon as a suitable minister for the colony and sent out to them. The arbitrators with great gravity declared that his recent offenses there gave them cause enough to deal with him as they had done; but these disclosures made him unfit ever to bear ministry any more, what repentance soever he should pretend.

From here Lyford went to Nantasket, on the Bay of the Massachusetts, where Oldham lived with some of his friends. Thence he removed to Naumkeag, since called Salem; but later, whether for hope of greater profit or what I know not, he forsook the friends who had stuck to him, and went down to Virginia, where shortly after he died; and so I leave him to the Lord. His wife afterwards returned to this country; thus much of this matter.

Though the storm had blown over, the effects which

followed it were serious; for the company of adventurers broke up in consequence, and the majority wholly deserted the colony as regards any further supplies. Furthermore, some of Lyford's and Oldham's friends fitted out a fishing ship on their own account, and arriving ahead of the ships that came to the plantation, took away their dock and other necessary preparations that they had made for their fishing at Cape Ann the year before at great expense and would not restore it unless they would fight for it. However, the Governor decided to send some of the settlers to help the fishermen build a new one, and let them keep it. This fishing ship also brought Lyford's and Oldham's contingent some supplies, but of little value; but they were unsuccessful in their fishing, and they could make no return for the supplies sent, so after this year their friends in England never looked after them again.

This ship also brought from some of the adventurers their reasons for having abandoned the colony, and offers of reuniting again upon certain conditions. They are long and tedious, and most of them have already been touched upon.

Their answer was in part as follows:

In charging us with having dissembled with His Majesty and the adventurers in our original declaration of general agreement with the French Reformed Church, you do us wrong, for we both hold with and practice the beliefs of the French and other Reformed Churches as published in the *Harmony of Confessions*, according to our means, in effect and substance. But in attempting to tie us to the French practices in every detail, you derogate from the liberty we have in Christ Jesus. The Apostle Paul would have none follow him but wherein he followed Christ;

much less ought any Christian or church in the world to do so. The French may err, we may err, and other churches may err, and doubtless do in many circumstances. The honor of infallibility, therefore, belongs only to the word of God and the pure testament of Christ, to be followed as the only rule and pattern for direction by all churches and Christians. It is great arrogance for any man or church to think that he or they have so sounded the word of God to the bottom as to be able to set down precisely a church's practices without error in substance or circumstance, and in such a way that no one thereafter may digress or differ from them with impunity. Indeed it is not difficult to show that the Reformed Churches differ from each other in many details.

The rest I omit for brevity's sake; and so leave these men and their doings, and return to the rest of the adventurers, who were friends of the company and stuck to them. I will first insert some of their letters; for I think it best to render their minds in their own words:

Letter to the Colonists at New Plymouth, from the Adventurers in England who remained friendly to them:

To our Loving Friends, etc.

Though what we feared has happened, and the evil we tried to avert has overtaken us, still we cannot forget you or our friendship and fellowship of some years' standing, and though its expression has been small, our hearty affection towards you, unknown by face, has been no less than to our nearest friends or even to ourselves. And though your friend Mr. Winslow can tell you the state of things here, lest we should seem to neglect you, to whom by a wonderful providence of God we are so nearly united, we have thought well to write and let you know what has happened here and the reasons for it, and our intentions and desires concerning you for the future.

The old basis of partnership is entirely dissolved, and we are left to bethink ourselves what course to take in the future, that your lives and our money be not lost.

The causes of these alterations are as follows: First and mainly, the many losses and crosses at sea and the abuses of seamen have incurred such heavy expenses for us that we could not continue without impoverishing ourselves, unless our means had been greater and our associates had stuck together. Secondly, there has been a faction against you, which, though influenced to abandon you mainly for want of money, pretended to charge you with being Brownists,[2] etc. But how you or we ought to turn all this to account remains to be considered; for we know the hand of God to be in all these things, and no doubt He would admonish us hereby to see what is amiss.

While we ourselves are ready to take every opportunity to further so hopeful an enterprise, it must rest with you to put it on its feet again. And whatever else may be said, let your honesty and conscience remain approved, and lose no jot of your innocence amidst your crosses and afflictions; and surely if you behave yourselves wisely and go on fairly, you will need no other weapon to wound your adversaries; for when your righteousness is revealed as the light, they, who have causelessly sought your overthrow, shall cover their faces with shame.

We think it only right that everything belonging to the common stock shall be kept together and increased, rather than dispersed for any private ends whatever; and that after your necessities are met, you shall send over such commodities as the country affords, to pay the debts and clear the engagements here, which amount to not less than £1400. Let us all endeavor to keep an honest course, and see what time will bring forth, and what God in His providence will work for us. We are still convinced that you

---

[2] For a discussion of Browne, see Introduction, pp. xii–xiii.

are the people who must make the settlement a success when all others fail and return; and your experience of God's providence and preservation of you is such that we hope your hearts will not fail you, though your friends should forsake you—which we ourselves will not do whilst we live and your honesty of purpose remains unchanged.

We have sent you some cattle, clothes, stockings, shoes, leather, etc. We have consigned them to Mr. Allerton and Mr. Winslow as our agents, at whose discretion they are to be sold in exchange for commodities. Go on, good friends, comfortably; pluck up your spirits and quit yourselves like men in all your difficulties, that, notwithstanding all the threats of men, your good work may continue; for inasmuch as it is for the glory of God and the good of our countrymen, it is a better course for a man to run than to live the life of Methuselah in wasting the plenty of a tilled land or eating the fruit of a grown tree.

With hearty salutations to you all, and hearty prayers for you all, we lovingly take our leaves, this 18th of Dec., 1624.

> Your assured friends to our power,
> J.S. W.C. T.F. R.H. etc.

This letter shows the state of affairs of the plantations at this time. They bought the goods, but at dear rates. The adventurers put 40 percent on them for profit and risk outward bound; and for risk on the goods sent back in payment, homeward bound, they added another 30 percent— in all 70 percent.[3] This seemed unreasonable to some, and too oppressive, considering the case of the purchasers. The cattle were most valuable; the other things were neither of the best quality nor at the best prices.

---

[3] Exorbitant rates of interest, current at this period, were a crushing burden to the Pilgrims in their efforts to work themselves free of debt.

They also sent over two fishing ships on their own account. One was the pinnace which was wrecked the previous year here and saved by the planters, and which, after she reached home, was attached by one of the Company for a private debt, and had now been sent out again on his account. The other was a large ship, well fitted, with an experienced captain and crew of fishermen, to make a fishing cruise, and then to go to Bilbao or Sebastian to sell her fish. The pinnace was ordered to load with corfish, and to bring home to England the beaver received for the goods sold to the plantation. The big ship was well laden with good dry fish, which at market prices would have yielded £1800. But as there was a rumor of war with France, the captain feared to carry out his orders, and on getting over, put first into Plymouth, and afterwards into Portsmouth, and so met with a heavy loss, being obliged to sell at lower prices.

The pinnace met with no better success. She was laden with a cargo of corfish caught on the banks, as full as she could float; and besides she had some 800 lbs. of beaver, as well as other furs to a good value, from the plantation. The captain, seeing so much lading, wished to put it aboard the bigger ship, for greater safety; but as Mr. Winslow, their agent in the business, was bound in a bond of £500 to send it to London in the small ship, there was some discussion between the captain and him about it. But he told the captain he must obey his orders about it, or ignore them at his peril. So the furs went in the small ship, and he sent bills of lading in both.

The captain of the big ship was so careful, both vessels being so well-laden, that he towed the small ship at his stern all the way over. So they went joyfully home together, and had such fine weather that he never cast her off till they were well within the England channel, almost in sight of Plymouth. But even there she was unhappily taken by a Turkish man-of-war, and carried off to Saller,[4] where the captain and crew were made slaves, and many of the beaver skins were sold for 4d. a piece. Thus all their hopes were dashed, and the joyful news they meant to carry home was turned to heavy tidings. Some thought this was the hand of God in punishment for their too great exaction of the poor colony; but God's judgments are unsearchable, nor dare I make bold with them. However, it shows us the uncertainty of all human things, and how foolish it is to take pleasure in them or trust to them.

In the big ship, Captain Standish was sent over from the settlement with instructions and letters both to their friends of the Company and to the honorable Council of New England. They requested the Company, since they only meant to let them have goods for sale, that they might have them upon easier terms, as they would never be able to bear such high interest or allow so much percent; and that they should send goods which were useful and suitable to them. They wished the Company to be informed of the contents of the letter to the Council of New England. This letter sought the Council's favor and help, and asked that the adventurers who had forsaken them might be brought to order and not keep the colony bound while they themselves went free; and that they might either stand by their former agreement, or else reach some fair conclusion by dividend or composition.

But he arrived at a very bad time, for the country was full of trouble, and the plague very deadly in London, so that no business could be done. However, he spoke with

---

[4] Sallee, on the Moroccan west coast.

some of the honored Council, who promised all possible help to the colony. Several of the friendly adventurers were so reduced by their losses last year, and now by the ship taken by the Turks, and the decreased profits on their fish, and such multitudes in London were dying weekly of the plague, that all trade was dead and little money was available; so that with great difficulty he raised £150 (and spent a good deal of it in expenses) at 50 percent, which he expended on trading goods and such other commodities as he knew they needed. He returned as passenger on a fishing ship, having made good preparations for the settlement that was afterwards made with the adventurers.

In the meantime it pleased the Lord to give the plantation peace and health and contented minds, and so to bless their labors that they had sufficient corn, and some to spare for others, besides other food. After harvest this year, they sent out a boat-load of corn forty or fifty leagues to the eastward, up a river called the Kennebec. The boat they sent was one of the two shallops their carpenter had built them the year before; for they had nothing bigger. They laid a little deck over her midships to keep the corn dry, but the men had to make the best of all weathers without shelter—and that time of year it begins to be rough. But God preserved them and gave them success. They brought home £700 worth of beaver, besides some other furs, having little or nothing else for trading with but this corn, which they themselves had raised out of the earth. This voyage was made by Mr. Winslow and some of the old standers, for they had no sailors.

"But they gathered up their spirits, and the Lord so helped them, whose worke they had in hand, as now when they were at the lowest they begane to rise againe . . ."

CHAPTER VII

[*1626*]

About the beginning of April they heard of Captain Standish's arrival, and sent a boat to fetch him home with the things he had brought. He was welcome; but the news he brought was sad in many regards; not only as to the losses which their friends had suffered, but also the tidings that Mr. John Robinson,[1] their old pastor, was dead, which saddened them much and not without cause. Their adversaries had been long plotting to hinder his coming hither; but the Lord had appointed him a better place. An account of his death is given in these few lines written to the Governor and Mr. Brewster.

---

[1] Robinson had been their pastor since 1609 and his death was a severe blow to the Pilgrims, who had been cheered and comforted by his letters full of sagacious advice, and inspired by the hope that he would be allowed to join them. In his later years Robinson had grown more tolerant and liberal, setting himself against narrow sectarianism. He was buried in St. Peter's Church in Leyden, just across from the Pilgrims' meeting place, and a tablet to his memory was set in its wall.

A letter from Roger White at Leyden to Governor Bradford and William Brewster at New Plymouth:

Loving and kind Friends,

I do not know whether this will ever come to your hands, or miscarry as my other letters have done. But because of the Lord's dealing with us here, I have had a great wish to write to you, knowing your desire to participate with us both in our joys and sorrows, as we do with you. This is to give you to understand that it has pleased the Lord to take out of this vale of tears your and our loving and faithful pastor, and my dear and reverend brother, Mr. John Robinson, who was ill for some eight days. He began to sicken on Saturday morning; yet next day (being the Lord's day) he taught us twice. The week after he grew daily weaker, but was without pain. The physic he took seemed to benefit him, but he grew weaker every day, though he remained sensible to the last. He fell sick on Feb. 22nd, and departed this life on March 1st. He suffered from a continual inward ague, but was free from infection, so that all his friends came to see him. If either prayers or tears or care could have saved his life, he had not gone hence. But he having faithfully finished his course, and performed the work which the Lord had appointed him here to do, now rests with the Lord in eternal happiness. Since his going our Church lacks a governor; yet we still continue by the mercy of God, and hold close together in peace and quietness; and so hope to do, though we are very weak. We wish (if such were the will of God) that you and we were again united, either there or here; but seeing it is the will of the Lord thus to dispose of things, we must labor with patience to rest contented, till it please the Lord otherwise to dispose. As for news, there is not much. In England we have lost our old King James,[2]

---

[2] James I of England died Mar. 27, 1625, to be succeeded by Charles I, from whom the Pilgrims could hope for even less protection.

who departed this life about a month ago; and here they have lost the old prince, Grave Maurice; both having departed this life since my brother Robinson. In England we have a new king, Charles, of whom there is great hope; here they have put Prince Henry in his brother's place. Thus with my love remembered, I take leave and rest,
                            Your assured loving friend,
                                    Roger White.
Leyden, April 28th, 1625.

Thus these two great princes and the colonists' old pastor left this world about the same time. Death makes no difference.

Captain Standish further brought them notice of the death of their early friend, Mr. Cushman,[3] whom the Lord took away also this year, and who had been their right hand with their friends, the adventurers, and for many years had undertaken all their business with them to great advantage. He had written to the Governor but a few months before of the serious illness of Mr. James Sherley, one of the chief friends of the plantation, who lay at the point of death, praising his love and helpfulness in everything, and much bemoaning the loss his death would be to them, for he was the stay and life of the whole business; also that he proposed to come over this year and spend the rest of his days with them. But he who thus wrote of another's illness, knew not his own death was so near. It shows that a man's ways are not in his own power, but in His hands, Who has the issue of life and death. Man may propose, but God doth dispose.

Count Maurice of Nassau, Prince of Orange, second son of William the Silent, died in April and was succeeded by his brother Count Frederick Henry.
[3] Deacon Robert Cushman died of the plague.

Their other friends from Leyden wrote many sad letters to them, lamenting the heavy loss of their pastor, and though they would gladly come to them, they saw no probability of it, but concluded that all their hopes were at an end; and besides, many, being aged, began to drop away by death.

They were greatly perplexed—and not without cause. But they took courage, and the Lord so helped them, Whose work they had in hand, that now when they seemed at the lowest ebb they began to rise again; and being stripped as it were of all human helps and props, by His divine providence they were not only upheld and sustained, but their example was both honored and imitated by others; as the sequel will show if the Lord spare me life and time to unfold it.

Having now no fishing business or other things to attend to besides their trading and planting, they set themselves to follow them with the best industry they could. The settlers, finding that their spare corn was a commodity worth six shillings a bushel, spared no pains in sowing it. The Governor and those appointed to manage the trade (for it was still retained for the general benefit, and none were allowed to trade for themselves) co-operated; so, lacking goods to trade with, and hearing that a settlement which had been at Monhegan and belonged to some merchants at Plymouth was to break up, and many useful goods were to be sold, the Governor and Mr. Winslow took a boat and some hands and went there. Mr. David Thomson, who lived at Piscataqua, learning their purpose, took the opportunity to go with them; but lest their competition for the goods should raise the prices, they agreed to buy them all and divide them equally between them. They also bought some goats, which they distributed amongst the colonists as they thought fit in exchange for corn. Their share of the goods came to above £400 sterling. That same spring a French ship had been wrecked at Sagadahoc, containing many Biscay rugs and other commodities, which had fallen into the hands of these people and some fishermen at Damariscove Islands, who had been taken into partnership; and these extras increased their share of the purchase to £500. This they made shift to pay for, chiefly with beaver and goods they had got the winter before, and what they had obtained that summer. Mr. Thomson having somewhat exceeded his resources, asked them to relieve him of some of his purchase; but they declined to take any but the French goods, and on the understanding that the merchant who was selling them, and who was a Bristol man, would take their bill to be paid next year; to which both parties agreed. By this means they were well furnished with articles for trading, and were able to take up some of their previous engagement, such as the money raised by Captain Standish and the balance of former debts. With these goods and their corn, when harvested, they traded profitably, and were able to meet their engagements punctually and get some clothing for the people, and still had some supplies in hand. But soon they began to be emulated, and others went and supplied the Indians with corn and beat down the price, giving them twice as much as they had done, and under-traded them with other articles too.

This year they sent Mr. Allerton to England, and gave him instructions to settle with the adventurers upon as good terms as he could, for which composition Captain Standish had paved the way the year before. They enjoined him not to conclude absolutely till they knew the terms and had well considered them, but to arrange preliminaries as well as he could, and refer the conclusion to them. They also gave him commission under their hands and seals to raise some money, provided it did not exceed the sum specified, for which they engaged themselves and instructed him how to expend it for the use of the plantation.

Finding that they ran great risks in going such long voyages in a small open boat, especially during the winter, they began to think how they could get a small pinnace. It was the more necessary since others were paying the Indians half as much corn again as they had formerly given, and in such a small boat they could not carry a quantity sufficient for their purposes. They had no shipbuilder among them, nor did they know how to get one at present; but they had an ingenious man who was a house carpenter, who had worked under the shipbuilder who died, when he was building their boats. So at their request he tried his skill, and took one of the biggest of their shallops, sawed her across the middle, lengthened her about five or six feet, strengthened her with timbers, built her up and decked her and made her a convenient and serviceable vessel, suitable for their use. They got her finished and fitted with sails and anchors for the coming year; and she did them service for seven years.

Thus passed the affairs of this year.

"For the present, excepte peace and union were preserved they should be able to doe nothing, but endanger to over throw all, now that other tyes and bonds were taken away."

CHAPTER VIII
[*1627*]

At the usual season of the arrival of ships, Mr. Allerton returned, and brought some useful goods with him according to the orders given him. As commissioned, he had raised £200, which he got at 30 percent. They got the goods safely home and in good condition. He told them, also, how with much ado he had arranged for a settlement with the adventurers, with the help of several of their faithful friends there. Of the agreement or bargain he had brought a draft with a list of their names annexed, drawn by the best counsel of law they could get, to make it binding. The body of it I insert here.

To all Christian people, greeting, etc.[1]

Whereas at a meeting on the 26th of October last, several persons whose names to the one part of these presents are subscribed in a schedule hereunto annexed, adventurers to New Plymouth in New England in America, agreed in

---

[1] By this document, six years after their arrival, the Pilgrims bought out all rights of the London company of adventurers in their joint enterprise, for the price of £1800, the money to be paid in instalments of £200 a year. Thus they made themselves masters of their own affairs, subject only to the authority of the English government.

consideration of the sum of one thousand and eight hundred pounds sterling to be paid (in manner and form following) to sell and make sale of all the stocks, shares, lands, merchandise, and chattels, whatsoever, to the said adventurers and their fellow adventurers to New Plymouth aforesaid, in any way accruing or belonging to the generality of the said adventurers aforesaid; as well as for any sum or sums of money or merchandise at any time heretofore adventured or disbursed by them howsoever; for the better setting forth and expression of the said agreement the parties to these presents subscribing, do for themselves severally, and as much as in them is, grant, bargain, alien, sell, and transfer, all the said shares, goods, lands, merchandise, and chattels, to them belonging as aforesaid to Isaac Allerton, one of the planters resident at New Plymouth aforesaid, assigned and sent over as agent for the rest of the planters there, and to such other planters at New Plymouth aforesaid as the said Isaac, his heirs or assigns, at his or their arrival, shall by writing or otherwise think fit to join or partake in the premises, their heirs and assigns, in as large, ample, and beneficial manner and form, to all intents and purposes, as the said subscribing adventurers here could or may do or perform. All which stocks, shares, lands, etc., to the said adventurers allotted, apportioned, or in any way belonging, the said adventurers do warrant and defend unto the said Isaac Allerton, his heirs and assigns, against them, their heirs and assigns, by these presents. And therefore the said Isaac Allerton, does, for him, his heirs and assigns, covenant, promise, and grant to and with the adventurers whose names are hereunto subscribed, their heirs, etc., well and truly to pay, or cause to be paid, to the said adventurers, or 5 of them, which were at that meeting aforesaid, nominated and deputed, viz.: John Pocock, John Beauchamp, Robert Kean, Edward Bass, and James Sherley, merchants, their heirs, etc., to and for the use of the generality of them, the sum of £1800 of lawful money of

England, at the place appointed for the receipts of money, on the west side of the Royal Exchange in London, by £200 yearly, and every year, on the feast of St. Michael, the first payment to be made A.D. 1628, . . . Also the said Isaac is to endeavor to procure and obtain from the planters of New Plymouth aforesaid, security, by several obligations, or writings obligatory, to make payment of the said sum of £1800 in form aforesaid, according to the true meaning of these presents. In testimony whereof to this part of these presents remaining with the said Isaac Allerton, the said subscribing adventurers have set their names, . . . And to the other part remaining with the said adventurers the said Isaac Allerton has subscribed his name, the 15th Nov., 1626, in the second year of his majesty's reign.

John White
John Pocock
Robert Kean
Edward Bass
William Hobson
William Pennington
William Quarles
Daniel Poynton
Richard Andrews
Newman Rookes
Henry Prowning
Richard Wright
John Ling
Thomas Goffe
Samuel Sharpe
Robert Holland
James Sherley
Thomas Mott
Thomas Fletcher
Timothy Hatherley
Thomas Brewer

John Thorned
Myles Knowles
William Collier
John Revell
Peter Gudburn
Emnu Alltham
John Beauchamp
Thomas Hudson
Thomas Andrews
Thomas Ward
Fria Newbald
Thomas Heath
Joseph Tilden
William Perrin
Eliza Knight
Thomas Coventry
Robert Alden
Lawrence Anthony
John Knight
Matthew Thornhill
Thomas Millsop

This agreement was approved by all the plantation, and consented to, though they did not know just how to raise the payment and meet other engagements and supply the yearly wants of the colony, since they were forced to raise money or purchase goods at such high interest to supply themselves with necessities. However, they undertook it, and seven or eight of the chief members became jointly bound for the payment of the £1800 on behalf of the rest, at the days set. It was a great risk as things stood at present. At the return of their agent it was absolutely confirmed on both sides, and the bargain was fairly engrossed on parchment, and many things put into better form by the advice of the most learned counsel they could get; and to prevent forfeiture of the whole for non-payment on any of the days, it ran thus: to forfeit thirty shillings a week if they missed the time.

Now there were some unsuitable people among them from the first who came from England, and others sent later by some of the adventurers, concerning whom the Governor and Council had seriously to consider how to settle things in regard to this new bargain, in respect of the distribution of things both for the present and future. For the present, unless peace and unity were preserved, they would be able to do nothing, but would endanger everything. So they decided to include all in the partnership—*i. e.* either heads of families or single young men of ability who were free and able to be helpful to the commonwealth; for, first, they had need of men for defense and carrying on business; secondly, most of them had borne their part in former miseries, and ought to be allowed to partake of the greater prosperity, if the Lord were pleased to give it.

So they called the company together and conferred

with them, and came to the conclusion that the trade should be managed as before, to help to pay the debts; and all eligible persons should be enrolled as purchasers, single free men to have a single share, and every father of a family to be allowed to purchase as many shares as there were members of his family—that is to say, one for himself, one for his wife, and one for every child that he had living with him. As for servants, they had none, except what their masters gave them out of theirs, or their deserts should gain them from the company afterwards. The shares were allotted accordingly, and everyone was to pay his proportion towards the purchase and all other debts which the profits derived from trading did not cover. This gave satisfaction to all.[2]

The cattle they had were divided first, in this proportion: a cow to six persons or shares, and two goats to the same, the stock being first equalized in value according to age and quality, and then drawn for by lots. Pigs, though more numerous, were dealt with similarly. Then they agreed that every person or share should have twenty acres of land allotted to them, besides the single acres they owned already. Those appointed to make the allotment were instructed to begin first on one side of the town, up to a certain distance, and then on the other side, similarly;

---

[2] By the arrangement here described, the trade of the colony was still to be kept as the business of the colony as a whole, since from the proceeds of it must be paid the yearly debt of £200 to the London adventurers, as well as other outstanding public expenses. But houses, livestock and land enough to enable each family to grow its own staple crops were now distributed to private owners. Later in the year, for reasons given below, the conduct of the trade and the payment of the public debts were put into the hands of a commission of five, with agents of their own choosing in London, for the space of six more years.

and to include only tillable land—or at least such of it as was along the water-side, as most of it was—and to leave the rest as common land. They were all to agree as to the fitness of it before the lots were drawn, to avoid dissatisfaction afterwards. For the same reason they agreed by mutual consent, before any lots were drawn, that those whose land was nearest the town should choose a neighbor or two whom they would allow to plant corn with them for four years; and afterwards they should be allowed to use as much of theirs for the same period if they wished. Every plot of twenty acres was to be laid out five acres in breadth along the water side and four acres in length, excepting nooks and corners which were to be measured to best advantage. But no meadows were to be laid out at all; nor were they for many years after, because of the scarceness of meadow land. If they had been given out now, it would have hindered later developments; so each season everyone was shown where to mow, according to the proportion of cattle he had, and the fodder he required.

This distribution gave general satisfaction, and settled men's minds. They gave the Governor and four or five leading men among them the houses they lived in; the other houses were valued, and equalized fairly, and everyone kept his own; so that he who had a better house made some allowance to him who had a worse, according to the valuation.

One thing which occurred at the beginning of the previous winter I have deferred mentioning till now, so that I might handle it altogether. A ship with goods and many passengers aboard, bound for Virginia, lost herself at sea, either through the incompetence of the captain, or his illness—for he was so ill with scurvy that he could only lie at the cabin door and give directions—and it seemed he was poorly helped by the mate and the crew; or perhaps the fear and unruliness of the passengers made them steer a course between the southwest and the northwest, so that they might make land the sooner. They had been six weeks at sea, and had no water or beer or wood left, having burnt up all their empty casks. One of the passengers had a hogshead of wine or two, which was almost used up, and they feared they would be starved at sea or wiped out by disease—and so they ran this desperate course.

But it pleased God that though they either only just avoided the shoals of Cape Cod, or else ran stumbling over them in the night they knew not how, they made right towards a small blind harbor which lies about in the middle of Manamoick Bay, to the south of Cape Cod; and about high water they touched upon a bar of sand that lies across it, but took no harm, the sea being smooth; so they put out an anchor. But towards the evening the wind sprang up at sea, and it was so rough that their cable broke and they were beaten over the bar into the harbor, where they saved their lives and their cargo, though much was injured by salt water, for in the storm they had sprung the butt-end of a plank or two and beat out their oakum; but they were soon over, and ran onto a dry flat within the harbor, close by the beach. So at low water they got out their goods and dried those that were wet, and saved most of their things without any great loss; nor was the ship so badly damaged but that she might be mended and made serviceable again. But though they were glad that they had saved their lives, when they had refreshed themselves a little they began to realize their condition, and not knowing where they were or what they should do they lost heart. Shortly after, they saw some Indians coming to them in canoes, which made them stand upon their guard. But when they heard some of the Indians speak English to them, they were relieved, especially when they asked if they were the Governor of Plymouth's men, or friends of theirs, and offered to guide them to the English settlement or carry their letters.

They feasted these Indians and gave them many presents, and sent two of their men and a letter with them to the Governor, and begged him to send a boat to them with some pitch and oakum and spikes and various other necessaries to mend their ship. They also asked him to help them with some corn and several other things they wanted, to enable them to continue their voyage to Virginia. They promised to pay for anything they received in any goods which they had aboard.

After the Governor had been informed by the messengers of their condition, he had a boat got ready with the supplies they needed, and as the other more responsible members of the colony were away trading, he went himself and took some trading goods, too, to buy corn from the Indians. It was no season of the year to go outside the Cape, but knowing where the ship lay, he coasted along the lower side of the Bay and put into a creek called Namskeket,[3] where it is not much above two miles overland to the bay where they were; and he had Indians ready to carry over anything to them. They were very glad of his arrival, and of the things to mend their ship and other necessaries. He also brought them as much corn as they wanted; and some of their sailors having run away among the Indians, he had them sent back to the ship, and so left

---

[3] Naumskachett creek is on the inside of the Cape, between Brewster and Orleans.

them well provided and very grateful for the courtesies shown them.

After the Governor left them, he went into some other harbors near there and loaded his boat with corn, which he traded, and then went home. He had not been home many days before he received word from them that in a violent storm, owing to the bad mooring of the ship after she had been mended, she was driven ashore again, and so beaten that she was wholly unfit to go to sea. So their request was that they might have leave to come to them and live with them, till they could convey themselves to Virginia. If they might have means to transport their goods, they would pay for it and for anything else with which the plantation could provide them. Considering their distress, all their requests were granted, and all help rendered them—their goods transported and they themselves accommodated in their houses as well as they could.

The chief among these people were a Mr. Fells and a Mr. Sibsie, who had a number of servants belonging to them, many of them Irish. Some others had a servant or two each; but most of the people were themselves servants and were engaged by the two men mentioned above, who owned most of the cargo. After they had arrived and were settled, the masters asked for some land to employ their servants upon, since it was likely to be the latter end of the year before they could get passage for Virginia, and they had now the winter before them. If they had opportunity to take passage before the crop was ripe, they would sell it standing. So they had ground allotted in convenient places, and Fells and some of them grew a great deal of corn, which they sold at their departure.

This Fells, amongst his other servants, had a maid-servant who kept his house and did his household affairs; and, as was intimated by some who were with him, he was suspected of keeping her as his concubine. Both of them were questioned as to this, but nothing could be proved and they stood upon their justification; so they were dismissed with admonition. But afterwards it appeared she was with child, so he got a small boat and ran away with her for fear of punishment. First he went to Cape Ann, and afterwards to the Bay of Massachusetts; but he could get no passage and was nearly wrecked, so he was forced to come back and submit himself. So they packed him away and those that belonged to him at the first opportunity, and dismissed all the rest as soon as they could, as there were many undesirable people among them, though there were also some who behaved themselves very well all the time they stayed. And the plantation benefited by selling them corn and other provisions in exchange for clothing, of which they had a variety, such as cloth, perpetuanes [4] and other stuffs, besides stockings and shoes and such like goods, which the planters stood in need of. So the advantage was mutual, and a couple of barks took them away at the latter end of the summer. Several of them have since acknowledged their gratitude from Virginia.

So that they might lose no opportunity of trading, the settlers decided to build a small pinnace at Manomet, a place on the sea twenty miles to the southward of them, towards which ran a creek, so that they could convey their goods to within four or five miles of it, and then transport them overland to their vessel, and so avoid rounding Cape Cod, with its dangerous shoals. By this means

---

[4] A woolen fabric made in England; so called because of its durability.

they could make voyages southward in much shorter time and with far less danger. For the safety of their vessel and goods they built a house and kept some servants there, who also planted corn and kept swine and were always ready to go out with the bark when needed. It was a satisfactory and profitable enterprise.

With the return of the ships they sent Mr. Allerton to England again, giving him full power under their hands and seals to conclude the former bargain with the adventurers, and sent them bonds for the payment of the money. They also sent what beaver they could spare to meet some of their engagements and to defray his expenses; but the high rates of interest left them little margin. He had orders to procure a patent for a suitable trading-house on the river Kennebec; for the settlers at Piscataqua and other places to the eastward of them and also the fishing ships competed with them for the trade of the Indians, and threatened by procuring a grant to exclude them from thereabouts—and they found they were so well furnished with goods for the purpose that they might take all the trade from them. They thought it essential to prevent this, and at least to preserve free trade for themselves in localities which they themselves had first discovered and developed.

This year they received letters and messengers from the Dutch colony, sent to them from the Governor there, written both in Dutch and French. The Dutch had traded to the south of them several years before they came, but had made no settlement there till four or five years after their arrival at New Plymouth. Their letters were as follows—it being their custom to be full of complimental titles.

I shall render it in English, leaving out the superfluous titles from the body of the letter.

The Dutch Colonists at Manhattan to the Settlers at New Plymouth:

Noble, worshipful, wise and prudent Lords, the Governor and Councilors residing at New Plymouth, our very dear friends:

The Director and Council of New Netherlands wish to your Lordships, worshipful, wise and prudent, happiness in Christ Jesus Our Lord, with prosperity and health in soul and body.

We have often before this wished for an opportunity to congratulate you on your prosperous and praiseworthy undertakings, and the government of your colony there; the more so, since we also have made a good beginning in the foundation of a colony here, and because our native country is not far from yours, and our forefathers many years ago formed friendship and alliance with your ancestors both for war and trade, confirmed under the hands of kings and princes. These have not only been confirmed by the king now reigning, but it has pleased His Majesty, upon mature deliberation, to make a new alliance to take up arms against our common enemy the Spaniards,[5] who seeks to usurp the lands of other Christian kings so that he may obtain his pretended monarchy over all Christendom, and so rule at his pleasure over the consciences of so many hundred thousand souls; which God forbid!

It appears that some of our people, who happened to go northward in their boat, met some Indians, who told them that they were within half a day's journey of your planta-

---

[5] In the first years of his reign Charles I, under the Duke of Buckingham's influence, made some vain attempts to help the Protestant cause on the Continent against the Catholic monarchies of Spain and Austria.

tion, and offered to take letters to you; so we could not forbear to salute you with these few lines, bearing our good will and service to you, in all friendly kindliness and neighborhood. If it should happen that any goods that come to us from our native country may be serviceable to you, we shall feel ourselves bound to accommodate you either for beaver or any other merchandise. Should we have no goods at present that you want, if you care to sell us any beaver, or otter, or such, for ready money, and let us hear in writing by this bearer, whom we have instructed to wait three or four days for your answer, we will depute someone to deal with you at any place you may appoint. In the meantime we pray the Lord to take you, our honored friends and neighbors, into His holy protection.

By appointment of the Governor and Council, etc.
ISAAC DE RASIÈRES,[6] Secretary.

From Manhattan, in the Fort of Amsterdam. March 9th, 1627.

To this they answered as follows:

From the Settlement at New Plymouth to the Dutch Colony at New Amsterdam:

To the honored, etc.

The Governor and Council of New Plymouth, wishes, etc. We have received your letters, expressing your good will and friendship towards us, but with over high titles, more than is our right, or it is fitting for us to receive. But for your good will and congratulations of our prosperity in these small beginnings of our poor colony we are much obliged to you, and acknowledge them with many thanks,

---

[6] Isaac de Rasières had come to New Netherlands in 1626, as secretary of the colony under Peter Minuit.

accepting them as a great honor to us and a sure proof of your love and good neighborhood.

This is also to give your worships to understand, that it is no small joy to us to hear that His Majesty has not only been pleased to confirm the ancient alliances and other contracts formerly made by his predecessors of famous memory, but has himself (as you say) strengthened them with a new bond, the better to resist the pride of that common enemy, the Spaniard, from whose cruelty the Lord keep us both, and our native countries. Now though this were sufficient to unite us together in love and good neighborhood in all our dealings, many of us are under further obligations for the courteous treatment we received in your country, having lived there for many years in freedom, as many of our friends do to this day; for which we and our children after us are bound to be grateful to your nation, and shall never forget it, but shall heartily desire your good and prosperity as our own, forever.

Your friendly offer to accommodate us with any merchandise you may have, either for beaver or otter or other wares, is also very acceptable, and we doubt not we shall shortly have profitable trade together. This year we are fully supplied with all necessaries, clothing, etc., though later we shall hope to deal with you, if your rates are reasonable. When you send to us again we shall like to know what price you give for beaver per pound, and otter per skin; and on what per cent you will deal for other commodities, and what you can supply us with; also what other goods from us would be acceptable to you, as tobacco, fish, corn, etc., and what prices you will give, etc.

We hope you will pardon us for our imperfect writing in your language, and take it in good part; through want of practice we cannot so well express what we understand, nor understand everything as full as we should. We humbly pray the Lord for His mercy's sake that He will take both us and you into His gracious keeping and protection.

By the Governor and Council of New Plymouth,

Your Worships' very good friends and neighbors, etc.
New Plymouth, March 19*th.*

After this there was much correspondence and other intercourse, and they traded profitably together for several years, till other things interrupted it, as will appear afterwards.

Before they sent Mr. Allerton to England this year, the Governor and some of the principal members seriously considered how best to discharge the many obligations which lay so heavily upon them, and also how, if possible, to bring over some of their friends at Leyden, who wished so much to come to them, and whose company they desired equally. To effect this, the leading men of the colony resolved upon a venturesome course, not knowing how to accomplish their objects otherwise. This was, that they should purchase the trade of the settlement (now owned jointly by the settlers, as a body, and by the adventurers) for a certain period, and in that time to undertake to pay the £1800, and all the rest of the debts of the plantation then owing, which amounted to about £600 more; the trade of the settlement to revert to the common ownership at the end of the period. Upon coming to this resolution they called the settlers together, and made it clear to them what all their debts amounted to, and upon what terms they should undertake to pay them in a given time. But their other objects they were obliged to conceal,[7] only

---

[7] That is, their plan to bring over more of the members left behind at Leyden, to which some of the settlers then in New Plymouth would be certain to object on the score of expense.

privately consulting some of their most trusted friends about it. So after some discussion with the colonists, it was agreed to, and the contract drawn up on the following condition.

Articles of agreement between the Colony of New Plymouth of the one part, and William Bradford, Captain Myles Standish, Isaac Allerton, etc., of the other part; and such others as they shall think good to take as partners in the trade for beaver and other furs and commodities, etc. Made July, 1627.

1. First it is agreed and covenanted between the said parties, that the aforesaid William Bradford, Captain Myles Standish, and Isaac Allerton, etc., have undertaken and do by these presents covenant and agree to pay, discharge, and acquit the said colony of all debts due for the purchase or otherwise, on the date of these presents.

2. The above said parties are to have and freely enjoy the pinnace lately built, the boat at Manomet, and the shallop called the bass-boat, with all implements belonging to them in the store of the said company; with the whole stock of furs, fells, beads, corn, wampum, hatchets, knives, etc., now in the store, or due to the same upon account.

3. That the above said parties have the whole trade to themselves, their heirs and assigns, with all the privileges thereof, as the said colony does now, and may use the same for six full years to come, to begin the last day of September next ensuing.

4. In further consideration of the discharge of the said debts, each member of the colony promises and covenants yearly to pay or cause to be paid to the above said parties during the full term of the above said six years, three bushels of corn or six lbs. of tobacco, at the choice of the parties.

5. The said parties shall during the aforesaid term ex-

pend £50 per annum in hose and shoes to be brought over for the colony's use, to be sold to them for corn at six shillings per bushel.

6. That at the end of the said term of six years, the whole trade shall revert to the use and benefit of the said colony as before.

7. Lastly, if the aforesaid parties, after they have acquainted their friends in England with these covenants, do thereupon resolve to perform them, and undertake to discharge the debts of the said colony, according to the true meaning and intent of these presents, they are then upon notice given to stand in full force; otherwise all things to remain as they were formerly, and a true account to be given to the said colony of the disposition of everything as usual.

Mr. Allerton took a copy of this agreement to England, and had orders to arrange with some of their special friends there to join with them in this trade upon the above conditions, and also to impart to them confidentially the other object that induced them to take this course, that is, to bring over some of their friends from Leyden, if possible; and to tell them that if any of them would join with them they would thankfully accept their partnership; and finally, by letter, gave them some grounds for their hope of accomplishing it with advantage for all.

"And Morton became lord of misrule, and maintained, as it were, a school of Athisme."

CHAPTER IX

[*1628*]

After Mr. Allerton's arrival in England, he informed the adventurers of his commission to make purchase of the trade of the colony for six years, and upon delivery of the bonds for the yearly payments it was finally concluded, and a deed engrossed in parchment was delivered to him under their hands and seals confirming it. He also arranged with some special friends among them, as instructed, to participate in the purchase, and to supply them with money at better rates, etc. Concerning this I insert here a letter from Mr. Sherley to the Governor throwing light on what followed.

James Sherley in England to Governor Bradford at New Plymouth:

Sir,
I have received yours of May 26th through Mr. Gibbs and Mr. Goffe, with the barrel of otter skins, for which I got a bill of store, and sold them for £78-12-0 sterling; and Mr. Allerton has received the money as will appear by the account. It is true, as you write, that your obligations are large, not only for the purchase but for the working stock you will require, which you cannot raise at 6 or 8 percent as here but must pay 30, 40 and even 50 percent. Were not your profits considerable, and God's blessing

on your honest endeavors more than ordinary, you could not long be masters of your affairs. And this, it seems, your honest and able agent, Mr. Allerton, has seriously considered. He tells me that you are willing to permit me and some few others to join with you as partners in the purchase; I thank you and all the rest, and gladly accept, and though absent, shall willingly be at such expense as you and the rest think proper. This year I am prepared to forego the £50 due and the two years' increase for the venture, which comes in all to £80, without making any condition for the profit—you with the rest to bear the risk outward and homeward. I have persuaded Mr. Andrews and Mr. Beauchamp to do the same, so that you will not have to bear the high rate of the previous two years. We leave it freely to yourselves to allow us what you please, and according as God shall bless us. Whatever course I take, Mr. Beauchamp is willing to do the same; and though he may have seemed rather harsh before, you will find he is now new molded. I also see by your letter that you desire me to be your agent here. I have ever found you such faithful, honest, and upright men, that I have resolved to do you all the good that lies in my power; so if you please to select so inadequate a man to perform your business, I promise to do the best I can with the ability the Lord has given me; and wherein I fail, blame yourselves that you did not make a better choice. As I am not in good health, and we are all mortal, I have advised Mr. Allerton to associate Mr. Beauchamp with me as your deputy, which is both necessary and advisable for you, and will cost you no more, for it is not the salary that induces me to undertake your business. Thus commending you and yours and all God's people to the guidance and protection of the Almighty, I ever rest,

> Your faithful, loving friend,
> JAMES SHERLEY.

London, Nov. 17th, 1628.

With this letter he sent a draft of power of attorney to be sealed and returned to them, authorizing them to act as their agents. As some trouble arose about it afterwards, I will insert it.

To all to whom these presents shall come, greeting; know ye that we, William Bradford, Governor of New Plymouth, in New England in America, Isaac Allerton, Myles Standish, William Brewster, and Edward Winslow, of New Plymouth aforesaid, merchants, do by these presents for us and in our names make, substitute, and appoint James Sherley, goldsmith, and John Beauchamp, salter, citizens of London, our true and lawful agents, factors, substitutes, and assigns; as well to take and receive all such goods, wares, merchandise whatsoever as to our said substitutes or either of them, or to the city of London, or other place of the Realm of England, shall be sent, transported, or come from us or any of us; as also to vend, sell, barter, or exchange the said goods, wares, and merchandise, so from time to time to be sent to such person or persons upon credit, or otherwise in such manner as to our said agents and factors jointly, or to either of them severally, shall seem proper. And further we make and ordain our said substitutes and assigns jointly and severally for us, and to our uses and accounts, to buy and consign for us and to us to New England aforesaid, such goods and merchandise to be provided here, and to be returned hence as by our said assigns or either of them shall be thought fit. And to recover, receive, and demand for us and in our names all such debts and sums of money, as now are or hereafter shall be due, incident, accruing, or belonging to us, or any of us, by any ways or means; and to acquit, discharge, or compound for any debt or sum of money, which now or hereafter shall be due or owing by any person or persons to us, or any of us. And generally for us and in our names to do, perform, and execute every act and thing which to our said assigns, or either of them, shall seem proper to do, as fully and effectually, to all intents and purposes, as if we or any of us were in person present. And whatsoever our said agents and factors jointly or severally shall do, or cause to be done, in or about the premises, we will and do, and each of us does ratify, allow, and confirm, by these presents. In witness whereof we have hereunto put our hands and seals.

Dated November 18th, 1628.

This was accordingly confirmed by the above named, and four more of the principal members, under their hands and seals, and delivered to them. Mr. Allerton had formerly received authority under their hands and seals for transacting their business, raising money, etc., and this deed he still retained while he was employed on these affairs. Their complete trust in him and their other friends made them remiss in canceling such previous deeds, which was a disadvantage to them later, as will appear in due course.

Mr. Allerton, having settled everything satisfactorily, returned to the colony in the early spring of the year with their supplies for trading, the fishermen with whom he came being accustomed to sail in the winter and get here betimes. He brought a fair stock of goods for the settlement, not subject to such high interest, and an account of the beaver sold and of the money expended for goods and the payment of other debts. He had discharged all engagements, except to Mr. Sherley, Mr. Beauchamp, and Mr. Andrews; and from them he also brought an account, which amounted to not above £400, for which he had given bonds. He had also made the first payment for the purchase, due this year, viz., £200, and brought them the bond for it, duly canceled. So they had now no foreign debts except £400, odd, and the balance of the yearly purchase money. They had some other debts over here, but they were without interest, and they were in a position to discharge them when they were due. To this pass the Lord had brought things for them.

Mr. Allerton also brought them notice that their friends referred to above, with some others who wished to join them in the trading and in the purchase, intended that a reasonable number of the congregation at Leyden should be sent over next year without fail, if the Lord pleased to bless their journey. He also brought them a patent for Kennebec;[1] but it was so inadequate that they were obliged to endeavor to renew and enlarge it the next year, and also that which they had at home, at great expense, as will appear. Hitherto Mr. Allerton had done them good and faithful service: would that he had so continued, or that they had now ceased employing him any longer in England. But of this more afterwards.

Having procured a patent for Kennebec, they erected a house in the most convenient place for trade up the river, and stocked it with goods for that purpose, both for winter and summer; not only with corn, but with such other commodities as the fishermen had traded to them, such as coats, shirts, rugs, blankets, biscuits, peas, prunes, etc. What they could not procure from England they bought from the fishing ships and so carried on their business as well as they could.

This year the Dutch visited them again. With kind letters from the colony they sent a variety of goods, such

---

[1] Now Augusta, Maine.

as sugar, linen, Holland finer and coarser stuffs, etc. Their secretary de Rasières came with them in their bark to Manomet, to the house the settlers had established there. He brought attendants, and his coming was heralded by trumpets. He requested them to send a boat to take him on to New Plymouth, as he could not travel so far overland. So they sent a boat to Manoanscussett,[2] and brought him to the plantation with most of his people. After some few days' entertainment he returned to his bark, and some of the leading settlers went with him and bought some of his goods. After this beginning they often sent over to them and had intercourse for many years.

Amongst other commodities they sold the Dutch a good deal of tobacco in exchange for linen, stuffs, etc.; and tobacco was profitably traded with them by the New Plymouth colony, till the Virginians learned of the Dutch settlement. But what became most profitable in time was the beginning they then made in the trade for wampum.[3] They bought £50 worth of it from the Dutch who told them how much they had sold of it at Fort Orange,[4] and assured them they would find it so at Kennebec. At first they could not sell it—in fact it was two years before they cleared this small quantity. Afterwards, when the Indians further inland began to know of it, for many years they could scarcely get enough for them.

---

[2] Manoanscusset was on the east side of the isthmus, near the site of the present town of Sandwich.

[3] The wampum, or wampampeake (white strings of money), was made from quahog and periwinkle shells, carved into beads and strung. It soon was in great demand among the Indians of the Cape, as de Rasières had predicted. This purchase proved to be a lucky stroke, for the wampum provided a currency basis for barter. Later it became legal tender, its value fixed by law.

[4] The present site of Albany.

This, with their other sources of supply, reduced their trade with the fishermen, and in the main also with the scattered settlers. It was strange to see the great change it wrought in a few years among the Indians themselves. The natives of these parts and in Massachusetts hitherto had none or very little of this wampum, except the sachems and some of the chiefs who wore a little of it for ornament. It was, however, largely made and used by the Narragansetts and Pequots, who grew rich and powerful, while the Indians here were poor and beggarly, and had no use for it. Nor did the English of New Plymouth or any of the other settlements, until told of it by the Dutch, so much as know what it was, much less that it was a commodity of such value. But after it grew to be valuable here, the local Indians took to it too, and learned how to make it, gathering the shells from the shores. It has remained a current commodity now for about twenty years, and it may prove a drug in time.

In the meantime it makes the tribes hereabouts rich and powerful and proud, and provides them with arms and powder and shot, through the depravity of some unworthy persons, both English, Dutch and French, and likely to be the ruin of many. Hitherto the Indians round here had no guns or other arms but their bows and arrows, nor for many years after; they scarcely dared handle guns, they were so afraid of them; and the very sight of one, though out of kilter, was a terror to them. But the Indians to the east who had dealings with the French got guns from them, and in time our English fishermen, with equal covetousness, followed their example. But upon complaint it pleased the King's Majesty to prohibit it by a strict proclamation, commanding that no sort of arms or munition should be traded to the Indians by his subjects.

Some three or four years before this there came over one Captain Wollaston, a man of fine qualities, with three or four others of some distinction, who brought with them a great many servants, with provisions and other necessaries to found a settlement. They pitched upon a place within Massachusetts, which they called, after their Captain, Mount Wollaston.[5] Among them was one Mr. Morton, who, it seems, had some small share with them in the enterprise, either on his own account or as an agent; but he was little respected amongst them and even slighted by the servants. Having remained there some time, and not finding things answer their expectations, Captain Wollaston took the majority of the servants to Virginia, where he hired out their services profitably to other employers. So he wrote up to Mr. Rasdell, one of the chief partners, who was acting as their merchant, to bring another party of them to Virginia for the same purpose. With the consent of Rasdell he appointed one Fitcher, as his deputy, to govern the remnant of the colony till one of them should return.

But Morton, in the others' absence, having more craft than honesty—he had been a kind of pettifogger of Furnival's Inn[6]—watched his opportunity when rations were scarce with them, got some drink and other junkets and made them a feast, and after they were merry began to tell them he would give them good counsel. "You see," says he, "that many of your comrades have been taken to Virginia; and if you stay till this Rasdell returns you too will be carried off and sold as slaves with the rest. So I

---

[5] Now Quincy.
[6] One of the smaller inns of chancery, a school and headquarters for lawyers. Actually, Morton was a member of Clifford's Inn.

would advise you to oust this Lieutenant Fitcher; and I, having a share in this settlement, will take you as partners, and you will be free from service, and we will trade, plant, and live together as equals, and support and protect one another,"—and so on. This advice was easily received; so they drove out Lieutenant Fitcher and would not allow him to come amongst them, forcing him to get food and other relief from his neighbors, till he could get passage to England.

They then fell to utter licentiousness, and led a dissolute and profane life. Morton became lord of misrule, and maintained, as it were, a school of atheism. As soon as they acquired some means by trading with the Indians, they spent it in drinking wine and strong drinks to great excess—as some reported, £10 worth in a morning! They set up a Maypole, drinking and dancing about it for several days at a time, inviting the Indian women for their consorts, dancing and frisking together like so many fairies—or furies rather—to say nothing of worse practices. It was as if they had revived the celebrated feasts of the Roman goddess Flora, or the beastly practices of the mad Bacchanalians. Morton, to show his poetry, composed sundry verses and rhymes, some tending to lasciviousness and others to the detraction and scandal of some persons, affixing them to his idle, or idol, Maypole. They changed the name of the place, and instead of calling it Mount Wollaston, they called it Merry Mount, as if this jollity would last forever.

But it did not continue long, for shortly after, Morton was sent back to England, as will appear. In the meantime, that worthy gentleman, Mr. John Endicott, arrived from England, bringing over a patent under the broad seal, for the government of Massachusetts.[7] Visiting this neighborhood, he had the Maypole cut down, and reprimanded them for their profaneness, admonishing them to improve their way of living. In consequence, others changed the name of their place again, and called it Mount Dagon.[8]

In order to maintain this riotous prodigality and excess, Morton, hearing what profit the French and the fishermen had made by trading guns, powder, and shot to the Indians, began to practice it hereabouts, teaching them how to use them. Having instructed them, he employed some of them to hunt and fowl for him, until they became far more able than the English, owing to their swiftness on foot and nimbleness of body, being quick-sighted, and knowing the haunts of all sorts of game. With the result that, when they saw what execution a gun would do and the advantage of it, they were mad for them and would pay any price for them, thinking their bows and arrows but baubles in comparison.

And here I must bewail the mischief that this wicked man began in this district, and which, continued by men that should know better, has now become prevalent, notwithstanding the laws to the contrary. The result is that

---

[7] Endicott led the Puritan group which was to be known as the Massachusetts Bay Colony, destined in time to absorb the Pilgrims. This group, which included Winthrop, Saltonstall, and other important Puritan figures, did not come with a royal charter, as Bradford states, but it was obtained later. Their grant overlapped territory previously assigned to others, including the Pilgrims. Cradock, chief promoter of this enterprise, wrote to Endicott: "We trust you will not be unmindfull of the mayne end of our plantation, by endevoring to bring the Indians to a knowledge of the Gospel." But this aim was a minor one; the colony was in reality a trading company, backed by rich merchants. See Introduction, p. xxiii.

[8] Dagon was the principal deity of the Philistines, the enemies of Israel. He is frequently mentioned in the Old Testament.

the Indians are stocked with all kinds of arms—fowling-pieces, muskets, pistols, etc. They even have moulds to make shots of all sorts—musket bullets, pistol bullets, swan and geese shot and smaller sorts. It is well known that they often have powder and shot when the English lack it and cannot get it, it having been bought up and sold to those who trade it to the Indians at a shilling per pound—for they will buy it at any price. This goes on while their neighbors are being killed by the Indians every day, or are only living at their mercy. They have even been told how gunpowder is made, and all the materials that are in it, and that they are to be had in their own land; and I am confident that if they could only get saltpeter they would make gunpowder itself.

Oh, the horror of this villainy! How many Dutch and English have lately been killed by Indians, thus furnished! and no remedy is provided—nay, the evil has increased. The blood of their brothers has been sold for profit; and in what danger all these colonies are is too well known. Oh! that princes and parliaments would take some timely steps to prevent this mischief and to suppress it, by exemplary punishment of some of those gain-thirsty murderers —for they deserve no better title—before their colonies in these parts are wiped out by the barbarous savages, armed with their own weapons by these traitors to their country. But I have forgotten myself, and have been too long on this digression; now to return.

Morton having taught them the use of guns, sold them all he could spare, and he and his associates determined to send for large supplies from England, having already sent for over a score by some of the ships. This being known, several members of the scattered settlements hereabouts agreed to solicit the settlers at New Plymouth, who then outnumbered them all, to join with them to prevent the further growth of this mischief, and to suppress Morton and his associates. Those who joined in this action, and afterwards contributed to the expense of sending him to England, were from Piscataqua, Naumkeag, Winnisimmett, Wessagusset, Nantasket, and other places where the English had settled. The New Plymouth colonists thus addressed by their messengers and letters, and weighing their reasons and the common danger, were willing to help, though they themselves had least cause for fear.

So, to be short, they first decided to write to Morton jointly, in a friendly and neighborly way, requesting him to desist, and sent a messenger with the letter to bring his answer. But he was so overbearing that he scorned all advice; he asked what it had to do with them; he would trade guns to the Indians in spite of them all, with many other scurrilous remarks, full of disdain. So they sent to him again and bade him be better advised and more temperate in his terms; that the country would not bear the injury he was doing; it was against their common safety and against the King's proclamation. He answered as haughtily as before, that the King's proclamation was no law, and asking what was the penalty. They replied: more than he could bear—His Majesty's displeasure. But he persisted, and insolently said that the King was dead, and his displeasure with him; that if they came to molest him, let them look to themselves; he would be prepared for them.

So they saw there was no way but to take him by force. They resolved to proceed and unanimously requested the Governor of New Plymouth to send Captain Standish and sufficient men to seize Morton. This was accordingly done; but he defended himself stiffly, closed his doors, armed his associates, and had dishes of powder and bullets ready on the table; and if they had not been overarmed with drink, more harm might have been done. They summoned him to yield, but they got nothing but scoffs from him. At length, fearing they would wreck the house, some of his crew came out—intending not to yield, but to shoot; but they were so drunk that their guns were too heavy for them. He himself, with a carbine overcharged and almost half filled with powder and shot, tried to shoot Captain Standish; but he stepped up to him and put aside his gun and took him. No harm was done on either side, except that one of his men was so drunk that he ran his nose upon the point of a sword that someone held in front of him on entering the house; but all he lost was a little of his hot blood.

Morton they took to New Plymouth, where he was kept till a ship went from the Isle of Shoals to England. In this he was dispatched to the Council of New England, with letters giving information of his behavior, entrusted to a representative sent at their common expense to inform their honors more particularly, and to prosecute him. But Morton fooled this man after he had left here, and though he went to England, nothing was done to him—he was not so much as rebuked, so far as was heard—and he returned the following year. Some of the worst of the party were dispersed, and some of the more decent were permitted to live in the house till he was heard from. But I have been too long about so unworthy a person and so bad a cause.[9]

---

[9] The story of Morton has been thoroughly treated in many histories and requires little comment here. Bradford's story does not agree in all details with other contemporary accounts. Undoubtedly Morton was loose-living and irreligious, and behaved scandal-

This year Mr. Allerton brought over a young man as minister to the colony, whether upon his own initiative or at the instance of some friends there, I do not know; but he was not sent by the orders of the church, for they had been so bitten by Mr. Lyford that they wished to know well whom they were inviting, beforehand. His name was Mr. Rogers; but they discovered that he was crazed in the brain; so they were obliged to go to the expense of sending him back again the next year; besides the cost of bringing him out, which was not small by Mr. Allerton's account, for provisions, clothing, bedding, etc. Mr. Allerton was much blamed for bringing such a man over, for they had expenses enough already.

In previous years Mr. Allerton had brought over some small quantities of goods upon his own account, and sold them for his private benefit, which was more than anyone had hitherto ventured to do. But as he had done them good service otherwise, and as he sold them among the people of the colony and their wants were thereby supplied, it was passed over. But this year he brought over a greater quantity, and they were intermixed with the goods of

---

ously. But although he was sent back to answer charges, no legal action was taken against him, and he returned to New England at the first opportunity—to the dismay of the people at Plymouth. His traffic with the Indians—and there is every reason to believe that he sold both firewater and firearms to them—jeopardized the colonist's very survival. In his *New English Canaan* he denounced the Pilgrims for making a great "shew of religion, but no humanity." He also accused them of sharing their spirituous liquors with the Indians. He loved hunting, was an adept at falconry, made boon companions of the Indians, male and female, and regarded New England as "nature's masterpiece." He was sent back to England a second time, returned to Plymouth in 1644, was arrested when he entered the Massachusetts Bay jurisdiction, imprisoned and fined. Two years later he died in Maine.

the colony, and all packed together, so that it could not be said which were theirs and which were his; so if any mischance had happened at sea, he could have laid the whole loss on them, if he had wished. And it seemed to result that what was most salable and could be sold promptly, he claimed was his! He also began to sell to others outside the settlement, which, considering their agreement, they disliked. But love thinks no evil, nor is suspicious; so they took his fair words for excuse, and decided to send him to England again this year, considering how well he had done formerly and how well he stood with their friends there; and particularly as some of their friends from Leyden were to be sent for, the arrangements for which he could, or might, assist in. It was also thought that, as the patent for Kennebec must be extended, as well as the one here, he would best be able to affect it, having begun it. So they gave him instructions and sent him to England once more. His instructions were to bring over no goods on their account, except £50 worth of hose, shoes, and linen, according to the conditions—besides some trading goods to a certain value; and in no case was he to exceed his instructions or run them into further expense. He was to arrange that their trading goods came over early, and whatever was sent on their account should be packed by itself, and marked with their mark; and no other goods were to be mixed with them. In fact, he requested them to give him such instructions as they thought fit, and he would follow them, to prevent any jealousy or further trouble. So they thought they had provided satisfactorily for everything.

*"And that here should be a resting place for so many
of them, when so sharp a scourge came upon their owne
nation."*

CHAPTER X

[*1629*]

Mr. Allerton arrived safely in England, and delivered the letters to their friends there, acquainting them with his instructions. He found them willing to join in the trading partnership and in the expense of sending over the Leyden people, some of whom had already left Holland and were prepared to come over, so they were sent off before Mr. Allerton was ready to leave. They took passage on the ships that came to Salem, which brought over many godly persons to begin the settlements and churches of Christ there and in the Bay of Massachusetts.[1] So their friends here were rewarded for their long delay with double blessing, in that they not only enjoyed them now, when so recently all their hopes had seemed to be blasted, but with them came other godly friends and Christian brethren, to plant a still larger harvest unto the Lord, for the increase of his churches and

---

[1] In April of this year five ships set sail for the Bay settlement, the largest fleet ever bound for New England. These colonists landed at Salem, then Naumkeag, and later pushed out to settle other points around the bay, including Boston.

people in these parts. It was to the astonishment of many and almost to the wonder of the world, that from so small a beginning such great things should ensue—as in due time was manifested; and that there should be a resting place for so many of the Lord's people here, when so sharp a scourge had come upon their own nation. But it was the Lord's doing, and it ought to be marvelous in our eyes.

I will here insert some of their friends' letters, which best express their own attitude towards these proceedings.

Two letters from James Sherley in England to Governor Bradford at New Plymouth:

Sir,

With this there are many more of our friends from Leyden coming over to you, whose arrival, though mostly a weak body, is the fulfillment, in part, of our purpose, so strongly opposed by some of the former adventurers. But God has His working in these things, which man cannot frustrate. We have also sent some servants in the ship *Talbot*, that sailed lately; but the Leyden contingent come in the *Mayflower*. Mr. Beauchamp and myself, with Mr. Andrews and Mr. Hatherley, have, with your good will, joined your partnership, etc.
May 25th, 1629.

Your power of attorney has been received, and the goods have been sold by your friend and agent, Mr. Allerton, I having been in Holland nearly three months, at Amsterdam and in other parts of the Low Countries. I see, also, the agreement you have made with the main body of the settlers, and think you have done very well, both for them, for you, and for your friends at Leyden. Mr. Beauchamp, Mr. Andrews, Mr. Hatherley, and myself so thoroughly approve of it, that we are willing to join you, and, God directing us, will assist you the best we possibly can. Indeed, had you not taken this course, I do not see how you could ever have accomplished the end originally aimed at. We know it must cause further delay in realizing profits, for most of those who we sent in May, and those now sailing, though honest and good people, are not likely to be helpful at present—indeed, for some time they will be an expense to you and us. Had you not taken this wise and astute course, the main body of your colonists would probably have grudged their coming. Again, as you say well in your letter, the burden being now on the shoulders of only a few, you will manage it the better, having no discontent or contradiction, but all lovingly joined together in affection and counsel, so that God will no doubt bless and prosper your honest labors and endeavors. So in all respects I consider you have been marvelously discreet and well-advised, and have no doubt it will give all parties satisfaction—I mean all who are reasonable and honest men, and make conscience of fulfilling their obligations to the uttermost, not with regard to their own private interests so much as the accomplishment of the good object for which this enterprise was first started. . . . Thus desiring the Lord to bless and prosper you and all yours, and all our honest endeavors, I rest,

Your unfeigned and ever loving friend,
JAMES SHERLEY.

London, March 8th, 1629.[2]

I have mentioned here the coming of both these companies from Leyden, though they actually came at two different times. The former party, numbering 35 persons, sailed in May, and arrived here about August, 1629; the

---

[2] By modern reckoning, 1630.

latter sailed at the beginning of March, and arrived here the latter end of May, 1630. Their expenses, according to Mr. Allerton's accounts, came to above £550 (in addition to their transportations from Salem and the Bay, where they and their goods were landed), viz.: their transportation from Holland to England, and their expenses while there, and their passages out here, with clothing provided for them. I find in the account for the one party 125 yards of kersey,[3] 127 ells of linen, 66 pairs of shoes, with many other particulars. The cost of the other party is reckoned by families, some £50, some £40, some £30,—more or less, according to numbers, etc. Besides all this expense, their friends here had to provide corn and other provisions for them till they could reap a crop, which was some time. Those that came in May had to be maintained upwards of 16 to 18 months; the others proportionately. All they could do in the meantime was to build houses and prepare land for planting next season. The expense of maintaining them all this time was little less than the former sum.

I make special note of this for various reasons: first, to show a rare example of brotherly love and Christian care in performing their promise to their brethren. Secondly, to prove that there was more than the work of man in these achievements—thus successfully to have persuaded such able friends to join them in the enterprise, and to stand by them so faithfully in the face of such risks, most of them never having seen their faces to this day; it must needs be, therefore, the special work of God. Thirdly, that these poor people here in a wilderness should, notwithstanding, be able in time to repay all their

---

[3] Kersey was a woolen cloth, usually ribbed; an ell was 45 inches.

engagements, and others unjustly put upon them through unfaithful service, besides other great losses which they sustained, all of which will be related if the Lord be pleased to give me life and time. In the meantime I cannot help but wonder at His ways and works towards His servants, and humbly desire to bless His holy name for His great mercies hitherto.

The Leyden people having come over, and several members of the general body of the settlers seeing how great the expense was likely to be, began to murmur at it, notwithstanding the burden lay on other men's shoulders— especially at paying the three bushels of corn a year, according to the agreement. But to satisfy them, it was promised that if they could do without it they would not demand it of them. And it never was paid, as will appear.

Mr. Allerton's proceedings about the enlarging and confirming of the patents, both at home and at Kennebec, are best explained in another letter of Mr. Sherley's. Though much time and money was expended, he left it unaccomplished this year, and came without them.

James Sherley in England to the New Plymouth Colony:

Most worthy and loving Friends,

Some of your letters I received in July, and some since through Mr. Pierce; but till our main business, the patent,[4] was granted, I could not settle my mind or pen to writing. Mr. Allerton was so turmoiled about it, that I neither would nor could have undertaken it, if I had been paid a thousand pounds; but the Lord so blessed his labors that he obtained the love and favor of important

---

[4] This patent, was made to William Bradford, his heirs and assigns, by the Council of New England, and was assigned by Bradford to the colony in 1640. See history of that year.

men of repute and position. He got granted from the Earl of Warwick and Sir Ferdinand Gorges all that Mr. Winslow desired in his letters to me, and more besides, which I leave him to relate. Then he sued to the King to confirm their grant, and to make you a corporation, and so to enable you to make and execute laws as freely as the government of Massachusetts. This the King graciously granted, referring it to the Lord Keeper to give order to the solicitor to draw it up, if there were a precedent for it. So the Lord Keeper furthered it all he could, and also the solicitor; but as Festus said to Paul: With no small sum of money obtained I this freedom.[5] For, by the way, many riddles had to be solved, and many locks must be opened with the silver, nay, the golden key! Then it came to the Lord Treasurer, to have his warrant for making you custom-free for a certain time; but he would not do it, and referred it to the Council Table. And there Mr. Allerton attended day by day, when they sat, but could not get his petition read; and as Mr. Pierce was waiting with all the passengers at Bristol, he was forced to leave the further prosecution of it to a solicitor. But there is no fear nor doubt but that it will be granted—for the chief of them are friendly; but he should certainly return by the first ship that comes, for if you had this confirmed, you would be in a position to govern with the power befitting your rank and position God has called you to, and to stop the mouths of the base and scurrilous individuals who are ready to question and threaten you in every action. Besides, if you are freed of customs dues for seven years inward and twenty-one outward, the expense of the patent will be soon covered; and there is no doubt of ultimately obtaining it. But such things must work by degrees,—they cannot be hastened; so we (I

---

[5] It was not the Roman governor Festus who said this but the chief captain of the garrison in Jerusalem. Acts xxii, 28.

write on behalf of all our partners here) beg you to urge Mr. Allerton to come, and his wife to spare him this one year more, to finish this important business, which will be so much for your good, and I hope for that of your posterity for many generations to come.

Thus much of this letter; it was dated March 19th, 1629; but the fact of the matter was (as came out later), it was Mr. Allerton's object to have an opportunity to be sent over again for purposes of his own; and with that idea he requested them to write thus. The extension of the patent might easily have been finished, omitting the clause about the customs (which was Mr. Allerton's and Mr. Sherley's device), it having passed the King's hand. But covetousness never brings anything home, as the proverb says; and this opportunity being lost, it was never accomplished, though a great deal of money was vainly and lavishly expended on it. But of this more in its place.

I almost omitted to mention that this year Mr. Allerton gave them great and just offense by bringing over the unworthy Morton, who had been sent home only the year before for his misdemeanors. He not only brought him over, but into the very town (as if to beard them), and lodged him at his own house, employing him as his secretary till he was forced to send him away. So he returned to his old nest in Massachusetts, where it was not long before his misconduct gave them proper cause to apprehend him, and he was again sent by them a prisoner to England, where he lay a good time in Exeter jail. For, besides his misdeeds here, he was strongly suspected of the murder of a man who had ventured money with him, when he first came to New England. A warrant had been sent from the Lord Chief Justice to apprehend him, by virtue of which the Governor of Massachusetts sent him to England; and as punishment for his misdemeanors there, they demolished his house, so that it might no longer be a roost for such unclean birds to nestle in. But he got free again, and wrote an infamous and scurrilous book full of lies and slanders against many godly men of the country in high position, and of profane calumnies against their names and persons, and the ways of God. After several years, when the war was at its height in England, he returned to the country, and was imprisoned at Boston, for the book and other things, having grown old in wickedness.

As for the rest of Mr. Allerton's instructions, enjoining him not to exceed the £50 worth of goods before mentioned, nor to bring any but trading commodities, he ignored them, and brought over many other kinds of retail goods, selling what he could by the way on his own account, and delivering them the rest, which he said were theirs. Of trading goods he brought scarcely any, making excuses that they had expended so much on the Leyden people, the patent, etc. As regards exceeding his instructions, he laid the responsibility on Mr. Sherley, etc. He promised that next year they should have whatever trading goods they sent for. In this way he put them off, and though Mr. Sherley had written somewhat bearing out his statements, he was probably overruled by Mr. Allerton to do so.

The following is a still further extract from his former letter, bearing on this:

I see what you write in your letters concerning the paying of our debts, which I confess are great, and need to be carefully watched. But let us not fulfill the proverb:

to spend a shilling on a purse and put sixpence in it; nor think by the expenditure of £50 a year to raise means to pay our debts; you need to be well supplied and fully provided—and, chiefly, lovingly to agree.

This shows that there was a kind of concurrence between Mr. Allerton and the adventurers in England about these things, and that they had more regard for his opinion than for the advice sent from here. This troubled them greatly here, not knowing how to help it, and being loth to make any breach. Another more private difficulty was that Mr. Allerton had married the daughter of their reverend elder, Mr. Brewster, who was beloved and honored by them, taking great pains in dispensing and teaching the word of God to them, and whom they were loth to grieve in any way; so they bore with much for that reason.

Again, Mr. Allerton procured such letters from Mr. Sherley, with such applause of his wisdom, care, and faithfulness, that as things stood, none seemed so fit to send as he. Besides, though private gain, I feel sure, was one cause of Mr. Allerton's doings, I think, or at least charity leads me to hope, that he intended to deal faithfully with his partners here in the main. But things fell out otherwise and missed their aim, and the settlement in general suffered considerably in consequence, as will appear.

Along the same lines was another plan of Mr. Allerton's and his friends, unknown to the other partners here, until it was so far proceeded with that they felt obliged to sanction it and join with them, though they did not like it and mistrusted the outcome. It is explained in another extract from Mr. Sherley's letter, as follows:

I wish to acquaint you that we have thought good to become partners in a separate venture with one Edward

Ashley—a man I think some of you know—but it only concerns the place for which he has a patent in Mr. Beauchamp's name. For this purpose we have supplied him plentifully with provisions, etc. If you wish to join us as partners in this, we are willing you should. Hearing how anxious Bristol men were to join the enterprise and supply him, expecting good profits, we thought it important that we should not to miss such opportunity. He, on his side, like a shrewd man, thought it better to join with those who already had a settlement to back him there, than with strangers. It is not known that you are in the partnership, but only we four, Mr. Andrews, Mr. Beauchamp, myself, and Mr. Hatherley, who entered upon it in view of the great loss we have already sustained in the first plantation there. But as I said before, if you wish to join with us, we are willing you should. Mr. Allerton had no power from you to make this new contract, nor was he willing to do anything without your consent. Mr. William Pierce joined with us because of landing Ashley and his goods there. He has a new boat with him, and boards to make another, with four or five strong fellows, one of whom is a carpenter. In case you are not willing to join us, fearing the expense and doubting the success, we beg of you to afford him all the help you can, either with men, goods, or boats, and we will pay you for anything that he has. We wish you to keep the accounts separate, even if you join us, because there are partners in this enterprise who are not in the other; so charge him with men's wages, boat-hire, or goods; and anything you receive from him, charge to the colony.

And now, loving friends and partners, if you join in Ashley's project, we having found the money to stock this business and the other, it seems reasonable that you should bear your share of the stock, if not in money, by security to that amount. I hope in God, by His blessing and your honest endeavor, it may soon be paid; but the term of the partnership is not long, so it behooves us all to make the best use of the time that we possibly can, and let everyone put his shoulder to the burden and it will be lighter. I know you will consider this carefully, and return a satisfactory answer. None of us would have risked this, except as a support to your own enterprise.

There is no likelihood of doing any good by attempting to buy the debts for the purchase of the old adventurers' shares. I know some would not forego their interest, so let it run its course; it is arranged they are to be paid yearly, and so I hope they will be, according to agreement. The Lord grant that our loves and affections may still be united and knit together; and so we rest your ever loving friends,

JAMES SHERLEY.
TIMOTHY HATHERLEY.

Bristol, March 19th, 1629.

This matter of buying the debts of the purchase was part of Mr. Allerton's instructions, and in many instances it might have been done to advantage for ready cash; but Mr. Sherley disliked it. The Ashley enterprise troubled them much, for though he had ability enough to manage the business, he was known to be a very profane young man; and he had for some time lived among the Indians as a savage, naked like them, adopting their manners and customs, and in the meantime acquiring their language; so they feared he might not keep straight, though he promised better things. As soon as he landed at the place intended, called Penobscot, some four score leagues from this place, he wrote (and afterwards came) desiring to be supplied with wampum, corn for the winter, and other things. They bethought them that these were their chief commodities, and would be continually needed by him, and it would thus be greatly to the prejudice of their own trade at Kennebec, if, though they did not join the partnership, they should still have to supply him; on the other hand, if they should both refuse to join the partnership and to supply him, they would greatly offend their friends in England, and might possibly lose them.

Again, Ashley and Mr. Allerton, laying their crafty wits together, might get supplies elsewhere; and whether they joined in it or not, they knew Mr. Allerton would do so, and then he would swim, as it were, between both, to the prejudice of both—but especially of themselves. They had reason to think this scheme was chiefly of his contriving, and Ashley was a fit tool. So, to prevent worse mischief, they resolved to enter the new partnership, and gave him supplies of what they could, and kept a watch on his doings as well as they could. To do so more effectively, they associated with him, as an equal, as it were, and not merely as a servant, a steady young man who had come from Leyden; and as he was discreet and could be trusted, they were able to give him such instructions as kept Ashley within bounds. So they replied to their friends in England that they accepted their offer and joined with them in Ashley's enterprise, but told them what their fears were in regard to him.

When they had received full account of all the goods sent over to them that year, they saw they were very short of trading goods, and that Ashley was far better supplied than themselves. They were even forced to buy supplies from the fishermen, and such things as cotton, kersey, and other cloth from Mr. Allerton himself, and so to dispose of a large part of their beaver at reduced rates over here, instead of sending it home to help discharge their debts. This vexed them greatly, but Mr.

Allerton assured them that next year they should have whatever they wrote for. Their engagements for this year were large indeed—when they came to know them, which was not till two years after; and were increased by Mr. Allerton raising large sums at Bristol at 50 percent again, which he insisted he was forced to do, otherwise he could have got no goods transported by the fishing ships in the spring—such was their ill will towards the trade of the colony. But whether this was any more than an excuse, some of them doubted; however, the burden lay on their shoulders, and they must bear it—as they did many other heavy loads before the end.

This necessity of paying 50 percent, and the difficulty of having their goods transported by the fishing ships early in the year during the best season for trade, put them upon another project. Mr. Allerton, after the fishing season was over, secured a bargain in salt at a good fishing place and bought it. It came to about £113, and shortly after he might have got £30 clear profit for it without any trouble. But Mr. Winslow and some of the other partners, coming that way from Kennebec in the bark, met Mr. Allerton and persuaded him not to sell the salt, but suggested keeping it for themselves and hiring a ship in the west country to come fishing for them on shares, as was the custom. Her salt being here already, and a dock built where it lay safely housed, instead of bringing salt, they might load her full of trading goods without paying freight, and receive them in plenty of time, which would be greatly to their advantage. On arrival at New Plymouth this plan was discussed, and approved by all but the Governor, who was against it, as they had always lost by fishing; but the rest were strongly in favor of it, believing that they might make good profits by the fishing; and even if they should only save a little, or actually lose something by it, the advantage of getting early supplies would be ample return. So he gave way, and it was referred to their friends in England, to allow or disallow it. Of this, more in its place.

Considering what had to be done about the patents and in what state it had been left, and owing to Mr. Sherley's earnest wish to have Mr. Allerton come over to finish it and complete the accounts, etc., it was decided to send him over again this year—though it was with some fear and jealousy. However, he made them fair promises to perform all their business according to their directions and to redeem his former errors. So he was accordingly sent with full instructions, and with long letters to Mr. Sherley and the rest, both about Ashley's business and their own; stating how essential it was that they be supplied with trading commodities, what they had suffered through want of them, and of what little use other goods were in comparison. They fully explained about the fishing ship that was to be hired and loaded with trading goods to supply both them and Ashley, and the advantages to be gained. It was left to their decision to hire and fit her out, or not; but under no circumstances to send one, unless she were loaded with trading goods. But what happened will appear in the account of next year's doings.

I almost omitted another occurrence at the beginning of this year. A Mr. Ralph Smith [6] and his wife and family had come over to the Bay of Massachusetts, and lived at present with some straggling people at Nantasket. A boat from here putting in there on one occasion, he earnestly

---

[6] Smith, suspected of Separatism, had been forbidden to stay in the Massachusetts Colony unless he conformed to the Established Church there.

begged them to give him and his family passage to New Plymouth, with such effects as they could take; he had heard that it was likely he might procure houseroom here for some time, till he might decide to settle here if permitted, or elsewhere, as God should dispose; he was weary of being in that uncouth place, and in such a poor house that it kept neither him nor his effects dry. So, as he was a grave man and they understood he had been a minister, they brought him, though they had no orders to do so. He was kindly entertained here and housed, and later he had the rest of his goods and servants sent for and exercised his gifts among them. Afterwards he was chosen to the ministry and remained there several years.

It was mentioned before, that several of those who came from Leyden sailed in ships that went to Salem, where Mr. Endicott had chief command. Diseases which had developed among the passengers at sea infected those ashore, and many died; some of scurvy, others of an infectious fever which was amongst them for some time, though our people, through God's goodness, escaped it. Whereupon Mr. Endicott wrote for help, understanding that one of them at New Plymouth had some skill as a physician,[7] and had cured several of scurvy and others of various diseases by letting blood and other means. So he sent to the Governor here, requesting him to send him to them. The Governor complied, and wrote to him, receiving a letter in reply. This letter, though brief, shows the beginning of their acquaintance; and as a manifestation of the truth and of the ways of God, I thought it fitting and profitable to insert it here.

---

[7] This was Samuel Fuller, physician and one-time butcher, who had more talent as a proselytizer than as medical practitioner.

Governor John Endicott at Salem to Governor Bradford at New Plymouth:

Right Worthy Sir,

It is an unusual thing that servants of one master and of the same household should be strangers! I assure you I do not desire it—nay, to speak more plainly, I cannot be so to you. God's people are all marked with one and the same mark, and sealed with one and the same seal, and have, in the main, one and the same heart, guided by one and the same spirit of truth; and where this is, there can be no discord—nay, there must needs be sweet harmony. And so I pray the Lord that we may, as Christian brethren, be united with you by a heavenly and unfeigned love; bending all our hearts and forces in furthering a work beyond our strength, with reverence and fear, and fastening our eyes always on Him Who is able to direct and prosper all our ways. I am much beholden to you for your kind love and care in sending Mr. Fuller among us, and rejoice at what I hear from him of your attitude towards the outward form of God's worship. It is, as far as I can gather, no other than is warranted by the evidence of truth, and the same which I have maintained and professed ever since the Lord in His mercy revealed Himself unto me—though very different from the common report of you that has been spread about. But God's children must look for no less here below; and it is the great mercy of God that He strengthens them to go through with it. I need not be tedious to you now, for, God willing, I purpose to see your face shortly. In the meantime I humbly take my leave of you, committing you to the Lord's blessed protection, and rest,

Your assured loving friend,
JOHN ENDICOTT.

Naumkeag, May 11th, 1629.

A second letter received this year shows the progress of their church affairs at Salem, which was the second church erected in these parts. Afterwards the Lord established many more in several places.

Charles Gott at Salem to Governor Bradford at New Plymouth:

Sir,

I make bold to trouble you with a few lines to inform you how it has pleased God to deal with us since you heard from us; how, notwithstanding all the opposition here and elsewhere, it has pleased God to lay a foundation which I hope is agreeable to His word in every way. It pleased the Lord to move the heart of our Governor to set apart July 10th as a solemn day of humiliation for the choice of a pastor and a teacher. The first part of the day was used for prayer and teaching, the latter part for the election, which was held in this way.[8] The persons nominated, who had been ministers in England, were questioned concerning their calling. They acknowledged there was a twofold calling: the one an inward calling, when the Lord moved the heart of a man to take that calling upon him, and fitted him with gifts for it; the second an outward calling from the people, when a body of believers join together in covenant, to walk in all the ways of God; every male member having a free voice in the choice of the officers, etc. Now, we being satisfied that these two men were so qualified, as the apostle tells Timothy:[9] A bishop must be blameless, sober, apt to teach, etc.,—I think I may say, as the eunuch said to Philip: What should hinder him from being baptized, seeing there was

---

[8] From a fuller copy of this letter in Bradford's letter-book, it appears that this election at Salem was the first time that a written ballot was used in America.
[9] I Timothy, III, 2.

water, and he believed.[10] So these two servants of God, giving full satisfaction by their answers and being thus fitted, we saw no reason why we might not freely vote for their election. Mr. Skelton was chosen pastor, and Mr. Higginson teacher; and they, accepting the choice, Mr. Higginson, with three or four of the gravest members of the church, laid their hands on Mr. Skelton, with prayer. After this there was imposition of hands on Mr. Higginson. Since then, Thursday (being as I take it the 6th of August) has been appointed for another day of humiliation, for the choice of elders and deacons, and for ordaining them.

And now, good Sir, I hope that you and the rest of God's people with you, who are acquainted with the ways of God, will say that herein a right foundation was laid, and that these two blessed servants of the Lord came in at the door, and not at the window. Thus I have made bold to trouble you with these few lines, desiring you to remember us. . . . And so rest,

At your service in what I may,

CHARLES GOTT.

Salem, July 30th, 1629.

---

[10] Acts, VIII, 36.

". . . and as one small candle may light a thousand, so the light here kindled hath shone to many, yea in some sorte to our whole nation."

CHAPTER XI

[*1630*]

Ashley, being well supplied, had quickly gathered a good parcel of beaver, and like a crafty pate he sent it all home, and would not pay for the goods he had from here, but let them stand charged against him and drew still more. Though they knew his object well enough, they let him go on and wrote about it to England. However, owing to the beaver they received there and sold (which appealed to them as business men) and Mr. Allerton's high praise of him, they were more eager to supply him than the colony, and even somewhat disparaged it in comparison.

They were also forced to buy him a bark, and equip her with a captain and men to transport his corn and provisions, of which he used large quantities; for the Indians of those parts grew no corn, and at harvest time, when the corn here is ready, the weather is so bad and the season so dangerous that a shallop is no good for the purpose.

This spring the settlers looked anxiously for timely supplies in the fishing ship which they expected, and for which they had been at the expense of keeping a dock. But no ship came, nor were any goods heard of. Later they learned that supplies had been sent to Ashley by a fishing ship, which puzzled them—the more so that they had received no letters from Mr. Allerton or Mr. Sherley. However, they carried on their business as well as they could. At last they heard of the arrival of Mr. Pierce at the Bay of Massachusetts, with passengers and goods. They sent a shallop at once, supposing he would have something for them. But he told them he had nothing, and that a ship had been sent out fishing, but after eleven weeks beating at sea she met with such foul weather that she was forced to return to England, and the season being over she gave up the voyage. Nor had he heard much about goods in her for the settlers, or that she belonged to them, though he had heard something of that kind from Mr. Allerton. But Mr. Allerton had bought another ship, in which he was coming, which was to fish for bass to the eastward, and was bringing goods, etc. These reports troubled them and much astonished them. Mr. Winslow having been eastward brought similar news with more particulars, and that probably Mr. Allerton would not arrive till late. At length, having an opportunity, they resolved to send Mr. Winslow to England with what beaver they had ready, to see how their business stood, being dubious about it, especially Mr. Allerton's behavior. They wrote letters, and gave him such instructions as they thought proper—and if he found things unsatisfactory he was to discharge Mr. Allerton from being agent and from dealing any more for them in the business, and he was to see how the accounts stood, etc.

About the middle of summer Mr. Hatherley, one of the partners, arrives at the Bay of Massachusetts, having come over in the ship that was sent fishing, called the *Friendship*. They sent to him at once, not doubting that now their goods had come, and they would know how everything stood. They found the news was true, that this ship had been so long at sea and her provisions had been so largely consumed or spoiled, that she abandoned the voyage. He himself had been sent over by the rest of the partners to see how things went here. He was at Bristol with Mr. Allerton in the ship they had bought, called the *White Angel,* which was all ready to set sail, when that night came a messenger to Mr. Allerton from Barnstable, and told him of the return of the fishing ship *Friendship,* and what had happened. He not knowing what to do, the ship lying there at his expense ready to set sail, got Mr. Hatherley to go and discharge her and take order for the goods.

To be short, they found Mr. Hatherley somewhat reserved and troubled, Mr. Allerton not being there, and not knowing how to dispose of the goods till he came; but he said he heard he had arrived by the *White Angel,* to eastward, and expected to meet him there. He told them there was not much for them in the *Friendship,*—only two parcels of Barnstable rugs, and two hogsheads of methiglin [1] in wooden flackets. When these flackets came to be examined, only six gallons of the two hogsheads remained, the rest having been drunk up under the name "leakage." For the rest, the ship was laden with goods for various gentlemen and others who had come to settle in Massachusetts, for which they had paid freight by the ton. This was all the satisfaction they could get at present. They took this small lot of goods and returned with the news, and a letter as obscure, as follows:

---

[1] Also called mead, a liquor made of honey and water, boiled and fermented.

James Sherley in England to the Colonists at New Plymouth:

Gentlemen, Partners, and loving Friends,

Briefly thus: we have this year fitted out both a fishing ship and a trading ship. The latter we have bought, and so have disbursed a great deal of money, as will appear by our accounts. This trading ship, the *White Angel*, is however to perform two duties: fishing for bass and trading; and lest, while Mr. Allerton is employed trading, the fishing might suffer by neglect of the sailors, we have begged our mutual friend, Mr. Hatherley, to go over with him, knowing he will be a comfort to Mr. Allerton, and that it will be a joy to you to see a careful, loving friend, and one who is a great stay to the business. If it should please God that one should die—as God forbid—the survivor would keep the accounts and the other matters straight. We have now spent large sums of money, as they will acquaint you. . . . When it was only four or five hundred pounds apiece, we did not trouble much about it, but left it to you and your agent, who without flattery deserves infinite thanks both from you and us for his pains. . . . But now that our ventures are double, nay treble for some of us, we have decided to send over our friend Mr. Hatherley, whom we pray you to entertain kindly. The main object of sending him is to examine the accounts and report on the condition of the business, about all of which we beg you to inform him fully. I will not promise, but shall endeavor to obtain the grant of your patent as desired, and that ere long. Pray do not take anything unkindly; I have not written out of suspicion of any unjust dealing. Be you all kindly saluted in the Lord, so I rest,

Yours in what I may,
JAMES SHERLEY.

March 25th, 1630.

It is not surprising that these things troubled them. First, there was this fishing ship which had been fitted out, laden with other goods and scarcely any of theirs, though their main object was that he should bring them ample supplies, and their special orders were not to fit out a ship except for this purpose; and now to have the expenses charged to their account, though clean contrary to their orders, was a mystery they could not understand—the more serious seeing that she had lost both her voyage and her provisions. Secondly, that another ship should be bought, and sent out on business never thought of by any here, much less intimated to their friends in England either by word or letter, was equally inexplicable. Bass fishing was never favored by them, and as soon as ever they heard of this project they foresaw loss. As for Mr. Allerton's trading for them, it never entered their thoughts. Thirdly, that their friends should complain of disbursements, and yet incur such great risks contrary to all orders seemed very strange—all these important projects being wrapped up in a brief and obscure letter. But amidst all their doubts they must have patience till Mr. Allerton and Mr. Hatherley arrived. In the meantime Mr. Winslow had gone to England, and the rest of them were forced to follow their employments as best they could.

At length Mr. Hatherley and Mr. Allerton came, and finding those at the settlement very depressed about it, Mr. Allerton told them that the *White Angel* did not belong to them, and had not been bought on their account; they need not have anything to do with her unless they wished. Mr. Hatherley confirmed this, and said that they wanted him to put in his share but he had refused. However, he questioned whether they would not charge her to the general account, if there were a loss—which he now saw was likely—seeing that Mr. Allerton had proposed the undertaking. As for the fishing ship, he told them they need not be anxious; and he produced her accounts, which showed that her first fitting out did not much exceed £600. On the failure of the first voyage, at her return, he had sold goods out of her in England, and applied the money to the second voyage, which, together with such goods and implements as Mr. Allerton would need for fishing, such as salt, nets, spikes, nails, etc., would amount to nearly £400. As for this second voyage it would show a profit on the freight of the goods and the sale of some cattle which would be paid for partly here and partly by bills in England. So the total loss, which would not be much above £200, would be all they would have to bear on this account.

Mr. Hatherley also told them he was sent over as the agent of those in England, and that whatever he and Mr. Allerton did jointly they would stand by; that they would not sanction what Mr. Allerton did alone, unless they wished; but what he (Mr. Hatherley) did alone they would guarantee. So they sold him and Mr. Allerton all the rest of their stock of goods, and gave them possession of them; and a statement was drawn up in writing and confirmed under both Mr. Allerton's and Mr. Hatherley's hands, to the above effect. Mr. Allerton being best acquainted with the people, sold all such goods as he had no need of for fishing, as nine shallop-sails made of good new canvas, and the ropes for them, all new, and several such useful things, for beaver, by Mr. Hatherley's permission. Thus they thought they had well provided for themselves.

However, those at the colony censured Mr. Allerton

for entering upon this project, doubting its success. Mr. Allerton brought to the town, after he had sold what he could elsewhere, a great quantity of other goods, besides trading commodities; as linen, bed-ticks, stockings, tape, pins, rugs, etc., and said they could have them if they wished. But they told him they had forbidden him before to bring any such things on their account, as it would injure their trade and reduce their returns. But he and Mr. Hatherley said if they would not take them, they would sell them themselves, and take corn for what they could not sell otherwise. They told them they might, if they had instructions to do so. These goods came to upwards of £500.

Mr. Allerton then went off on his bass fishing; and Mr. Hatherley, as ordered, after examining the affairs of the settlement, about all of which they informed him fully, asked for a boat to go and visit the trading house at Kennebec and Ashley at Penobscot. They accordingly supplied him with a boat and men for the voyage and acquainted him thoroughly with everything. He was fully satisfied and now saw plainly that Mr. Allerton played his own game, not only to the great detriment of the partners at the colony who employed and trusted him, but to that of the partners in England also, by prejudicing them against the settlement, assuring them that they would never be able to recoup themselves for their great expenses, if they would not follow his advice and support his projects.

Mr. Hatherley disclosed, besides, a further scheme in connection with this ship, the *White Angel*. It appeared that as she was well fitted with good ordnance, and known to have made a great fight at sea, in which she came off victorious, they had agreed with Mr. Allerton that after she had brought her cargo of goods here and had loaded with fish, she would go to Oporto, and there be sold, freight, ordnance, and all. But this was prevented, partly by the advice given by their friends here to Mr. Allerton and Mr. Hatherley, showing how it might ruin their friends in England, who were men of property, should it become known—and in the interests of the colony they utterly disallowed it, and protested against it; and partly by their ill success, for they had arrived too late to do any good with the fishing, and had brought such a drunken crew that neither Mr. Allerton nor anyone else could keep them in order, as Mr. Hatherley and everyone could see to their shame.

Ashley also was caught in a trap before Mr. Hatherley returned, for trading powder and shot to the Indians. He was apprehended by those in authority, who would have confiscated over a thousand weight of beaver, but that the Governor here showed a bond under Ashley's hand, to the amount of £500, not to trade any arms or ammunition to the Indians or otherwise misbehave himself. It was proved, besides, that he had committed uncleanness with Indian women—things feared at the outset. So their goods were freed, but he was sent home in custody. To make an end of him, after some time of imprisonment in the Fleet,[2] by means of friends he was set at liberty, and intended to come over again, but the Lord prevented it; for he had an offer made to him by some merchants to go to Russia, owing to his skill in the beaver trade, which he accepted, and on returning home was drowned at sea. This was his end.

Mr. Hatherley, fully conversant with the state of affairs,

---

[2] Fleet Street prison, in London.

was satisfied, and able to inform them how things stood between Mr. Allerton and the colony. In fact, he discovered that Mr. Allerton had got the better of him too, and had taken possession of the things for which Mr. Hatherley stood jointly responsible to the partners here, as concerned the *Friendship*, besides most of the freight money, and some of his own private property. About this, however, more will appear in due course. He returned to England and they sent a good quantity of beaver with him to the rest of the partners; so both he and it were very welcome to them.

Mr. Allerton was busied with his own affairs and returned with his *White Angel*, being no longer employed by the plantation. But these troubles were not ended till many years after, nor fully realized for a long time, being folded up in obscurity and kept in the clouds to the great loss and vexation of the colony. In the end, for peace' sake, they were forced to bear the unjust burden of them almost to their undoing, as will appear if God give me life to finish this history.

They sent letters by Mr. Hatherley to the partners in England, to show them how they had settled with Mr. Hatherley and Mr. Allerton for the *Friendship*'s account, and that they both affirmed that the *White Angel* did not belong to them in any way, and that therefore their account must not be charged with it. They also wrote to Mr. Winslow, their agent, that he, too, should protest against it in their names, should any such thing be intended and that they would never permit it. They also signified that they dismissed Mr. Allerton wholly from being their agent, or from having anything to do with any of their business.

This year John Billington the elder, one of those who

came over first, was arraigned, and both by grand and petty jury found guilty of willful murder by plain and notorious evidence, and was accordingly executed.

This, the first execution among them, was a great sadness to them. They took all possible pains in the trial, and consulted Mr. Winthrop, and the other leading men at the Bay of Massachusetts recently arrived, who concurred with them that he ought to die, and the land be purged of blood. He and some of his relatives had often been punished for misconduct before, being one of the profanest families among them. They came from London, and I know not by what influence they were shuffled into the first body of settlers. The charge against him was that he waylaid a young man, one John Newcomin, about a former quarrel, and shot him with a gun, whereof he died.

Having by good fortune a letter or two that came into my hands concerning the proceedings of their reverend friends at the Bay of Massachusetts, who had lately come over, I thought it not amiss to insert them here, before concluding this year.

Sir,

Being at Salem on Sunday, the 25th of July, after the evening service Mr. Johnson received a letter from the Governor, Mr. John Winthrop, saying that the hand of God was upon them at Boston and those at Charlestown, visiting them with sickness and taking many from amongst them, the righteous suffering with the wicked in these bodily judgments. He desired the godly here to take into consideration what was to be done to pacify the Lord's wrath, etc. It was concluded that the Lord was to be sought in righteousness; and to that end, the 6th day (Friday) of this present week has been set apart that they may humble themselves before God and seek Him in His ordinances.

On that day such godly persons as are amongst them and known to each other will at the end of the service publicly make known their godly desire and practice it, viz., that they solemnly enter into covenant with the Lord to walk in His ways. As those who have agreed to keep this day live at three different places, each settlement having men of ability among them, they decided to form themselves into three distinct bodies, not intending to proceed hastily to the choice of officers, or the admission of others to their society, except a few well-known to them, promising afterwards to receive by confession of faith such as appear to be qualified. They earnestly beg the church at New Plymouth to set apart the same day, for the same purpose, beseeching the Lord to withdraw the hand of correction from them, and to establish and direct them in His ways. And though the time be short, we pray you to be instigated to this godly work, as the cause is so urgent, whereby God will be honored and they and we shall undoubtedly receive sweet comfort. Be you kindly saluted, etc.

Your brethren in Christ, etc.

Salem, July 26th, 1630.

A member of the New Plymouth Settlement, staying at Charlestown, to a friend at New Plymouth:

Sir,

I have the sad news to impart that many here are sick and many dead—the Lord in mercy look upon them. Some here have entered into church covenant.[3] The first four were the Governor, Mr. John Winthrop, Mr. Johnson, Mr. Dudley, and Mr. Wilson; since then five more have joined, and others are likely to follow daily. The Lord increase them both in number and in holiness, for His sake. There is a gentleman here, Mr. Coddington, a Boston man,

---

[3] That is, joined together to form a new church.

who told me that Mr. Cotton's [4] advice at Hampton was that they should take counsel of those at New Plymouth, and should do nothing to offend them. There are many honest Christians desirous to see us, some because of the love they bear us and the good opinion they have of us; others to see if we are so unworthy as they have heard. We have a name for holiness, and love towards God and his saints; the Lord make us more and more worthy of it, and that it may be more than a name or else it will do us no good. Be you lovingly saluted, and all the rest of our friends. The Lord Jesus bless us, and the whole Israel of God. Amen.

Your loving brother, etc.

Charlestown, Aug. 2nd, 1630.

Thus out of small beginnings greater things have grown by His hand Who made all things out of nothing, and gives being to all things that are; and as one small candle may light a thousand, so the light enkindled here has shone to many, yea, in a sense, to our whole nation; let the glorious name of Jehovah have all the praise.

---

[4] This is the only mention by Bradford of the famous Puritan preacher, John Cotton. Both he and Mr. Coddington came from Boston, England. Coddington was later banished because of his sympathy for Anne Hutchinson, and became governor of Rhode Island.

"Wherefore, even amongst friends, men had need be carfull whom they trust, and not lett things of this nature lye long unrecaled."

CHAPTER XII
[*1631*]

Ashley being taken away by the hand of God, and Mr. Allerton discharged from his employment, their business began to run smoothly again, since they were better able to guide it, Penobscot being now wholly in their control; for though Mr. William Pierce had a share in it, as things stood he was glad to have his money repaid him and resign. Mr. Winslow sent them over some supplies from England as soon as he could, and when he arrived some time later, he brought a large supply of suitable goods with him by means of which their trading could be carried on successfully. Neither his representations nor the letters they wrote succeeded in preventing Mr. Sherley and the rest from charging both the Friendship and the White Angel to the general account, which was the cause of continual contention thereafter.

I will now insert a letter of Mr. Winslow's on the subject.

Edward Winslow in England to Governor Bradford at New Plymouth:

Sir,
It chanced by God's providence that I received and brought your letters per Mr. Allerton from Bristol to

London; and I fear what the outcome will be. Mr. Allerton intended to fit out the ship again for fishing. Mr. Sherley, Mr. Beauchamp, and Mr. Andrews disclaim responsibility, protesting that but for us they would never have risked one penny; Mr. Hatherley takes no decided stand on either side. As to what you write about him and Mr. Allerton taking the *White Angel* upon themselves on behalf of the partners here, the others insist that they never gave any such orders, nor will they make it good; if those two like to be responsible for the account, well and good. What the upshot will be, I do not know. The Lord so direct and assist us that He may not be dishonored by our dissensions. I hear from a friend that I was much blamed for telling what I heard in the spring about the plans for selling the ship in Spain; but if I had not told you what I heard so peremptorily reported—and which I offered to prove at Bristol—I should certainly have been unworthy of my employment. As to the power of attorney, given so long ago to Mr. Allerton, what we feared has happened; Mr. Sherley and the others have got it and will not surrender it, that being the instrument of our agents' credit to procure such sums. I expect bitter words, hard thoughts, and sour looks from several for writing this, as for reporting the former information. I would I had a more thankful task, but I hope a good conscience will make it comfortable, etc.

Nov. 16th, 1631.

Thus far he.

The deed mentioned above was given under their hand and seal when Mr. Allerton was first employed by them, and its return was requested when they first began to suspect him. He told them it was among his papers, but he would find it and give it them before he went. When he was ready to go, it was demanded again. He said he had not found it, but it was among his papers which he was taking with him, and he would send it by the boat coming from the eastward; and then again it could not be found, but he would look it up at sea. Whether Mr. Sherley had it before or after this is not certain; but having it, he would not let it go, and keeps it to this day. So even among friends, men need to be careful whom they trust, and not let things of this nature lie long unrecalled.

James Sherley in England to Governor Bradford at New Plymouth:

Sir,

I have received your letter through our friends Mr. Allerton and Mr. Hatherley, who, blessed be God, have arrived safely at Bristol. Mr. Hatherley has come to London, but Mr. Allerton I have not yet seen. We thank you, and are very glad you dissuaded him from the Spanish voyage, and that he did not fulfill his intentions; for we all utterly disliked the project, as well as the fishing of the *Friendship*. We wished him to sell the salt, and were unwilling to have him undertake so much business, partly because of previous failure, and partly because we were loth to disburse so much money. But he assured us this would repay us, and that the colony would be long in doing so; nay, I remember that he even doubted if by your trading there you could meet your expenses and pay us, and for this very reason he induced us to undertake that business with Ashley, though he was a stranger to us. . . .

As to the cost of the fishing ship we are sorry it proves so heavy, and are willing to take our share of it. What Mr. Hatherley and Mr. Allerton have proposed no doubt they themselves will make good; we gave them no authority to make any composition to separate you from us in this or any other scheme. Furthermore, I think you have no cause to forsake us, for we involved you in nothing but what your agent advocated and you in your letters desired. If he exceeded your authority, I hope you will not blame us, much less leave us in the lurch, now that our money is expended. . . . But I fear neither you nor we have been properly dealt with; for, as you write, surely one half of £4000—nay a quarter—in commodities, despatched in seasonable time, would have provided you more effectively. Yet, in spite of all this and much more that I might write, I cannot but think him honest, and that his intentions were good; but the wisest may fail. Well, now that it has pleased God to give us hope of agreeing, doubt not but we shall all endeavor to adjust these accounts fairly, as soon as we possibly can. I suppose you sent over Mr. Winslow as we Mr. Hatherley, to certify each other how the state of things stood. We have received some satisfaction upon Mr. Hatherley's return, and I hope you will receive the same upon Mr. Winslow's return.

Now to answer your letter more particularly; I shall be very brief. The charging of the *White Angel* to your account could not be more surprising to you than the purchase of her was to us; for you commissioned [1] that what he did you would stand by; we gave him no such commission, yet for his credit and your sakes paid the bills he charged us with. . . . As to my writing that she was to fulfill two purposes, fishing and trading, believe me I never so much as thought of any private trading, nor will I countenance any; for I was always against it, and used these very words: It will reduce the profits of the settlement and ruin it.

The rest of the letter I omit as it is not very pertinent. It was dated Nov. 19th, 1631. In another letter, dated Nov.

---

[1] His commission was abused; he never had any authority for such undertakings, as they well knew, nor had the adventurers in England any authority to pay this money—nor would they have paid a penny of it if they had not had some other object in view. (B.)

24th, in answer to the general letter on the same subject, there are these words:

As to the *White Angel* about which you write so earnestly, saying we thrust her upon you contrary to the intentions of the purchaser, we say you forget yourselves and do us wrong. We will not take upon us to divine what the thoughts or intentions of the purchaser were; but what he spoke we heard, and that we will affirm and make good against anyone, viz., that unless she were bought, Ashley could not be supplied, and if he were not supplied we could not recoup ourselves for our losses on your account.

From another of his dated Jan. 2nd, 1631: [2]

We propose to keep the *Friendship* and the *White Angel*, as regards last year's voyages, on the general account, hoping that together they will produce profit rather than loss and cause less confusion in our accounts and less disturbance in our intercourse. As for the *White Angel*, though we laid out the money and took bills of sale in our own names, none of us had so much as a thought of separating from you in any way this year, because we did not wish the world (I may say Bristol) to see any breach between Mr. Allerton and you, or between him and us, and so disgrace him in his proceedings. We have now let him the ship at £30 per month, by charter-party, and secured him in a bond of £1000 to perform the contract and bring her back to London, if God please. What he takes in her for you shall be marked with your mark, and bills of lading shall be taken and sent in Mr. Winslow's letter, who is this day riding to Bristol about it. So in this voyage we deal with him as strangers, not as partners. He has turned in three books of accounts, one for the company, another for Ashley's business, and the third for the *White Angel* and

---

[2] By modern reckoning, 1632.

Friendship. The books, or copies of them, we propose to send you, for you may discover the errors in them more readily than we could. It can be reckoned how much money he has had from us, and you can charge him with all the beaver he had from you. The total sum, as he has it, is £7103-7-1. Of this he has expended, and given to Mr. Vines and others, about £543. You will know from your books whether you had the goods he charges to you. This is all I can say at present concerning the accounts. He expected to complete them in a few hours; but he and Straton and Fogg were over a month at them; but he could not wait till we had examined them for fear of losing his fishing voyage—which I fear he has already done. . . .

We bless God Who put it into our minds to send to each other; for had Mr. Allerton gone on in that risky and expensive way one year more, we should not have been able to meet his expenditure; nay, both he and we must have lain in the ditch and sunk under the burden. . . . Had there been an orderly course taken and your business better managed, by the blessing of God yours would have been the ablest colony we know of, undertaken by Englishmen. . . .

Thus far of these letters of Mr. Sherley's.

A few observations about former letters, and then I will give the simple truth of the things in controversy between them—at least as far as good evidence can show.

1. It seems clear that Ashley's business and the buying of the ship and the resultant plans were first contrived by Mr. Allerton.

2. Though Mr. Allerton may not have intended to wrong the plantation, his own private ends led him astray; for it became known that in the first two or three years of

his employment as agent he had made £400, and put it into a brewery of Mr. Collier's in London. Again, Mr. Sherley and he had private dealings; and yet I believe, as he mentioned above, that Mr. Sherley did not countenance any private trading which he thought would injure the colony.

3. Considering all they had done for the settlement, in former risks and recent disbursements, when Mr. Allerton's proposals turned out unsuccessful, they thought it fair that the colony should bear them, and so took advantage of such power as Mr. Allerton formerly had as their agent, to let these losses devolve upon them.

4. As for Mr. Allerton, with pity and compassion I may say with the apostle Timothy (I Tim. vi, 9, 10): "But they that will be rich fall into temptation and a snare . . . and pierce themselves through with many sorrows . . . for the love of money is the root of all evil." God gave him to see the evil of his ways, that he may find mercy in repentance for the wrongs he has done.

As to the two ships, the truth as far as could be learned was this. The idea of fitting out the fishing ship—the *Friendship*—came first from the colony, but was left to them in England to carry out or not, as they thought best. But when it was fully considered, and the plan seemed hopeful and profitable, it was suggested: why might they not do it for themselves to cover their losses, and without letting the colony share in it? If their supplies reached them in time, that was sufficient. So they hired her and fitted her out, and freighted her as full as she could carry, with the goods of passengers belonging to Massachusetts, which rose to a good sum of money, and intended to send the New Plymouth settlement their goods in the other ship. Mr. Hatherley confirmed the following upon oath before the Governor and Deputy Governor of Massachusetts, Mr. Winthrop and Mr. Dudley: that the *Friendship* was not intended for the joint partnership, but for the private account of Mr. James Sherley, Mr. Beauchamp, Mr. Andrews, Mr. Allerton, and himself. This deposition was taken under their hands at Boston, Aug. 29th, 1639, as may be seen, besides other testimony.

As for the *White Angel*, though she was first bought, or at least the price arranged, by Mr. Allerton at Bristol, Mr. Sherley need not have disbursed the money against his will. That she was not intended for the general partnership appears from various evidence. The bills of sale were made out in their own names, without any reference to the colony at all; namely, Mr. Sherley, Mr. Beauchamp, Mr. Andrews, Mr. Denison, and Mr. Allerton—Mr. Hatherley would not join them in this. Mr. Allerton took oath to the same effect concerning the *White Angel* before the Governor and Deputy, on September 7th, 1639, and deposed that Mr. Hatherley and himself, on behalf of them all, agreed to free all the rest of the New Plymouth partners from the losses of the *Friendship* for £200.

Concerning Mr. Allerton's accounts, they were so lengthy and intricate that they could not understand them, much less correct them, and it was two or three years before they could unravel them even imperfectly. I know not why, but he took upon himself to keep all the accounts, though Mr. Sherley, their agent, was to buy and sell all their goods, and did so usually; but it was Mr. Allerton who passed in accounts for all disbursements—goods bought, which he never saw, the expenses for the Leyden people incurred by others in his absence, for the patents, etc.—in connection with all of which he made it appear that the balance owing to him was over £300, and demanded payment. However, on examination he was found to be over £2000 debtor to them, besides I know not how much that could never be cleared up, interest unaccounted, etc. Then they were obliged to pass bills for expenses that were intolerable. The fees for the patent came to above £500–all for nothing; £30 given at a clap, and £50 spent on a journey, etc. No wonder Mr. Sherley said that if their business had been better managed they might have been the richest English colony at that time. He even screwed up his poor old father-in-law's account to above £200, when, alas! he, poor man, never dreamed that what he had received could be near that value, believing that many of the things brought over had been given by Mr. Allerton as presents to him and his children.[3] Nor did they come to nearly that value in fact, the prices being inflated by interest.

This year Mr. Sherley, too, sent over a cash account, showing what Mr. Allerton had received from them and disbursed, for which he referred to his accounts; besides an account of beaver sold, which Mr. Winslow and others had taken over, and a large supply of goods which Mr. Winslow had brought back, and all the disbursements for the *Friendship* and *White Angel,* and anything else he could charge the partners with. In these accounts of Mr. Sherley's some things were obscure and some twice charged. They made them debtor to the total amount of £4770-19-2, besides £1000 still due for the purchase yet unpaid, and notwithstanding all the beaver and goods that both Ashley and they had shipped over.

---

[3] Allerton, it will be remembered, had married a daughter of Elder Brewster's.

Into such huge sums had Mr. Allerton run them in two years, for at the end of 1628 all their debts did not much exceed £400, as will be remembered; now they amounted to as many thousands! In 1629, when Mr. Sherley and Mr. Hatherley were at Bristol, they wrote a long letter in which they gave an account of the debts and the sums that had been disbursed; but Mr. Allerton begged and entreated them to omit it. So they blotted out two lines in which the sums were mentioned, and wrote over them so that not a word could be read, to which they have since confessed. They were thus kept hoodwinked, until now they found themselves deeply in debt.

To mend matters, Mr. Allerton now wholly deserted them; having brought them into the briars, he leaves them to get out as best they can. But God crossed him mightily, for having hired the ship from Mr. Sherley at £30 a month, he set out again with a drunken crew and so overloaded her that she could not bear sail, and they were forced to put into Milford Haven and reload her, which lost them the season and resulted in a less profitable voyage than the year before. Having reached this country, he sold trading commodities to any that would buy, to the serious detriment of the colony; but what was worse, what he could not sell outright he sold on credit, and formed a disreputable company of traders to cover every hole and corner even up the Kennebec, to take away the trade from the settlement's house there, on the patent for which he had wasted so much of their money. Not content with this, he did all he could to reduce its value to the colony and ruin them; he took partners, and set up a trading house beyond Penobscot, to cut off the trade there too.

But the French, seeing that it would injure them, came

down on them before they were well settled and ousted them, killing two of their men and taking all the goods, to a considerable value, the loss being mostly, if not all, Mr. Allerton's. The rest of the men were sent into France and this was the end of that project. Those to whom he sold on credit, being loose and drunken fellows, for the most part, cheated him of all they got into their hands. Afterwards, when he came to New Plymouth, the church called him to account for these and other gross miscarriages. He confessed his fault, and promised better ways, and that he would wind himself out of the tangle as soon as he could, etc.

This year Mr. Sherley must needs send them out a new accountant. He had made mention of such a thing the year before, but they wrote him that their expenses were so great already that he need not increase them in this way, and that if they were dealt with fairly and had their accounts properly sent in from there, they could keep their accounts here themselves. Nevertheless, he sent them over a man they could not well refuse, as he was a younger brother of Mr. Winslow's—Mr. Josias Winslow—whom they had been at considerable expense to instruct in London before he came. He came over in the *White Angel* with Mr. Allerton, and there began his first employment.

This year their house at Penobscot was robbed by the French, and all their goods of any value was taken, up to £400 or £500 at least. The captain in charge of the house and some of the men with him had gone westward with their vessel to fetch a supply of goods which had been brought over for them. In the meantime came a small French ship into the harbor, and amongst the company was a false Scot. They pretended they had just come in from sea, and did not know where they were; that their vessel was very leaky, and asked if they might haul her ashore and mend her. They used many French compliments, and in the end, seeing only three or four servants and understanding from this Scotchman that the captain and the rest were away from home, they began praising their guns and muskets that lay in racks on the wall, and took them down to look at them, asking if they were loaded. And when they had hold of them, one of them presents a gun ready charged at the servants and another a pistol, and bid them quietly deliver up their goods. Some of the men were carried aboard, and others had to help carry the goods. When they had taken what they wanted, they set them at liberty and went their way, with this mock: to tell their captain when he returned that some of the Isle of Rey gentlemen had been there.

This year Sir Christopher Gardiner, a descendant of that Bishop of Winchester who was so great a persecutor of God's Saints in Queen Mary's days,[4] and a great traveler, who had received the honor of knighthood at Jerusalem, being made Knight of the Sepulchre there, came into these parts under pretense of forsaking the world and living a godly life. He was not willing to perform any mean employment, or to take any pains for his living; and some time after he offered to join the churches in several places. He brought over with him a servant or two and a comely young woman, whom he called his cousin, but it was suspected that, after the Italian manner, she was his con-

---

[4] Stephen Gardiner, Catholic bishop of Winchester and chancellor under Queen Mary, was one of those responsible for the fanatical policy of persecuting and burning Protestants that made her reign one of the most unpopular in English history.

cubine. Having been living in Massachusetts, for some misbehavior which he should have answered for there, he fled from authority and got among the Indians of these parts. He was pursued, but they could not get him, though they promised a reward if he were found.

The Indians came to the Governor here and told where he was, and asked if they might kill him. He told them by no means, but if they could capture him and bring him here, they would be paid for their pains. They said he had a gun and a rapier and he would kill them if they attempted it, and the Massachusetts Indians had said they might kill him. But the Governor told them they must not kill him, but watch their opportunity and seize him. So they did; for coming upon him by the riverside, he got into a canoe to escape, and while he was covering them with his gun to keep them off, the stream carried the canoe against a rock and tumbled both him and his gun and rapier into the water. But he got out, and having a little dagger by his side, they dare not close with him. So they got some long poles and soon beat the dagger out of his hands, when he was glad to yield, and they brought him to the Governor. But his arms and hands were badly swollen and very sore with the blows they had given him. So he treated him kindly and sent him to a lodging where his arms were bathed and anointed, and he was quickly well again. The Governor blamed the Indians for beating him so much, but they said they only whipped him a little with sticks!

In his lodging, those who made his bed, found a little notebook that had slipped out of his pocket by accident, in which was a memorandum of the day he was reconciled to the Pope and the Church of Rome, and in what university he took his scapula [5] and such and such degrees. This was handed over to the Governor here, who sent the Governor of Massachusetts word of his capture. He was sent for, and the notes were handed over to the Governor there, who was very grateful. After Sir Christopher got to England he showed his malice; but God prevented him.

Governor Winthrop at Boston to Governor Bradford at New Plymouth:

Sir,

It has pleased God to bring Sir Christopher Gardiner safely to us, with his dependents. And though I never intended to take any harsh measures with him, but to treat him as his position demanded, I let him know your kind words about him, and that he will speed the better for your mediation. It was a special providence of God to bring those notes of his into our hands. Please instruct all that are aware of them not to inform anyone, for that may frustrate the use to be made of them. The good Lord our God Who has always ordered things for the good of His poor churches here, direct us in this aright, and dispose it to a good issue. I am sorry we put you to so much trouble about this gentleman, especially at this busy time, but I knew not how to avoid it. I must again beg you to let me know what expense and trouble any of your people have been at on his account, that it may be recompensed. So, with the true affection of a friend, desiring all happiness to you and yours, and to all my worthy friends with you, whom I love in the Lord, I commend you to His grace and providence, and rest,

Your most assured friend,
JOHN WINTHROP.

Boston, May 5th, 1631.

---

[5] Academic medal.

Anent this I will take the liberty to show what occurred through this man's malice, complying with others. And though I do not doubt it will be more fully dealt with by honored friends whom it more directly concerned and who have more exact knowledge of the matter, I will give a hint of it here, showing God's providence in preventing the injury that might have resulted. The information I received was in a letter from my much honored and beloved friend, Mr. John Winthrop, Governor of Massachusetts.

Governor Winthrop at Boston to Governor Bradford at New Plymouth:

Sir,

Upon a petition presented by Sir Christopher Gardiner, Sir Ferdinand Gorges, Captain Mason, etc., against you and us, the cause was heard before the lords of the Privy Council, and was afterwards reported to the King, the success of which makes it evident to all that the Lord has care of His people here. The passages are admirable, but too long to write. I heartily wish for an opportunity to impart them to you; they cover many sheets of paper. But the conclusion was (against all expectation) an order for our encouragement, and much blame and disgrace upon the adversaries. This calls for much thankfulness from us all, which we purpose, the Lord willing, to express in a day of Thanksgiving to our merciful God. I do not doubt but that you will consider whether it is not fitting for you to join in it. As He humbled us by our recent correction, so He has now lifted us up by an abundant rejoicing in our deliverance from so desperate a danger; and the instrument whereby our enemies hoped to ruin us He has mercifully turned to our great advantage, as I shall further acquaint you when opportunity serves.

The following is the order of the Privy Council:

Jan. 19th, 1632.
At the Court of Whitehall

Present

Sigillum LORD PRIVY SEAL
EARL OF DORSET
LORD VISCOUNT FALKLAND
LORD BISHOP OF LONDON

LORD COTTINGTON
MR. TREASURER
MR. VICE CHAMBERLAIN
MR. SECRETARY COOKE

MASTER SECRETARY WINDBANK

Where His Majesty has lately been informed of a great distraction and much disorder in that plantation in the parts of America called New England, which if they be true and suffered to run on, would tend to the great dishonor of this kingdom and the utter ruin of that plantation. For prevention whereof and for the orderly settling of the government according to the intention of those patents which have been granted by His Majesty and by his late royal father King James, it has pleased His Majesty that the lords and others of his most honorable Privy Council should take the same into consideration. Their lordships in the first place thought fit to make a committee of this board to examine the information; which committee, having called several of the principal adventurers in the plantation, and heard those that are complainants against them, most of the things informed being denied and remaining to be proved by parties that must be called from that place, which would require a long lapse of time; and at present their lordships finding the adventurers occupied in the dispatch of men, victuals, and merchandise for that place, all of which would be at a standstill if the adventurers should be discouraged or suspect that the state had no good opinion of the plantation; their lordships not laying the fault or fancies (if any be) of some individuals upon the general government of the principal adventurers, which in due time is to be further enquired into, have thought fit in the meantime to declare that the appearances were so fair and the hopes so great, and that the country would prove both so beneficial to this kingdom and so profitable to the particular adventurers, that the adventurers had cause to go on cheerfully with their undertakings, and rest assured that if things were carried on as was claimed when the patents were granted, and as by the patents is appointed, His Majesty would not only maintain the liberties and privileges heretofore granted, but supply anything further that might tend to the good government, prosperity, and comfort of his people there of that place. . . .

WILLIAM TRUMBALL.

"And also the people of the plantation begane to grow in their outward estate, by reason of the flowing of many people into the cuntrie, espetially into the Bay of the Massachusetts."

CHAPTER XIII

[*1632*]

Mr. Allerton returned to England, little regarding his bond of £1000 to perform his contract; for though bound to take the ship to London and to pay £30 per month for her hire, he did neither, for he stopped at Bristol to fit her out again there; and this he did three times. She had been ten months on the former voyage, but he never paid a penny for her hire. It would seem he knew well enough how to deal with Mr. Sherley —he, though he must needs foist her upon the general account, disposing of her as he pleased. And though Mr. Allerton had thus broken his contract in every way, Mr. Sherley goes and sells him both the ship and all her accounts from first to last in a bond of £2000—in effect he might as well have given her to him—and not only this, but as good as gives him sanctuary, for he allows him one year to prepare his account and present it to the partners here, and another year to make payment of what should be due upon the account. In the meantime he wrote earnestly to them not to hinder him in his business, or delay him for the sake of the accounts, etc. The result was that in the interim he collected all the money due for freight and any other amounts belonging to her or the *Friendship*, as his own private debts; and, after all, sold ship, ordnance, fish, and other lading in Spain, as he had first planned, and what became of the money he best knows. Meanwhile their hands were tied and they could do nothing but look on, till he had transferred everything to other men's hands, except a few cattle and a little land and a few things he had here at New Plymouth, and so ultimately removed all his belongings, as he had already done himself, from hence.

Mr. Hatherley came over again this year upon his own business, and began to make preparations to settle in the country. As appeared later, he had closed out his share in the business and remained a partner in name only, nor did he trouble about their affairs in any way, except as regards his engagements in connection with the *Friendship*. In connection with that, and some dealings between Mr. Allerton and him, and some debts that Mr. Allerton owed him on private transactions, he drew up an account of over £2000, and tried to thrust it upon the partners here on the ground that Mr. Allerton had been their agent. But they told him they had been fooled long enough in that way, and showed him that it was no concern of theirs. As for the debts of the *Friendship* he must expect to meet them.

Mr. Pierce did the same thing, Mr. Allerton having got into his debt also in their private dealings. However, the partners here easily shook off these worries! but Mr. Allerton brought much trouble and vexation upon himself, as he had upon others, for Mr. Denison sued him for the money he had disbursed for one-sixth share in the *White Angel*, and recovered it with damages.

Though the partners were thus plunged into heavy engagements and unjust debts, the Lord prospered their trading and they made large returns yearly and would soon have freed themselves if they had been fairly dealt with otherwise. The settlers, too, began to grow in prosperity, through the influx of many people to the country, especially to the Bay of Massachusetts. Thereby corn and cattle rose to a high price, and many were enriched and commodities grew plentiful. But in other regards this benefit turned to their harm, and this accession of strength to weakness. For as their stocks increased and became more saleable, there was no longer any holding them together; they must of necessity obtain bigger holdings, otherwise they could not keep their cattle; and having oxen they must have land for plowing. So in time no one thought he could live, unless he had cattle and a great deal of land to keep them, all striving to increase their stocks. By this means they were quickly scattered all over the Bay, and the town in which they had lived compactly until now was left very thinly peopled, and in a short time almost desolate.

If this had been all the ill that resulted, it would have been small in comparison with the rest; but the church also was disunited, and those who had lived so long together in Christian and comfortable fellowship must now part and suffer many divisions. First, those who lived on their lots on the other side of the Bay, called Duxbury, owing to the trouble of bringing their wives and children to public worship and church meetings here, growing to a considerable number, sued to be separated and become a distinct body. So they were allowed to separate about this time, though very unwillingly. To prevent any further scattering from this place and weakening of it, it was thought best to give out some good farms in the neighborhood to special persons who would promise to live at New Plymouth, likely to be helpful to the church and commonwealth, and so tie the lands to New Plymouth as farms for its inhabitants, so that their cattle and their plowed land might be kept there by servants, and they retain their dwellings here. So some special lands were granted at a place called Green's Harbor,[1] where no allotments had been made in the former division, very well-meadowed and suitable for raising cattle. But alas! this remedy proved worse than the disease; for within a few years those who had thus got footing there seceded from the church, partly deliberately, and partly by wearing out the rest with importunity and pleas of exigency, so that they either had to let them go or live in continual contention. Others again, thinking themselves impoverished or for want of accommodation, broke away on one pretense or another, thinking their own imagined necessity or the example of others sufficient warrant. This I fear will be the ruin of New England—at least of the churches of God there—and will provoke the Lord's displeasure against them.

This year Mr. William Pierce came over and brought goods and passengers in a ship called the *Lyon*, which belonged chiefly to Mr. Sherley and the rest of the London partners, those here having nothing to do with her. Besides some beaver which they had sent home earlier in the year, they sent in this ship upwards of £800 worth and some otter skins. They sent, also, copies of Mr. Allerton's accounts, requesting them to examine them and rectify such things as they should find amiss in them, as they were

---

[1] Now Marshfield.

better acquainted with the goods bought and the disbursements made there than they could be here. With these they sent a book of exceptions to his accounts, where they could specify them, and did not doubt but they in England might add to them. They showed them how much Mr. Allerton was debtor to the general account, and as they had now put the ship *White Angel* wholly in his control and had tied their hands here, they requested them to call him to account. But it pleased God that the ship taking these papers, on her way to Virginia before going home, was wrecked on the coast not far from Virginia and their cargo was lost. This was the first loss they had sustained of that kind. But Mr. Pierce and the men saved their lives and also the letters, and got to Virginia and so safely home.

Copies of the accounts were therefore sent over again to England.

The following is part of Mr. Pierce's letter from Virginia. It was dated Dec. 25th, 1632, and came to their hands on April 7th, before they had heard anything from England:

William Pierce in Virginia to the New Plymouth Colony:

Dear Friends,

The news of this fatal stroke that the Lord has brought upon me and you will probably come to your ears before this comes to your hands, and therefore I need not enlarge on particulars, etc. Almost all my worldly belongings have been taken away—and yours also in a great measure, by this and your various former losses. It is time to look about us, before the wrath of the Lord break forth in utter destruction. The good Lord give us all grace to search our hearts and try our ways and turn unto the Lord and humble ourselves under His mighty hand, and seek atonement. . . . Dear friends, know that all your beaver and books of account are swallowed up in the sea; your letters remain with me and shall be delivered if God bring me home. But what more should I say? By this we have lost our worldly goods—yet a happy loss if our souls are gainers. There is more in the Lord Jehovah than ever we had in this world. O that our foolish hearts could be weaned from things here below, which are vanity and vexation of spirit; and yet we fools catch after shadows, that fly away and are gone in a moment! . . . Thus with my continual remembrance of you in my poor desires to the Throne of Grace, beseeching God to renew His love and favor towards you all, in and through the Lord Jesus Christ, both in spiritual and temporal good things, as may be most to the glory and praise of His name and your everlasting good, so I rest,

Your afflicted brother in Christ,
WILLIAM PIERCE.

Virginia, Dec. 25th, 1632.

"When they came up the river, the Dutch demanded what they intended, and whither they would goe . . ."

CHAPTER XIV

[*1633*]

This year Mr. Edward Winslow[1] was chosen governor. By the first return of ships they received letters from Mr. Sherley about Mr. Allerton's further ill-success and the loss by Mr. Pierce, with many sad comments. But there was little hope of getting anything out of Mr. Allerton or of their accounts being either eased or rectified by them over there. They saw plainly that the burden of it all would be thrown upon their backs. The special passages of his letters I will insert here, for though I am weary of this tedious and uncomfortable subject, yet for the truth's sake I am compelled to fully ventilate matters which have resulted in so much trouble and so many hard censures on both sides. I do not wish to be partial to either side, but to disclose the truth as nearly as I can in their own words, and so leave it to the unbiased judgment of any who shall come to read them.

---

[1] Winslow had great talent as a negotiator, and was often chosen to treat with the Indians, as well as to be the Pilgrims' emissary to England. His election as governor was in recognition of his ability and loyalty.

James Sherley in London to the Colony at New Plymouth:

Loving Friends,

My last was sent in the *Mary and John* by Mr. William Collier. I then certified you of the great and unseasonable loss you and we had, in the wreck of Mr. Pierce and his ship the *Lyon*; but the Lord's holy name be blessed, Who gives and takes as it pleases Him; His will be done, Amen. I then related to you that fearful accident, or rather judgment, the Lord pleased to lay on London bridge by fire, and therein gave you an idea of my great loss; the Lord I hope will give me patience to bear it, and faith to trust in Him and not in the slippery and uncertain things of this world.

I hope Mr. Allerton is nearly with you by this time; but he had many disasters here before he got away. The last was a heavy one; his ship, while getting out of the harbor at Bristol in stormy weather, was driven so far ashore that it cost him over £100 to get her afloat again. His condition was so lamentable that I could not but afford him some help, as did some who were strangers to him; besides, your goods were in her, and if he had not been assisted he must have given up his voyage, and loss could not have been avoided on all sides. When he first bought her I think he would have made a saving match if he had sunk her and never set sail in her! I hope he sees the Lord's hand against him, and will leave off these voyages. I think we did well in parting with her; she would have been a clog to the account, time and again, and though we shall not get much by way of satisfaction, we shall lose no more. And now, as I have written before, pray wind up all the accounts with him there; here he has nothing but many debts, which he owes in various quarters. Besides, not a man here will spend a day, nay scarcely an hour, on the accounts but myself, and that business will require more time and help than I can afford. I need not say any more; I hope you will do what will be best and will be just with him, to which add mercy and consider his intentions, though he failed in many particulars, which now cannot be helped. . . .

Tomorrow or next day at furthest we are to pay £300, and Mr. Beauchamp is out of the town, so I must do it. O, the grief and the trouble that mad Mr. Allerton has brought upon you and us! I cannot forget it, and to think of it draws many a sigh from my heart and tears from my eyes. And now the Lord has visited me with another great loss, but I can bear it with more patience than those which I have foolishly pulled upon myself. . . .

And in another letter there is this passage:

By Mr. Allerton's fair propositions and large promises I have overrun myself; indeed grief hinders me from writing, and tears will not suffer me to see; therefore as you love those who ever loved you and the colony, think of us. Oh, what shall I say of that man who has abused your trust and wronged our loves! But to lament now is too late, nor can I complain of your backwardness, for I know it lies as heavy on your hearts as it does on our purses. Had the Lord sent Mr. Pierce safely home, it had eased both you and us of some of those debts. The Lord I hope will give us patience to bear these crosses and that great God Whose care and providence is everywhere, and especially over those who desire truly to fear and serve Him, direct and guide, prosper, and bless you, so that you may have the power, as you have the will, to take off this heavy burden which now lies upon me for your sakes—and, as I hope, for your ultimate good and that of many thousands more. For had not you and we joined together, New England might have been scarcely known, and would not, I feel sure, be inhabited by such honest English people as it now is. The Lord increase and bless them. . . . So with my continual prayers for you all, I rest

                        Your assured loving friend,
June 24th, 1633.   JAMES SHERLEY.

Though Mr. Sherley became more alive to his own condition by these losses, and complained the more sadly and unreservedly of Mr. Allerton, no steps were taken to help them here—not so much as to examine and rectify the accounts, by which probably some hundred of pounds might have been deducted. But probably they saw that the more there was taken off the account the less would come to them in England.

But to come to other things. Mr. Roger Williams,[2] a godly and zealous man, with many rare qualities but a very unstable judgment, who settled first in Massachusetts but owing to some discontent left there, came here about this time, where he was made welcome according to their poor ability. He exercised his gifts among them, and after some time was admitted as a member of the church; and his teaching was highly approved, and for its benefit I still bless God and am thankful to him even for his sharpest admonitions and reproofs, so far as they agreed with the truth. This year he began to hold some strange opinions, and from opinion proceeded to practice. This caused some controversy between the church and him, and in the end some discontent on his part, so that he left them somewhat abruptly. Afterwards he applied for his dismissal, to transfer himself to the church at Salem, which was granted,

---

[2] Roger Williams was for a time assistant to the Rev. Ralph Smith at Plymouth. His stand for complete freedom of religious belief and his subsequent history as founder of the colony of Rhode Island are well known.

with some caution to them about him. But he soon fell into more trouble there, to the disturbance of church and government. I need not give particulars, for they are too well known to all; though for a time the church here received some hard censure through him and at the hands of those who afterwards smarted themselves. But he is rather to be pitied and prayed for; so I shall leave the matter, and desire the Lord to show him his errors and return him to the way of truth, and give him a settled judgment and constancy therein; for I hope he belongs to the Lord and that He will show him mercy.

Having already had intercourse with the Dutch, as will be remembered, they, seeing the New Plymouth people settled here in such a barren quarter, told them of a river which they called Fresh River, now known by the name of Connecticut River, which they had often recommended to them as a fine place for both agriculture and trade, and wished them to make use of it. But their hands then being full, they let it pass. Afterwards, a tribe of Indians who came there were driven out by the Pequots, who usurped their territory; and the banished tribe often begged them to go there, and said they could do plenty of trade, especially if they could keep a house there. So, having a good stock of goods, and being obliged to look out how they could better themselves and help to meet their heavy engagements, they began to explore in that dirction and to trade with the natives. They found it a fine place, though at first they did little trade; but the Indians put it down to the season of the year and the fear they were in of their enemies. So they tried several times, not unprofitably; but they saw that the surest way would be to keep a house there to receive the trade when it came down from inland.

The Indians, not seeing them very active in establishing

themselves, solicited the Massachusetts colony similarly—for their object was to be restored to their country again. But those in the Bay, who had but lately arrived, were not fitted for it. However, some of the chief of them proposed to join with the partners here to trade jointly with them up the Connecticut River, which they were willing to agree to, with the idea that they should share equally in the building and the stock. A time of meeting was appointed in Massachusetts, and some of the principal men here were appointed to deal with them, and went accordingly. But the Massachusetts people entertained many fears of danger and loss and the like, which were seen to be the main causes of their disinclination, though they alleged that they were not provided with trading goods, etc. So the New Plymouth people offered at present to put in sufficient for both, provided they would become responsible for the half, and meantime prepare for next year. They confessed that more could not be expected, but thanked them and told them they did not care to do it. So they said they hoped it would be no offense to the Massachusetts colony if they went on without them. They said there was no reason against it; and so this partnership fell through. So the New Plymouth colonists in due time made a beginning there, and were the first English to discover the place and build it, though they were little better than forced out of it afterwards, as will appear.

The Dutch now began to repent, and hearing of their preparations, endeavored to prevent them, and getting in a little before them established a small fort [3] with two

---

[3] In June, 1633, the Dutch had bought from the Indians a strip of land on the present site of Hartford on which to build their blockhouse.

pieces of ordnance, threatening to stop their passage. But having prepared a small frame of a house and having a big new bark, they stowed the frame in her hold, together with boards to cover and finish it and nails and all other necessaries. This was intended as a defense against the Indians, who were much offended that they had brought back and restored the right sachem of the place called Natawanute; so they encountered a double danger in this attempt, both from the Dutch and the Indians. When they came up the river the Dutchmen demanded what they intended and whither they would go; they answered, up the river to trade—their orders being to go and settle above them. They bid them stop or they would shoot, and stood by, their ordnance ready loaded. They replied that they had orders from the Governor of New Plymouth to go up the river to such a place, and, shoot or not, they must obey their orders and proceed; and that they would not harm them, but they must go on. So they passed on, and though the Dutch threatened them they did not shoot.

Coming to the place appointed,[4] they clapped up their house quickly, landed their provisions and left the men, sending the bark home. Afterwards they palisaded their house and fortified themselves better. The Dutch sent home word to Manhattan, asking what they should do, and in process of time they sent a troop of about seventy armed men in warlike formation, with colors displayed, to attack them; but seeing them strongly established, and that it would cost blood, they came to parley and returned in peace. They did the Dutch no wrong, for they took not a foot of any of the land they had bought, but went

---

[4] This was at the point where the Farmington River empties into the Connecticut, now the site of Windsor. The house which was brought in the boat was the first frame house put up in Connecticut.

to a place above them, and bought the tract of land which belonged to their friends the Indians, whom they took with them, and with whom the Dutch had nothing to do. So this was their entrance there; and they deserved to continue to hold it, and not, later, to have been thrust out by friends, as in a way they were, as will be seen. But of these matters, more in another place.

It pleased the Lord this year to visit them with an infectious fever of which many fell very ill, and upwards of twenty persons died, men, women and children, and several of their oldest friends who had lived in Holland. Amongst them were Thomas Blossom, Richard Masterson, with some others; and in the end, after he had helped others much, Samuel Fuller, their physician, who had been a great help and comfort to them, not only in his profession, but also as a deacon of the church, a godly man, always ready to serve his fellows. He was much missed after his death, and he and the rest of their brethren who died were much lamented by them. This brought much sadness and mourning among them, and caused them to humble themselves and seek the Lord; and towards winter it pleased the Lord that the sickness ceased. This disease also swept away many of the Indians from the adjoining parts.

The spring before, especially the month of May, there had been a quantity of a great sort of fly, as large as wasps or bumble bees,[5] which came out of holes in the ground, filling all the woods, and eating the verdure. They made such a constant yelling noise that the woods rang with them, till they were ready to deafen the hearers. They have not been heard or seen before or since by the English. The Indians told them that sickness would

---

[5] These were the seventeen-year locusts.

follow, and so it did, in June, July, and August, during the greatest heat of the summer.

It pleased the Lord to enable them this year to send home a great quantity of beaver, besides paying all their expenses and debts here in the country, which was a great encouragement to their friends in England. Of beaver they sent 3366 lbs., and much of it was coat beaver, which yielded twenty shillings per lb., and some of it more; and 346 otter skins, which also sold at a good price—fourteen and fifteen shillings per lb. Thus much of the affairs of this year.

"And they sent Capten Standish to give them true information . . . and to procure Mr. Alden's release."

CHAPTER XV

[*1634*]

This year Mr. Thomas Prince [1] was chosen Governor.

Mr. Sherley's letters were very brief in answer to theirs this year. I will not copy any extracts from them, but will mention the subjects of one or two of them. First, he hopes they will not take offense at anything he wrote previously, professing his affection for them as before, etc. Secondly, as to Mr. Allerton's accounts, he is convinced the colony must suffer and that to no small figure; that they have cause enough to complain, but it is now too late; that Allerton had failed them all and himself, in his aims, and that he feared God in consequence would fail him, and it would not be strange if he fell into worse ways, etc. Thirdly, he blesses God and is thankful to Him for the good return made this year. This is the effect of his letters, other things being of a more private nature.

I now enter upon one of the saddest things that befell

---

[1] Prince came over in 1621; three years later he married a daughter of Elder Brewster's. He was governor in 1634, 1638, and, after the death of Bradford, from 1657 to his death in 1673.

them since they came; and before I begin, it will be necessary to quote that part of their patent which gave them rights at Kennebec.

The said Council has further given, granted, bargained, sold, enfeoffed, allotted, assigned, and made over, and by these presents do clearly and absolutely give, grant, bargain, sell, alien, enfeoff, allot, assign, and confirm unto the said William Bradford, his heirs, associates, and assigns, all that tract of land or part of New England in America aforesaid, which lies within or between, and extends itself from the utmost limits of Cobiseconte,[2] which adjoins the river of Kennebec, towards the Western ocean, and a place called the Falls of Nequamkeck[3] in America aforesaid; and the space of fifteen English miles on each side of the said river, commonly called Kennebec river, and all the said river called Kennebec that lies within the said limits and bounds, eastward, westward, northward, and southward, last above mentioned; and all lands, grounds, soils, rivers, waters, fishing, etc. And by virtue of the authority to us derived by his said late Majesty's letters patent, to take, apprehend, seize, and make prize of all such persons, their ships and goods, as shall attempt to inhabit or trade with the savage people of that country, within the several precincts and limits of his or their several plantations, etc.

Now it happened that one Hocking, belonging to the settlement at Piscataqua, went with a bark and some commodities to trade on the Kennebec, and must needs transgress their limits and even go up the river above their house towards the Falls, and intercept the trade that should have come to them. The man in charge of the

---

[2] Now Gardiner, Maine.
[3] Near Winslow, Maine.

place forbade him and begged him not to do them the injury of infringing their rights, which had cost them so dear. He replied he would go up and trade there in spite of them, and remain there as long as he pleased. The answer was that in that case he would be forced to remove him or apprehend him. Whereupon Hocking bid him do his worst, and went up and anchored there. So the captain took a boat and some men and followed him, and again urged him to depart. But all in vain; he could get nothing from him but ill words. So, as it was just the season for trade to come down, and if he allowed him to remain there and take it from them, all their previous expense would be wasted, he consulted with his men, who being willing, he decided to sever the boat from her anchorage, and let her drift down the river with the stream, but commanded his men not to shoot on any account unless he commanded them. He spoke to Hocking again, but all in vain; then he sent a couple of men in a canoe to cut his cable, which one of them did. Thereupon Hocking took up a gun which he had put ready, and as the bark drifted down past the canoe he shot the man in the head and killed him instantly. One of his comrades who loved him well, could not restrain himself, and making aim with his musket shot Hocking dead on the spot. This is a true account of what happened. The rest of the men took the vessel home, with these sad tidings. Now Lord Say and Lord Brook, with some other eminent men, had an interest in this settlement, so the people wrote home to them in such terms as to exasperate them as much as possible, leaving out all the extenuating circumstances, and making it appear that Hocking had been killed without provocation, suppressing the fact that he had killed a man first. So their Lordships were much offended, till they were fully informed of the details.

The news of this spread quickly, with the worst light put upon it, and reached their neighbors in Massachusetts. Their own bark came home to New Plymouth, bringing a true report of it, and all were deeply and naturally affected by it. Not long after, they had occasion to send their vessel to the Bay of Massachusetts; but the colony there was so incensed at the occurrence that they imprisoned Mr. Alden, who was aboard and had been at Kennebec but had taken no part in the affair, having only gone up to take supplies. They freed the boat, but kept Mr. Alden for some time. This was thought strange here, and they sent Captain Standish, with letters, to give them full information and to procure Mr. Alden's release. I will give a letter or two which refer to these things.

Two letters from Thomas Dudley at Newtown to William Bradford at New Plymouth:

Good Sir,

I have received your letter through Captain Standish, and am unfeignedly glad of God's mercy towards you in the steady recovery of your health. Concerning the matter you write of, I thought I would send a word or two in answer to yourself, leaving your Governor's letter to be answered by our court, to which with myself it is directed. I presume, until I hear further, that your patent may warrant your resistance of any Englishmen trading at Kennebec, and that the blood of Hocking and the man he slew will be required elsewhere, at his hands. But with yourself and others I grieve for their deaths. I think, also, that your general letters will satisfy our courts, and make them cease from meddling further in the matter. Upon that same letter I have liberated Mr. Alden, with his sureties; but that I may not seem to neglect the opinion of our court, I have bound Captain Standish to appear on June 3rd at our next court, to make affidavit for the copy of the patent and to testify to the circumstances of Hocking's provocations, both of which will tend to prove your innocence. If any offense has been taken at what we have done, let it be better considered, I pray you; and I hope the more you think of it, the less blame you will impute to us. At least you ought to be just in distinguishing between those whose opinions concur with your own, and others—though I can truly say I have spoken with no one on the subject, even those who blame you most, who had not always heretofore declared their good will towards your colony. Referring you further to the report you have from Captain Standish and Mr. Alden, I leave you for the present with God's blessing, wishing you perfect recovery of your health and long continuance of it. I desire to be lovingly remembered to Mr. Prince—your Governor, Mr. Winslow, and Mr. Brewster, whom I would see if I could. The Lord keep you all. Amen.

  Your very loving friend in our Lord Jesus,
    THOMAS DUDLEY.

Newtown,[4] *May 22nd, 1634.*

Sir,
 I am deeply sorry for the news that Captain Standish and others of your colony and my beloved friends are bringing with them to New Plymouth, in which I suffer with you, because of the difference of my opinion from

---

[4] The name was changed to Cambridge when Harvard College was founded there, in 1638.

that of others who are godly and wise amongst us here, reverence for whose judgments causes me to suspect my own ignorance. But I cannot alter it until I am convinced otherwise. I did not intend to show your letter to me, but to do my best to reconcile the differences as best I could; but Captain Standish demanding an answer to it publicly in court, I was forced to produce it, which made the breach the wider, as he will tell you. I proposed to the court that they should answer the letter from Mr. Prince, your Governor; but the court ruled that it required no answer, since it was itself an answer to a former letter of ours. Pray inform Mr. Prince of this, and others whom it concerns, so that they may not impute neglect or ill manners to me on this score. The recent letters I have received from England cause me to fear [5] that some trials are likely to fall upon us shortly, and this unhappy dispute between you and us, and between you and Piscataqua, will hasten them, if God with an extraordinary hand does not help us. To reconcile this for the present will be very difficult; but time cools distempers, and a common danger approaching us both will necessitate our uniting again. I pray you therefore, Sir, set your wisdom and patience to work, and exhort others to do the same, that things may not proceed from bad to worse, making our divisions like the bars of a palace; but that a way of peace may be kept open, where the God of peace may have entrance at His own time. If you are wronged, it is to your honor to bear it patiently; but I go too far in needlessly putting you in mind of such things. God has done great things for you, and I desire His blessings may be multiplied upon you more

---

[5] There was cause enough for these fears, which were concerned with the underhand work of some enemies to the churches here, which resulted in the issue by the King of a new Commission for Regulating Colonies, signed April 28th, 1634 (B.)

and more. I will commit no more to writing, but commending myself to your prayers, I rest

Your truly loving friend in our Lord Jesus,

THOMAS DUDLEY.

June 4th, 1634.

This shows what troubles arose and how hard they were to allay; for though they were heartily sorry for what had happened, they considered they had been unjustly injured and provoked, and that their neighbors, who had no jurisdiction over them, exceeded their bounds thus to imprison a member of their settlement and bring the question before their Court. But being assured of their Christian love, and convinced that it was done out of godly zeal, that religion might not suffer nor sin be in any way concealed or countenanced—especially the guilt of blood, of which all should be very conscientious—they endeavored to appease them as best they could, first by giving them the truth of it all; secondly by their willingness to refer the case to any indifferent judgment here, and to answer it elsewhere when they should be called upon to do so; and further, by asking Mr. Winthrop and other respected magistrates there, for their advice and direction. This mollified them and brought things to a comfortable end at last.

The advice given them by Mr. Winthrop and others was that from their court at New Plymouth they should write to the neighboring settlements, especially to that at Piscataqua and theirs in Massachusetts, appointing a meeting at some suitable place, to deliberate on the subject, full powers being delegated to those attending the meeting from the various colonies, but nothing to be done which should infringe the liberties of any of them. The law of God being that for conscience' sake that priests should be consulted with, it was thought desirable that the ministers of every colony should be present to give their advice on points of conscience. Though this suggestion seemed dangerous to some,[6] they were so well assured of the justice of their cause and the equity of their friends, that they agreed to it and appointed a time, of which notice was given a month beforehand, viz.: to Massachusetts, Salem, Piscataqua, and others, requesting them to produce any evidence they could in the case. The place of meeting was Boston.

But when the day came, there only appeared some of the magistrates and ministers of Massachusetts and of New Plymouth. As none had come from Piscataqua or other places, Mr. Winthrop and the others said they could do no more than they had done, and the blame must rest with them. So they opened up a fair discussion of the subject, and after all evidence had been fully sifted, the opinion of each of the magistrates and ministers was demanded, with the result that though all wished the trouble had never occurred, they could not but lay the blame and guilt on Hocking's own head. Whereupon such grave and godly counsels and exhortations were given as they thought fitting, both for the present and future, which were received with love and gratitude, with promises to endeavor to profit by them. And so it ended, and their love and concord renewed. Further, Mr. Winthrop and Mr. Dudley wrote very effectually

---

[6] The Plymouth colonists always feared the interference of ministers in secular affairs—one of the chief differences between them and the Massachusetts Bay people. The latter colony was to develop into a theocracy, with the ecclesiastics sharing in the functions of government.

on their behalf to Lord Say and others interested, which with their own letters, and Mr. Winslow's further declarations when in England, satisfied them fully.

They sent Mr. Winslow to England this year, partly for this object, and partly to notify the partners in England that the period of their contract for the company's trade here having expired, they instructed him to close the accounts with them, and to find out how much they still remained debtors to the account, and what further course would be best to pursue.[7] The outcome of it all will appear in next year's narrative. They sent over with him a substantial cargo which was very acceptable to them: in beaver 3738 lbs., mostly coat beaver which sold at twenty shillings per lb.; and 234 otter skins at fourteen shillings per skin. So altogether it arose to a large sum of money.

Early this year, they sent a boat to trade with the Dutch colony, where they met with a Captain Stone, who had lived in Christophers, one of the West Indian Islands, and had now been sometime in Virginia and had come up from there. He kept company with the Dutch Governor, and in some drunken fit got his leave to seize their boat, just as they were ready to leave and had finished trading, having £500 worth of goods aboard. There was not the least provocation or ground for such an act, but having made the Governor so drunk that he could scarcely utter an intelligible word, he urged him to do it and got the answer, "as you please." So he got aboard, most of their men being ashore, and with some of his own men made the rest weigh anchor, set sail, and

---

[7] The six-year period, for which the trade of the colony had been put into the hands of Bradford and his associates, was now over.

carry her away towards Virginia. But several of the Dutch sailors ashore, who had often been at New Plymouth and kindly entertained there, said to each other: "Shall we allow our friends to be wronged in this way, and have their goods carried away before our faces whilst our Governor is drunk?" They vowed they would not permit it, and got a vessel or two, and chased him and brought him back again, and delivered them their boat and goods.

Afterwards Stone came to Massachusetts, and they commenced an action against him for it; but by the mediation of friends it was allowed to lapse. Later, Stone came with some other gentlemen to New Plymouth and was friendly entertained by them with the rest, but revenge boiled in his breast, and some thought that on one occasion he intended to stab the Governor, and put his hand to his dagger for that purpose; but by God's providence and the vigilance of those at hand, it was prevented. Afterwards, returning to Virginia in a pinnace with a Captain Norton and some others, for some unknown reason they must needs go up the Connecticut River. What they did, I know not; but the Indians came aboard and knocked Stone on the head as he lay in his cabin; this was his end. They also killed all the others, but Captain Norton defended himself for a long time against them in the cook-room, till, by accident, the gunpowder which he had put ready in some open vessel before him took fire and it so burnt and blinded him that he could no longer make resistance, and was killed by them, though they much commended his valor.

I must now relate a strange occurrence. There was a tribe of Indians living on the upper parts of the Connecticut River, a long way from the colony's trading house there, who were enemies of the Indians that lived in the neighborhood, who stood in some fear of them, for they were a warlike tribe. About a thousand of them had enclosed themselves in a fort, which they had strongly palisaded. Three or four Dutchmen went up in the beginning of winter to live with them, to get their trade and prevent them from bringing it down to the English or from getting friendly with them. But their enterprise failed, for it pleased God to afflict these Indians with such a deadly sickness, that out of 1,000 over 950 of them died, and many of them lay rotting above ground for want of burial, and the Dutchmen almost starved before they could get away, kept there by the ice and snow. But about February, with much difficulty they reached the trading house of the New Plymouth people, by whom they were kindly treated, for they were almost exhausted with hunger and cold. After being refreshed by them for several days, they got to their own place, and the Dutch were very grateful for this kindness.

This spring, too, the Indians who lived around their trading house fell sick of smallpox, and died most miserably. A more terrible disease cannot attack them; they fear it worse than the plague, for usually it spreads amongst them broadcast. For want of bedding and linen and other comforts, they fall into a lamentable condition. As they lie on their hard mats, the pox breaks and matters and runs, their skin sticking to the mats they lie on, so that when they turn, a whole side will flay off at once and they will be all one gore of blood, dreadful to behold; and then, what with cold and other hardships, they die like rotten sheep. The condition of these natives was indeed lamentable. They were swept so generally by the disease that in the end they were unable to help one another, or to make a fire or fetch a little water to drink, or to bury their dead. They would keep up as long as they could, and when there was no other means to make a fire, they would burn the wooden dishes they ate their food in, and their very bows and arrows. Some would crawl out on all fours to get a little water and sometimes die by the way, not being able to get home again. But the people of the English trading house, though they were at first afraid of the infection, seeing their woeful condition and hearing their pitiful cries, had compassion on them, and daily fetched them wood and water and made them fires and got them food whilst they lived, and buried them when they died. Very few of the Indians escaped, notwithstanding that they did what they could for them at great risk to themselves. The chief Sachem himself died, and almost all his friends and relatives; but by the marvelous goodness and providence of God not one of the English was so much as ill, or in the least degree tainted with the disease, though they did these services for them daily for many weeks. The mercy they showed them in this way was greatly appreciated by all the Indians who knew or heard of it, and earned their gratitude; and their masters at New Plymouth highly commended and rewarded them for it.

"Some of the neighbours in the Bay, hereing of the fame of the Conightecute River, had a hankering mind after it, and now understanding that ye Indeans were swepte away with ye late great mortalitie . . . they begane now to prosecute it with great egernes."

CHAPTER XVI

[*1635*]

Mr. Winslow was welcomed by them in England, the more so owing to the large consignment of fur he brought with him, which came safely to hand and was well sold. He was given to understand that all the accounts would be cleared up before his return, and all former differences settled, and that the account of the *White Angel* would not be charged to them. Being called upon to answer some complaints made against the country at the Council, more particularly concerning their neighbors at the Bay than themselves, which he did to good effect, at the same time furthering the interests of the colonies as a whole as regards the encroachments of the French and other strangers, with a view to preventing them for the future, he took the opportunity of presenting this petition to their honors, the Commissioners for the Plantations.

To the Right Honorable the Lords Commissioners for the Plantations in America:

The humble petition of Edward Winslow on behalf of the Plantations in New England:

Humbly shows your lordships, that whereas your petitioners have settled in New England under His Majesty's most gracious protection, now the French and Dutch endeavor to divide the land between them; for which purpose the French on the east side entered and seized upon some of our houses and carried away the goods, killed two men in another place, and took the rest prisoners with their goods; and the Dutch on the west also made entry along the Connecticut River, within the limits of His Majesty's letters patent, where they have raised a fort and threaten to expel your petitioners who are also established on the same river, maintaining possession for His Majesty to their great expense and the risk of both their lives and goods.

In tender consideration whereof your petitioners humbly pray that your lordships will either procure their peace with those foreign states, or else give special warrant to your petitioners and the English colonies, to defend themselves against all foreign enemies. And your petitioners shall pray, etc.

This petition was well received by most of them, and Mr. Winslow was heard several times by them and appointed to attend for an answer from their lordships, having shown how this might be done without any expense or trouble to the state, simply giving the leading men there authority to undertake it at their own cost and in such a way as would avoid public disturbance. But this interfered with both Sir Ferdinand Gorges' and Captain Mason's plans, with whom the Archbishop of

Canterbury [1] was in league; for Sir Ferdinand Gorges, by the Archbishop's favor, was to have been sent over to the country as Governor General, and was about to conclude this project. The Archbishop's intention was to send over officials with him, furnished with episcopal power to disturb the peace of the churches here, overthrow their proceedings, and stop their further growth. But it fell out by God's providence, that though in the end they prevented this petition from taking any further effect, his plot with Sir Ferdinand came to nothing.

So when Mr. Winslow went before the Board to have his petition granted, he found that the Archbishop had checked it. However, hoping to obtain it nevertheless, he went to the Board again; but he found that the Archbishop, Sir Ferdinand, and Captain Mason had procured Morton, the man referred to previously,[2] to present complaints. Mr. Winslow answered them to the satisfaction of the Board, who checked Morton and rebuked him sharply, and also blamed Sir Ferdinand Gorges and Mason for countenancing him. But the Archbishop had a further object, and began to cross-question Mr. Winslow about many things. He accused him of preaching in the church publicly—with which Morton had charged him, affirming that he had seen and heard him do it; to which Mr. Winslow answered that sometimes, for want of a minister, he had endeavored to assist in the edification of his brethren. The Archbishop then questioned him

---

[1] William Laud was Archbishop of Canterbury under Charles I from 1633 until his execution by the Puritan party in Parliament in 1645. He was a strong supporter of the king's authority, and attempted to force the episcopal form of church government on all Englishmen everywhere.

[2] See above, pp. 244-249.

about marriage; to which he replied that as a magistrate he had occasionally married some of the people, pointing out to their lordships that marriage was a civil institution, and that he nowhere found in the word of God that it belonged to the ministry, and furthermore for a long time they had no minister; besides, it was now no new idea, for he himself had been married in Holland by the magistrates in their Stadt-house.

To be short, in the end the Archbishop, by his vehement importunity, got the Board at last to consent to his commitment; so he was imprisoned in the Fleet, and lay there about seventeen weeks before he could get released. This was the end of the petition; but the scheme of the others was frustrated too, which was no small blessing to the people over here. The expense to this colony was heavy, though it was undertaken as much or more in the interests of others. Indeed, Mr. Winslow was chiefly urged to the business by them, and the colony knew nothing of it till they heard of his imprisonment, though it had to bear the whole expense.

As to their own business, whatever Mr. Sherley's intention was before, he now declared plainly that he would neither take the *White Angel* from the general account, nor present any further account till he had received more goods; that though a fair supply had been sent over this time, they were mostly without notes of the prices, and not as properly invoiced as formerly. This Mr. Winslow said he could not help, because of his imprisonment. However, Mr. Sherley, Mr. Beauchamp, and Mr. Andrews sent over a letter of attorney under their hands and seals to recover what they could from Mr. Allerton on the *White Angel's* account, but they sent neither the bonds nor contracts, nor such other evidence as they had, to enable those at New Plymouth to act upon it. I will here insert a few passages from Mr. Sherley's letters about these things.

James Sherley in London to the Colony at New Plymouth:

I have received your letter of July 22nd, 1634, through our trusty and loving friend, Mr. Winslow, and your large parcel of beaver and otter skins. Blessed be our God, both he and it arrived safely. We have sold it in two parcels; the skins at fourteen shillings per lb., and some at sixteen; the coat at twenty shillings per lb. I have not sent the accounts over this year; I refer you to Mr. Winslow for the reason; but be assured that none of you shall suffer through not having them, if God spare me life. You say the six years have expired during which the people put the trade of the colony into your and our hands, for the discharge of the heavy debts which Mr. Allerton needlessly and unadvisedly ran us into; but it was promised that it should continue till our disbursements and engagements were met. You think this has been done already; we know otherwise. . . . I doubt not we shall lovingly agree, notwithstanding all that has been written on both sides about the *White Angel*. We have now sent you a letter of attorney, giving you power in our names (and to shadow it the more we say for our uses) to obtain what is possible from Mr. Allerton towards meeting the great expense of the *White Angel*. He certainly gave a bond, though at present I cannot find it; but he has often affirmed with great protestations that neither you nor we should lose a penny by him, and I hope you will find he has enough to meet it, so that we shall have no more trouble about it. Notwithstanding his unkind treatment of you, in the midst of justice remember mercy, and do not all you might do. . . . Let us get out of debt, and then let us survey the matter reasonably. . . . Mr. Winslow has undergone an unjust imprisonment but I am convinced it will result to your general advantage. I leave it to him to tell all particulars. . . .

Your loving friend,

London, Sept. 7th, 1635.   JAMES SHERLEY.

This year they sustained another great loss from the French. Monsieur d'Aulnay,[3] coming into the harbor of Penobscot, having invited several of the chief men belonging to the house aboard his vessel, got them to pilot him in; and after getting the rest into his power, he took possession of the house in the name of the King of France. By threats and otherwise he made Mr. Willett, their agent there, approve of the sale of the goods to him, of which he fixed the prices himself, making an inventory, though with many omissions. But he made no payment for them, saying that in due course he would do so if they came for it. As for the house and fortifications, he would not allow anything for them, claiming that it was not built on their own land. So, turning them out, with many compliments and fine words, he let them have their shallop and some provisions to bring them home.

When they got home and related the occurrence they were much disturbed about it, for the French had robbed this house once before, at a loss to them of above £500, and now to lose house and all vexed them greatly. So they decided to consult with their friends at the Bay, who now had many ships there, and if they approved of it, they intended to hire a fighting ship and try to beat out the French and regain their property. Their plan was ap-

---

[3] D'Aulnay had been commissioned by the Chevalier de Razilly, governor of Acadia, to drive out English settlers east of Pemaquid.

proved of, if they themselves would bear the expense. So they hired a fine ship of over 300 tons, well fitted with ordnance, and agreed with the captain, one Girling, that he and his crew should deliver them the house, after they had overcome the French, and give them peaceable possession of it, with all such trading commodities as should be found there, giving the French fair quarter if they would yield. In consideration of which services he was to have 700 lbs. of beaver, to be delivered to him there when he had completed his bargain; but if he did not accomplish it, he was to lose his labor and have nothing. With him they sent their own bark, and about twenty men under Captain Standish, to help him if necessary, and to put things in order if the house were regained; and then to pay Girling the beaver, which was aboard their own bark.

So they piloted him there, and brought him safely into the harbor. But he was so rash and heady he would take no advice, nor give Captain Standish time to summon them to surrender, as his orders were. If he had done so, and they had parleyed, seeing their force, the French would probably have yielded. He did not even have patience to place his ship where she could do execution, but began to shoot at a distance like a madman, and did them no harm at all. At last, when he saw his own folly, he was advised by Captain Standish and brought her well up and placed a few shots to some purpose. But now, when he was in a position to do some good, his powder was used up, so he was obliged to draw off again. He consulted with the Captain how he could get further supplies of gunpowder, for he had not enough to carry him home; so he told him he would go to the next settlement and endeavor to procure him some, and did so. But

Captain Standish gathered from intelligence he received that he intended to seize the bark and take the beaver, so he sent him the powder and brought the bark home. Girling never attacked the place again and went on his way; which ended the business.

Upon the ill success of their plans, the Governor and his assistants here notified their friends at the Bay, and pointed out that the French were now likely to fortify themselves more strongly, and become undesirable neighbors to the English. In reply they wrote to them as follows.

From the Colony of Massachusetts to that of New Plymouth:

Worthy Sirs,

After reading your letters and considering the importance of their contents, the court has jointly expressed their willingness to assist you with men and ammunition, to accomplish your ends with the French. But as none of you here have authority to conclude anything with us, nothing can be done for the present. We desire you, therefore, with all convenient speed to send someone of trust, with instructions from yourselves to make such an agreement with us as may be useful to you and fair to us. So in haste we commit you to God, and remain,

Your assured loving friends,

JOHN HAYNES, Governor	WILLIAM CODDINGTON
RICHARD BELLINGHAM, Deputy Governor	WILLIAM PINCHON
	ATHERTON HOUGH
JOHN WINTHROP	INCREASE NOWELL
THOMAS DUDLEY	RICHARD DUMER
JOHN HUMPHREY	SIMON BRADSTREET

Newtown, Oct. 9th, 1635.

Upon receipt of this they at once deputed two of their people to treat with them, giving them full power to conclude an agreement according to the instructions they gave them, which were to this purpose: that if the Massachusetts Colony would afford such assistance as, together with their own, was likely to effect the desired end, and also bear a considerable part of the expense, they would go on; if not, having lost so much already, they must desist and wait such further opportunity to help themselves as God should give. But the conference resulted in nothing, for when it came to an issue the others would go to no expense. They sent the following letter, and referred them to their messengers.

Richard Bellingham, Deputy Governor of Massachusetts, to the Governor of New Plymouth:

Sir,

Having seriously considered the great importance of your business with the French, we gave our answer to those whom you deputed to confer with us about the voyage to Penobscot. We showed our willingness to help, by procuring you sufficient men and ammunition. But as for money, we have no authority at all to promise, and should we do so it might be only to disappoint you. We also think it would be proper to seek the help of the other Eastern colonies; but that we leave to your own discretion. For the rest we refer you to your deputies, who can report further details. We salute you, and wish you all success in the Lord.

    Your faithful and loving friend,
    RICHARD BELLINGHAM, Deputy,
    In the name of the rest of the Committee.
Boston, Oct. 16th, 1635.

Not only was this the end of their suggested co-operation, but some of the merchants of Massachusetts shortly after started trading with the French, and furnished them both with provisions and ammunition, and have continued to do so to this day. So it is the English themselves who have been the chief supporters of the French; and the colony at Pemaquid, which is near them, not only supplies them, but constantly gives them intelligence of what is passing among the English—especially among some of them. So it is no wonder that they still encroach more and more upon the English, and supply the Indians with guns and ammunition to the great danger of the English settlers, whose homes are scattered and unfortified. For the English are mainly occupied with farming, but the French are well fortified and live upon trade. If these things are not looked to and remedied in time, it may easily be conjectured what will result.

This year, on the 14th or 15th of August, a Saturday, there was such a fearful storm of wind and rain as none living hereabouts, either English or Indians, ever saw. It was like those hurricanes and typhoons that writers mention in the Indies. It began in the morning, a little before day, and did not come on by degrees, but with amazing violence at the start. It blew down several houses and unroofed others; many vessels were lost at sea, and many more were in extreme danger. To the southward the sea rose twenty feet, and many of the Indians had to climb trees for safety. It took off the boarded roof of a house which belonged to the settlement at Manomet and floated it to another place, leaving the posts standing in the ground; and if it had continued much longer without the wind shifting it would probably have flooded some of the inhabited parts of the country. It blew down many hundred thousands of trees, tearing up the stronger by the roots, and breaking the higher pine trees off in the middle; and tall young oaks and walnut trees of a good size were bent like withes, a strange and fearful sight. It began in the southeast, and veered different ways. It lasted, though not at its worst, for five or six hours. The marks of it will remain this hundred years in these parts, where it was most violent. There was a great eclipse of the moon the second night after.

Some of their neighbors at the Bay, hearing of the fame of the Connecticut River had a hankering after it, as mentioned before. Understanding that the Indians had been swept away by the recent mortality, fear of whom was the chief obstacle to them before, they now began to explore it with great eagerness. The New Plymouth people there had most trouble with the Dorchester settlers about it; for they set their minds on the place which the New Plymouth colony had not only purchased from the Indians, but where they had actually built, and the Dorchester people seemed determined, if they could not remove them altogether, at any rate to leave them only an insignificant plot of land round the house, sufficient for a single family. This attempt not only to intrude themselves into the rights and possessions of others, but in effect to oust them, was thought to be most unjustifiable. Many were the letters that passed between them about it.

I will first insert a few lines written from their own agent from there.

Jonathan Brewster at Matianuck to the Governor of New Plymouth:

Sir,
The Massachusetts men are coming almost daily, some by water and some by land, as yet undecided where to

settle, though some evidently have a great liking for the place we are in, which was bought last. Many of them are looking for what this river will not afford, except at the place where we are, namely, a site for a great town, with commodious dwellings for many, not far apart. What they will do I cannot yet inform you. I shall do what I can to withstand them. I hope they will hear reason; that we were here first and entered the district with much difficulty and danger, both in regard to the Dutch and the Indians, and bought the land at great expense, and have since held possession at no small trouble, and kept the Dutch from encroaching further, though but for us they would have possessed it all and kept out all others. . . . I hope these and similar arguments will stop them. It was your will that we should use them and their messengers kindly and so we have done and do daily, to our great expense. The first party of them would have almost starved had it not been for this house, and I was forced to supply twelve men for nine days. Those who came last I entertained as best we could, helping them with canoes and guides. They got me to go with them to the Dutch, to see if I could arrange that some of them should have quiet settling near them; but they peremptorily refused them. I also gave their goods house-room according to their earnest request, and Mr. Pinchon's letter on their behalf, which I thought well to send you, enclosed. What trouble and cost will be further incurred I know not, for they are coming daily, and I expect those back again from below, where they have gone to view the country. All this should surely, in the judgment of all wise and understanding men, give us just claim to hold and keep our own.

        Thus with my duty remembered, I rest,
                Yours to be commanded,
                      JONATHAN BREWSTER.

Matianuck, July 6th, 1635.

After a thorough view of the place, they began to pitch upon the land near the house belonging to the New Plymouth people, which occasioned much expostulation between them and much agitating correspondence.

But lest I should be tedious, I will forbear the details and come to the conclusion. To make any forcible resistance was far from their minds—they had enough of that at Kennebec—and to live in continual contention with their friends would be uncomfortable. So for peace' sake, though they considered they suffered injury, they thought it better to let them have it, getting as good terms as possible; so they fell to treaty. First, since there had been such long disputes about it, they insisted they must first acknowledge that they had no right to it, or else they would not treat with them about it at all. This being granted, the conclusion reached was as follows: that the people of New Plymouth should retain their house and have the 16th part of all that they bought from the Indians; and the others should have all the rest of the land, leaving such a portion for the settlers of Newtown as the New Plymouth colony reserved for them. This 16th part was to be taken in two places—one in the neighborhood of the house, the other near the Newtown settlement. Further, they were to pay to the New Plymouth colony the proper proportion of what had been disbursed to the Indians when purchased. In this way the controversy was ended; but the injustice was not so soon forgotten. The Newtown people dealt more fairly, only wishing to have what could be conveniently spared.

Among the other business that Mr. Winslow had to do in England, he had orders from the church to bring over some able and fit person as their minister. Accordingly he had procured a godly and worthy man, a Mr. Glover;

but it pleased God that when he was ready for the voyage, he fell sick of fever and died. Afterwards, when Mr. Winslow was ready to sail, he became acquainted with a Mr. Norton, who was willing to come over, but would not engage himself to settle permanently at New Plymouth until he had an opportunity of judging of it; so he arranged that if, later, he preferred to be elsewhere, he would repay the money expended for him, which came to about £70, and be at liberty to move. He stayed about a year with them, and was much liked by them; but he was invited to Ipswich, where there were many rich and able men, and several of his acquaintances, so he went to them and is their minister. About half the expense was repaid, the rest he was allowed to keep for his services amongst them.

"Now the Pequents . . . being fallen out with the Dutch, lest they should have over many enemies at once, sought to make freindship with the English of the Massachusetts . . . and sent both messengers and gifts unto them . . ."

CHAPTER XVII

[*1636*]

Mr. Edward Winslow was elected Governor this year.

The previous year, seeing from Mr. Winslow's later letters that no accounts would be sent, they had resolved to keep the beaver and send no more till they had them, or some further agreement had been come to. At least, they decided to wait till Mr. Winslow came back and they could arrive at what was best. When he came, though he brought no accounts, he persuaded them to send the beaver, and was confident that upon receipt of it and his letters they would have the accounts next year; and though they thought his ground for hope was weak, they yielded to his importunity, and sent it by a ship at the latter end of the year, which took 1150 lbs. of beaver and 200 otter skins, besides many small furs, such as 55 mink, two black fox skins, etc.

This year, in the spring, came a Dutchman who had intended to trade at the Dutch fort, but they would not permit him. So, having a large stock of trading goods, he came here and offered them for sale. They bought a good quantity that were very suitable, such as Dutch roll, kettles, etc., amounting to the value of £500, for payment of which they gave bills on Mr. Sherley in England, having already sent the parcel of beaver mentioned above. By another ship this year they again sent a further considerable quantity, which would reach him and be sold before any of these bills came due. The quantity of beaver then sent was 1809 lbs. and 10 otter skins; and shortly after the same year, they sent by another ship, of which one Langrume was captain, 719 lbs. of beaver, and 199 otter skins, concerning which Mr. Sherley writes as follows.

James Sherley in London to the New Plymouth Colony:

I have received your letters with eight hogshead of beaver, by Edward Wilkinson, captain of the *Falcon*. Blessed be God for its safe arrival. I have also seen and accepted three bills of exchange. . . . But I must acquaint you that the Lord's hand is heavy upon this kingdom in many parts, but chiefly in this city with His judgment of the plague. Last week's bill was 1200 deaths, and I fear this will be more, and it is much feared that it will be a winter sickness. It is incredible the number of people who have gone into the country in consequence—many more than went out during the last plague. So there is no trading here; carriers from most places are forbidden to enter; and money, though long due, cannot be obtained. Mr. Hall owes us more than would pay these bills, but he, his wife, and all, are in the country, 60 miles from London. I wrote to him, he came up, but could not pay us. I am sure that if I were to offer to sell the beaver at eight shillings per lb., I could not get the money. But when the Lord shall please to cease His hand, I hope we shall have better and quicker markets; so it shall lie by in the meantime.

Before I accepted the bills, I acquainted Mr. Beauchamp and Mr. Andrews about them, that no money could be got, and that it would be a great discredit to you to refuse the bills—none having ever been dishonored—and a shame to us, with 1800 lbs. of beaver lying by, and more already owing than the bills came to, etc. But it was useless; neither of them would lift a finger to help. I offered to put up my third part, but they said they neither could nor would, etc. However, your bills shall be met; but I did not think they would have deserted either you or me at this time. . . . You will expect me to write more fully and answer your letters, but I am not a day each week at home in town. I take my books and all to Clapham; for here it is the most miserable time that I think has been known in many ages. I have known three great plagues, but none like this. And that which should be a means to pacify the Lord and help us is denied us, for preaching is put down in many places—not a sermon in Westminster on the Sabbath, nor in many towns about us; the Lord in mercy look upon us. Early in the year there was a great drought, and no rain for many weeks, so that everything was burnt up—hay at £5 a load; and now there is nothing but rain, so that much summer corn and late hay is spoilt. Thus the Lord sends judgment after judgment, and yet we cannot see or humble ourselves, and therefore may justly fear heavier judgments, unless we speedily repent and turn unto Him, which the Lord give us grace to do if it be His blessed will. Thus desiring you to remember us in your prayers, I ever rest

Your loving friend,
James Sherley.

Sept. 14th, 1636.

This was all the answer they had from Mr. Sherley, which made Mr. Winslow's hopes fail him. So they decided to send no more beaver till they came to some settlement. But now there came letters from Mr. Andrews and Mr. Beauchamp, full of complaints, surprised that nothing had been sent over to meet the amounts due them, and that it appeared by the account sent in 1631 that they were each of them out about £1100 apiece, and all this time they had not received one penny towards it; and now Mr. Sherley was trying to get more money from them, and was offended because they refused him. They blamed them here very much that all was sent to Mr. Sherley and nothing to them. The partners here wondered at this, for they supposed that much of their money had been paid in, and that each of them had received a proportionate quantity yearly out of the large returns sent home. They had sent home since the account was received in 1631—which included all and more than all their debts, with that year's supplies—goods to the following amount:

Nov. 18th, 1631.
  By Mr. Pierce 400 lbs. of beaver; otter 20 skins
July 13th, 1632.
  By Mr. Griffin 1348 lbs. of beaver; otter 147 skins
1633.
  By Mr. Graves 3366 lbs. of beaver, otter 346 skins
1634.
  By Mr. Andrews 3738 lbs. of beaver; otter 234 skins
1635.
  By Mr. Babb 1150 lbs. of beaver; otter 200 skins
June 24th, 1636.
  By Mr. Wilkinson 1809 lbs. of beaver; otter 10 skins
1636.
  By Mr. Langrume 719 lbs. of beaver; otter 199 skins
  Total—12530 lbs. of beaver; otter 1156 skins.

All these quantities were safely received and well sold, as appeared by letters. The coat beaver usually sold at twenty shillings per lb., and sometimes at twenty-four shillings; otter skins at fifteen shillings, and sometimes sixteen shillings each—I do not remember any under fourteen shillings. It may be that the last year's shipment fetched less; but there were some small furs not reckoned in this account, and some black beaver at high rates, to make up any such deficit. It was calculated that the above parcels of beaver came to little less than £10,000 sterling, and the otter skins would pay all the expenses and, with other furs, make up besides whatever might be short of the former sum. When the former account was passed, all their debts, those of the *White Angel* and *Friendship* included, came to but £4770. They estimated that all the supplies sent them since, and bills paid for them, could not exceed £2000; so that their debts should have been paid with interest.

It may be objected: how came it that they did not know the exact amount of their receipts, as they did of their returns, but had to estimate them? Two things were the cause of it; the first and principal was that the new accountant,[1] who was pressed upon them from England, wholly failed them and could never render them any accounts. He trusted to his memory and loose papers, and let things run into such confusion that neither he nor anyone else could bring things to rights. Whenever he was called upon to perfect his accounts, he desired to have so long, or such a time of leisure, and he would finish them. In the interim he fell very ill, and in conclusion he could make no account at all. His books, after a brief good beginning, were left altogether imperfect, and of his papers,

---

[1] The accountant, Josias Winslow, had been with them since 1632.

some were lost and others so confused that he knew not what to make of them himself when they came to be examined. This was not unknown to Mr. Sherley; and the colony came to smart for it to some purpose, both in England and here, though it was not their fault. They reckon they have lost in consequence some hundred of pounds for goods sold on credit, which were ultimately a dead loss for want of clear accounts to call for payment. Another reason of the mischief was, that after Mr. Winslow was sent into England to demand accounts and to take exception to the *White Angel*, no prices were sent with their goods and no proper invoice of them; everything was confused, and they were obliged to guess at the prices.

They wrote back to Mr. Andrews and Mr. Beauchamp, and told them they wondered they could say that they had sent nothing home since the last accounts; they had sent a great deal, and it might rather be wondered how they could send so much, besides all the expenses here and what the French had captured, and what had been lost at sea when Mr. Pierce's ship was wrecked off the coast of Virginia. What they had sent was sent to them all, to them as well as Mr. Sherley, and if they had not looked after it, it was their own faults; they must refer them to Mr. Sherley who had received it, from whom they should demand it. They also wrote to Mr. Sherley to the same purpose, and what the others' complaints were.

This year, two shallops going to Connecticut with goods from Massachusetts, belonging to those who had gone there to settle, were wrecked in an easterly storm, coming into the harbor at night. The boatmen were drowned and the goods were driven all along the shore and strewn up and down at high-water mark. But the Governor had them collected and an inventory made of them, and they were washed and dried. So most of the goods were saved and restored to the owners. Afterwards, another boat from the same place and bound for the same destination, was wrecked at Manoanscusett, and the goods that came ashore were preserved for them. Such misfortunes the Connecticut settlers from Massachusetts met with in their beginnings, and some thought them a correction from God for their intrusion there, to the injury of others. But I dare not be so bold with God's judgments as to say that it was so.

In the year 1634, the Pequots, a warlike tribe that had conquered many of its neighbors and was puffed up with numerous victories, were at variance with the Narragansetts, a great neighboring tribe. These Narragansetts held correspondence and were on terms of friendship with the English of Massachusetts. The Pequots, being conscious of the guilt of the death of Captain Stone,[2] whom they knew to be an Englishman, and of those who were with him, and having fallen out with the Dutch, lest they should have too many enemies at once, wished to make friends with the English of Massachusetts and sent messengers and gifts to them, as is shown by some letters from the Governor there, as follows.

Governor Winthrop of Massachusetts to the New Plymouth Colony:

Dear and Worthy Sir,
To let you know something about our affairs. The Pequots have sent to us desiring our friendship, and offering much wampum and beaver, etc. The first messengers

---
[2] For the murder of Captain Stone in 1634, see above, pp. 322–323.

were dismissed without answer; with the next we had several days' conference, and taking the advice of some of our ministers, and seeking the Lord in it, we concluded a peace and friendship with them on these conditions: that they should deliver to us the men who were guilty of Stone's death. . . . If we desired to settle in Connecticut they should give up their right to us, and we should trade with them as friends—the chief thing aimed at. To this they readily agreed; and begged that we should mediate a peace between them and the Narragansetts, for which purpose they were willing that we should give the Narragansetts part of the present they would bestow on us— for they stood so much on their honor that they would not be seen to give anything of themselves. As for Captain Stone, they told us there were but two left who had a hand in his death and that they killed him in a just quarrel, for he surprised two of their men, and bound them, and forced them to show him the way up the river. He went ashore with two others, nine Indians secretly watching him; and when they were asleep that night they killed him and the others to free their own men; and some of them going afterwards to the pinnace, it was suddenly blown up. We are now preparing to send a pinnace to them.

In another of his he writes thus:

Our pinnace has lately returned from the Pequots; they did little trade and found them a very false tribe, so they mean to have no more to do with them. I have many other things to write you.

Yours ever assured,
JOHN WINTHROP.

Boston, 12th of the first month, 1634.

After these occurrences, and as I take it, this year, John Oldham, so often mentioned before, now an inhabitant of Massachusetts, went trading with a small vessel, weakly manned, into the south parts, and upon a quarrel between him and the Indians was killed by them, as was before noted, at an island called by the Indians, Munisses, but since by the English, Block Island.[3] This, with the death of Stone and the trifling of the Pequots with the English of Massachusetts incited the latter to send out a party to take revenge and require satisfaction for these wrongs; but it was done so superficially, and without acquainting those of Connecticut and their other neighbors with the project that little good came of it. Indeed, to their neighbors it did more harm than good, for some of the murderers of Oldham fled to the Pequots, and though the English went to the Pequots and had some parley with them, they only deluded them, and the English returned without doing anything effective. After the English had returned, the Pequots watched their opportunity to kill some of the English as they passed in boats or went out fowling; and next spring even attacked them in their homes, as will appear. I only touch upon these things, because I have no doubt they will be more fully covered by those who have more exact knowledge of them, and whom they more properly concern.

This year Mr. Smith resigned his ministry, partly by his own wish, thinking it too heavy a burden, and partly at the persuasion of others. So the church looked out for someone else, having often been disappointed in their hopes before. But it pleased the Lord to send them an able and godly man, Mr. John Rayner, meek and humble in

---

[3] Named for the Dutch captain, Adrian Block, who is presumed to have discovered it in 1614. Oldham, it will be remembered, had been a troublemaker in New Plymouth and had been expelled from that colony in 1625.

spirit, sound in the truth, and every way unreprovable in his life and conversation. After some time of trial they chose him as their minister, the fruits of whose labors they enjoyed many years with much comfort, in peace and good agreement.

"Those that scaped the fire were slaine with the sword; some hewed to peeces, others rune throw with their rapiers, so as they were quickly dispatchte, and very few escaped."

CHAPTER XVIII

[1637]

𝓘n the early part of this year the Pequots openly attacked the English in Connecticut, along the lower parts of the river, and killed many of them as they were at work in the fields, both men and women, to the great terror of the rest; then they went off in great pride and triumph, with many high threats. They also attacked a fort at the river's mouth, though strong and well defended; [1] and though they did not succeed there, it struck those within with fear and astonishment to see their bold attempts in the face of danger. This made them stand upon their guard everywhere and prepare for resistance, and they earnestly solicited their friends and neighbors in Massachusetts to send them speedy aid, for they looked for more forcible onslaughts. So Mr. Vane, who was then Governor, wrote from their General Court to those here, asking them to join with them in this war, which they were cordially willing to do, but took the opportunity to

---

[1] This was the fort built in 1636 by Lion Gardiner at Saybrook and defended by him.

write to them about some previous events, as well as the present trouble, and pertinent to it. The succeeding Governor's answer I will here insert.

Governor John Winthrop at Boston to the New Plymouth Colony:

Sir,

The Lord having so disposed that your letters to our late Governor have fallen to my lot to answer, I could wish I had more freedom of time and thought so that I might do it more to your and my own satisfaction. But what is waiting now can be supplied later. As for the matters which you and your Council submit to our consideration, we did not think it advisable to make them so public as by bringing them to the cognizance of our General Court. But having been considered by our Council, this answer we think fit to return to you.

1. Whereas you signify your willingness to join us in this war against the Pequots, though you cannot bind yourselves without the consent of your General Court, we acknowledge your good feeling towards us, which we never had cause to doubt, and await your full resolution in the course.

2. Whereas you consider this war concerns us and not you, except incidentally, we partly agree with you; but we suppose that in case of peril you will not act upon that consideration any more than we should do in like case. We suppose you look upon the Pequots and all other Indians as a common enemy, who though he may vent the first outburst of his rage upon some one section of the English, nevertheless, if he succeed, will thereupon pursue his advantage to the undoing of the whole nation. Therefore, in soliciting your help, we do so with respect to your own safety as well as ours.

3. Whereas you desire that we should bind ourselves to

help you on all similar occasions, we are convinced you cannot doubt it; but as we now deal with you as an independent colony, recognizing that we cannot involve you in this campaign against your consent, so we desire the same freedom of decision if at any time you make a similar call upon us; and whereas it is objected that we refused to aid you against the French, we consider the cases are not quite equivalent, though we cannot wholly excuse our failing you on that occasion.

4. Whereas you object that we began the war without consulting you, and have since managed it contrary to your advice; the truth is that our first intentions being only against Block Island and the enterprise seeming of small difficulty, we did not so much as consider taking advice or looking for aid. When we had decided to include the Pequots, we sent to you at once or very shortly after, and by the time your answer was received it seemed unadvisable for us to change our plans.

5. As for our people trading at Kennebec, we assure you it has not been with our permission; and what we have provided to meet such cases at our last court Mr. Winslow can inform you.

6. Whereas you object to our trading and corresponding with your enemies the French, we answer you are misinformed. Except for some letters which have passed between our late Governor and them, of which we were cognizant, we have neither traded nor encouraged our people to trade with them; and only one or two vessels taking letters had permission from our Governor to go there.[2]

Several other objections have been made to us privately by our worthy friend, to which he has received some answer; but as most of them concern particular discourtesies

---

[2] By this means they furnished them with supplies, and have continued to do so. (B.)

or injuries from individuals here, we cannot say more than this: that if the offenders are exposed in the right way, we shall be ready to do justice as the cases require. In the meantime we desire you to rest assured that such things are done without our knowledge and are not a little grievous to us.

Now as to joining us in this war, which only concerns us to the same extent as it does yourselves, viz., the relief of our friends and Christian brethren who are now first in danger. Though you may think us able to carry it through without you—and if the Lord please to be with us, so we may—nevertheless three things we offer for your consideration, which we think will have some weight with you.

First, if we should sink under this burden, your opportunity of seasonable help would be lost in three respects; you could then only reinforce us or secure yourselves there at three times the risk and expense of the present undertaking; the suffering we should have borne, if through your neglect, would much reduce the acceptableness of your help afterwards; those amongst you who are now full of courage and zeal would be dispirited and less able to support so great a burden.

Secondly, it is very important to hasten the conclusion of this war before the end of this summer; otherwise the news of it will discourage both your and our friends from coming over to us next year, besides the further risk and loss it would expose us to, as yourselves may judge.

Thirdly, if the Lord please to bless our endeavors, so that we end the war or succeed in it without you, it may breed such ill thoughts in our people towards yours, that it will be thereafter difficult to entertain such opinion of your good will towards us as is fitting in neighbors and brethren. What ill consequences might result on both sides wise men may well fear, and would rather prevent than hope to redress. With hearty salutations to yourself and all your council and other good friends with you, I rest,

                Yours most assured in the Lord,
                      JOHN WINTHROP.

Boston, the 20th of the third month, 1637.

In the meantime the Pequots, especially the winter before, had sought to make peace with the Narragansetts, and used very pernicious arguments to persuade them: the English were strangers and were beginning to overspread their country, and would deprive them of it in time, if they were allowed thus to increase; if the Narragansetts were to assist the English to subdue them, the Pequots, they would only make way for their own overthrow, for then the English would soon subjugate them; but if they would listen to their advice, they need not fear the strength of the English, for they would not make open war upon them, but fire their houses, kill their cattle, and lie in ambush for them as they went about the country— all of which they could do with but little danger to themselves. By these means they easily saw the English could not long hold out, but would either be starved or forced to leave the country. They urged these and similar arguments so strongly that the Narragansetts were wavering and half-minded to make peace with them and join them against the English. But when they reconsidered what wrongs they had suffered from the Pequots, and what an opportunity they now had, with the help of the English, to repay them, revenge was so sweet to them that it prevailed over everything else. So they resolved to join the English against them; and they did so.

The court here agreed to send fifty men at their own expense, and with all possible speed got them armed, with sufficient leaders and a bark to carry their provisions and supply all their needs. But when they were ready to march with a contingent from the Bay, they had word that the enemy were as good as vanquished, and there would be no need of them.

I shall not take upon myself to describe in detail what had occurred, because I expect it will be done fully by those who best know the circumstances; I will only touch upon them in general. From Connecticut, where they were most alive to the present danger and all that it threatened, they raised a party of men, and another party met them from the Bay at a place where the Narragansetts were to join them. The Narragansetts were anxious to be gone, before the English were well rested and refreshed, especially some of them that had arrived last, for they wanted to come upon the enemy suddenly and undiscovered. A bark belonging to New Plymouth had just put in there, having come from Connecticut, and urged them to profit by the Indians' keenness, and to show themselves as eager as they were, for it would encourage them, and promptness would result to their great advantage.

So they proceeded at once, and arranged their march so that they reached the fort of the enemy,[3] in which most of their chief men were, before day. They approached it in utter silence, and both the English and Indians surrounded it, so that they should not escape. They then made the attack with great courage, speedily forcing an entrance to the fort and shooting amongst them. Those that entered first met with fierce resistance, the enemy shooting and grappling with them. Others of the attacking party ran to their houses and set them on

---

[3] The site of the Pequot fort was at modern Mystic.

fire, the mats catching quickly and, all standing close together, the wind soon fanned them into a blaze—in fact, more were burnt to death than killed otherwise. It burnt their bowstrings and made their weapons useless, and those that escaped the fire were slain by the sword—some hewn to pieces, others run through with their rapiers, so that they were quickly dispatched and very few escaped. It is believed that there were about 400 killed. It was a fearful sight to see them frying in the fire, with streams of blood quenching it; the smell was horrible, but the victory seemed a sweet sacrifice, and they gave praise to God Who had wrought so wonderfully for them, thus to enclose their enemy and give them so speedy a victory over such a proud and insulting foe. The Narragansett Indians all this while stood round, but kept aloof from danger and left the whole execution to the English, except to stop any who broke away; but they mocked their enemies in their defeat and misery, calling out to them when they saw them dancing in the flames a word which in the language of the vanquished Indians signified, O brave Pequots! and which was used by them in their prayers, and in their songs of triumph after victory.

After this attack had been thus fortunately concluded they marched to the waterside, where they met with some of their vessels, by which they were refreshed with food and other necessaries. But during their march the remnant of the Pequots who had escaped collected in a body, intending to take advantage of them at a neck of land they had to cross; but when they saw the English prepared for them, they kept aloof, so they neither did any harm nor received any. After refreshing themselves and taking further counsel, they resolved to follow up their victory and make war upon the rest; but most of the

Narragansett Indians forsook them, and those that they kept with them for guides they found very unwilling, either from envy, or because they saw the English would profit more by the victory than they were willing they should, or perhaps deprive them of the advantage of having the Pequots become tributary to them.

For the rest of these events, and the further campaign against the Pequots, I will relate them as given in a letter from Mr. Winthrop to the Governor here.

Governor John Winthrop at Boston to the Governor of New Plymouth:

Worthy Sir,

I received your loving letter, and am anxious to express my affection for you, but lack of time forbids. My desire is to acquaint you with the Lord's mercies towards us, in prevailing against His and our enemies, that you may rejoice and praise His name with us. About 80 of our men coasted along towards the Dutch plantation, sometimes by water but mostly by land, and met here and there with some Pequots, whom they slew or took prisoners. They captured two sachems and beheaded them, and not hearing of Sassacus, the chief sachem, they gave a prisoner his life to go and find him. He went and brought them word where he was; but Sassacus suspecting him to be a spy, fled, after he had gone, with some twenty more to the Mohawks, so our men missed him. However, they divided themselves and ranged up and down as the providence of God directed them, for their Indian allies had all gone, except three or four, who did not know how to guide them, or else would not.

On the 13th of the month they chanced upon a large band of the tribe, eighty men and two hundred women and children, in a small Indian town close by a hideous swamp,[4] which they all slipped into before our men could get to them. Our captains had not yet come up; but there were Mr. Ludlow and Captain Mason with some ten of their men, and Captain Patrick with some twenty or more of his, the noise of whose shooting attracted Captain Trask with fifty more. Then order was given to surround the swamp, which was about a mile round; but Lieutenant Davenport and some twelve more, not hearing the command, rushed into the swamp among the Indians. It was so thick with shrubwood and so boggy that some of them stuck fast and were wounded by many shots. Lieutenant Davenport was dangerously wounded near the armhole, and another man was shot in the head, and they were so weak that they were in great danger of being captured by the Indians. But Sergeant Riggs and Jeffrey and two or three more rescued them and killed several Indians with their swords. After they had been brought out the Indians desired parley. Through Thomas Stanton, our interpreter, terms were offered: that if they would come out and yield they should have their lives, except such as had had their hands in English blood. Whereupon the sachem of the place came out and an old man or two and their wives and children, and after that some other women and children; and they parleyed for two hours till it was night. Then Thomas Stanton was sent to them again to call them out; but they said they would sell their lives there, and forthwith shot at him so fiercely that if he had not cried out and been rescued at once, they would have killed him.

Then our men cleared the swamp with their swords, till the Indians were cooped up in so narrow a compass that they could kill them more easily through the thickets. So they stood all night about twelve feet apart from each other, the Indians coming close up to our men and shooting their arrows so that they pierced their hatbrims, their

---
[4] Near Fairfield.

sleeves, their stockings, and other parts of their clothes; but so miraculously did the Lord preserve them that not one of them was wounded except the three who had so rashly entered the swamp. Just before day it grew very dark, and some of the Indians who were still alive got through between our men, though they stood not more than twelve or fourteen feet apart; but they were soon discovered, and some were pursued and killed. Upon searching the swamp next morning they found nine slain, and some they pulled up whom the Indians had buried in the mire; so they think that of all the band not twenty escaped. Afterwards they found some who had died of their wounds while in flight.

The prisoners were divided, some being sent to the people of the Connecticut River, and the rest to us. Of these we are sending the male children to Bermuda [5] with Mr. William Pierce, and the women and female children are distributed through the towns. In all, there have now been killed and taken prisoners about 700. The rest are scattered, and the Indians in all quarters are so terrified that they are afraid to give them sanctuary. Two of the sachems of Long Island came to Mr. Stoughton and offered themselves as tributaries, under their protection; and two of the Neepnett sachems have been here to seek our friendship. Among the prisoners we have the wife and children of Mononotto, the former a modest looking woman of good behavior. It was by her mediation that the two English girls were spared from death and used kindly;[6] so I have taken charge of her. One of her first requests was that the English should not abuse her body, and that her children might not be taken from her. Those that had been wounded were soon brought back by John

---

[5] But they were taken to the West Indies. (B.)
[6] Two young girls had been taken prisoners by the Pequots in a raid on the English settlement at Wethersfield; they were eventually rescued by a Dutch trader.

Galop, who came with his shallop in a happy hour to bring them food and take the wounded to the pinnace where our chief surgeon was, with Mr. Wilson, about eight leagues off. Our people are all in good health, the Lord be praised, and although they had marched in their arms all day and had been in the fight all night, they professed they were so fresh that they could readily have started off on another such expedition.

This is the substance of what I received, though I am forced to omit several considerable circumstances. So, being much pressed for time—the ships sailing in four days, taking Lord Ley [7] and Mr. Vane—I will break off and with hearty salutations, I rest

Yours assured,
JOHN WINTHROP.

P. S.—The captain reports we have killed thirteen sachems; but Sassacus and Mononotto are still living. *28th of the fifth month,* 1637.

That I may make an end of the matter, this Sassacus, the Pequot's chief sachem, having fled to the Mohawks, they cut off his head and executed some other of their leaders, whether to satisfy the English or the Narragansetts—who as I have since heard hired them to do it—or for their own advantage, I do not know; but thus the war ended. The rest of the Pequots were utterly routed. Some of them submitted themselves to the Narragansetts and lived under them; but others betook themselves to the Monhiggs, under their sachem, Uncas,[8] with the ap-

---

[7] Lord Ley, eldest son of the Earl of Marlborough, had come over to see the country. Sir Harry Vane was ex-governor of the Massachusetts Bay Colony.

[8] Uncas is the hero of James Fenimore Cooper's *Last of the Mohicans* and other *Leather Stocking Tales*. The Pequot tribe was nearly exterminated as a result of this war.

probation of the English of Connecticut, under whose protection Uncas lived, he and his men having been faithful to them in the war, and having done them very good service. But it so vexed the Narragansetts that they had not the whole sway over them, that they never ceased plotting and contriving how to subjugate them; and when they found they could not attain their ends, owing to English protection, they tried to raise a general conspiracy against the English, as will appear later.

They received letters again from Mr. Andrews and Mr. Beauchamp in England, saying that Mr. Sherley neither had paid nor would pay them any money, nor give them any account. They were very vexed, blaming them still that they had sent everything to Mr. Sherley and none to themselves. Now, though they might have justly referred them to their former answer and insisted upon it, and some wise advisers urged them to do so, nevertheless, as they believed they were really out substantial sums of money, especially Mr. Andrews, they resolved to send them what beaver they had on their hands; but they delayed doing so till next year. Mr. Sherley's letters were to this purpose: that as the other partners had abandoned him in the payment of former bills, so now he told them he would abandon them in this; and, believe it, they should find it true. And he was as good as his word, for they could never get a penny from him or bring him to account, though Mr. Beauchamp sued him in Chancery. But they all turned their complaints against the New Plymouth partners, where there was least cause; indeed they had suffered most unjustly. They discharged Mr. Sherley from his agency, forbade him to buy or send over any more goods for them, and urged him to come to an end with their affairs.

"It pleaseth God, in these times, so to blesse ye cuntry with such access and confluence of people into it, as it was therby much inriched . . ."

CHAPTER XIX

[*1638*]

This year Mr. Thomas Pierce was chosen Governor. Amongst other enormities that occurred this year three men were tried and executed for robbery and murder. Their names were Arthur Peach, Thomas Jackson, and Richard Stinnings. There was a fourth, Daniel Crose, who was also found guilty, but he escaped and could not be found. Arthur Peach was the ringleader. He was a strong and desperate young man, and had been one of the soldiers in the Pequot war, and had done as good service as any there, always being one of the first in any attack. Being now out of means and loth to work, and taking to idle ways and company, he intended to go to the Dutch colony, and had lured the other three, who were servants and apprentices, to go with him. But there was also another cause for his going away secretly in this manner; he had not only run into debt, but he had seduced a girl, a maidservant in the town, and fear of punishment made him wish to get away, though this was not known till after his death. The other three ran away from their masters in the night and could not be heard of, for they did not go by the ordinary route, but shaped such a course as they thought would evade pursuit. Finding themselves somewhere between the Bay of Massachusetts and the Narragansetts' country, and wishing to rest, they made a fire a little off the road by the wayside, and took tobacco.

At length there came a Narragansett Indian by, who had been trading at the Bay, and had some cloth and beads with him. They had met him the day before, and now he was returning. Peach called him to come and drink tobacco with them, and he came and sat down. He had told the others he would kill the Indian and take his goods. The others were afraid; but Peach said, "Hang the rogue, he has killed many of us." So they let him do as he would, and when he saw his opportunity, he took his rapier and ran the man through the body once or twice, and took from him five fathoms of wampum and three coats of cloth; and then they went their way, leaving him for dead. But the Indian managed to scramble up when they had gone, and made shift to get home.

By this means they were discovered, and the Indians caught them; for wanting a canoe to take them over the water, and not thinking their act was known, by the sachem's command they were taken to Aquidneck Island, and were there accused of the deed, and examined and committed upon it by the English. The Indians sent for Mr. Williams and made grievous complaint; and the friends and relatives of the injured native were ready to rise in arms and incite the rest to do the same, believing they would now find the Pequot's words were true: that the English would turn upon them. But Mr. Williams pacified them, and told them they should see justice done upon the offenders, and went to the wounded man and took Mr. James, the physician, with him. The man told him who did it and how it was done. The physician found his wounds mortal, and that he could not live, as he testified upon oath before the jury in open court. He died shortly after.

The Governor of the Bay was acquainted with it, but referred it to New Plymouth, because the act was committed in his jurisdiction; but he urged that by all means justice should be done, or it would cause a war. Nevertheless, some of the more ignorant colonists objected that an Englishman should be put to death for an Indian. So at last the murderers were brought home from the island, and after being tried and the evidence produced, they all in the end freely confessed to all the Indian had accused them of, and that they had done it in the manner described. So they were condemned by the jury, and executed. Some of the Narragansett Indians and the murdered man's friends were present when it was done, which gave them and all the country satisfaction. But it was a matter of much sadness to them here, as it was the second execution since they came—both being for willful murder.

This year they received more letters from England, full of renewed complaints, on the one hand that Mr. Beauchamp and Mr. Andrews could get no money or accounting from Mr. Sherley, on the other that the latter should be importuned by them, retorting that he would account with those here and not with them, etc. So, as had been decided before, viz., that if nothing came of their last letters, they would then send them what fur they could, thinking that when some good part had been paid to them, Mr. Sherley and they would more easily agree about the remainder—they now sent to Mr. Andrews and Mr. Beauchamp through Mr. Joseph Young in the *Mary and Anne* 1325 lbs. of beaver divided between them. Mr. Beauchamp returned an account of his share, showing that he made £400 sterling out of it, freight and all expenses paid. But Mr. Andrews, though he had the larger and better half, did not make so much out of his through his own indiscretion, and yet charged the loss, which was about £40, to them here. They sent them more by bills and other payments, which was received and acknowledged by them and divided between them, such as for cattle of Mr. Allerton's which were sold, and the price of a bark which belonged to the stock and was sold, amounting to £434 sterling. The total value was thus £1234 sterling, except what Mr. Andrews had lost on his beaver, and which was made good otherwise. But this did not stay their clamors, as will appear hereafter.

It pleased God about this time to bless the country with such an influx of people that it was much enriched, and cattle of all kinds stood at high prices for many years. Cows were sold at £20, and some at £25 apiece, sometimes even at £28. A cow-calf usually fetched £10; a milchgoat £3 and sometimes £4; and she-kids thirty shillings and often £2 apiece. By this means the original settlers who had stock began to increase in wealth. Corn also commanded a high price, viz., six shillings a bushel. So other trading began to be neglected, and the old partners, having forbidden Mr. Sherley to send them any more goods, abandoned their trade at Kennebec, and as things stood, decided to follow it no longer. But a few of them were loth that it should all be lost by closing it entirely, so they joined with some others and agreed to give the colony about one-sixth of the profits from it; and with the first fruits of this the colony built a house for a prison. The trade at Kennebec has since been continued to the great benefit of the place; for as some well foresaw, such high prices for corn and cattle could not long continue, and the revenue got by trade would be much missed.

This year, about the 1st or 2nd of June, there was a fearful earthquake. Here it was heard before it was felt. It began with a rumbling noise or low murmur, like remote thunder; it came from the northward and passed southward. As the noise approached, the earth began to shake, and at length with such violence that platters, dishes, and other things standing on shelves came clattering down, and people were afraid for the houses themselves. It happened that at the time several of the chief citizens of the town were holding a meeting in a house, conferring with some of their friends who were about to move from the place—as if the Lord would hereby show His displeasure at their thus shaking apart and removing from one another. It was very terrible for a while, and as the men sat talking in the house, some women and others were just out of doors, and the earth shook with such violence that they could not stand without catching hold of the posts and palings near by. But the violence did not last long. About half an hour after, or less, came another noise and shaking, but not so severe as before and not lasting long. Some ships along the coast were shaken by it; but it was not only felt near the sea, for the Indians noticed it inland. So powerful is the mighty hand of the Lord as to make both the earth and the sea to shake, and the mountains to tremble before Him when He pleases; and who can stay His hand?

It was observed that the summers for several years after

this earthquake were not so hot and seasonable for the ripening of corn and other fruits as formerly, but were colder and more moist and subject to early and untimely frosts, so that often much Indian corn failed. Whether this was the cause, I leave it to naturalists to judge.

"... *many of them grew aged and saw many changes were like to befall; so as they were loath to leave these intanglements upon their children and posteritie* ..."

CHAPTER XX

[1639 - 1640]

I will combine these two years, because there occurred but little of interest outside of the ordinary affairs of the colony. New Plymouth had several times granted land for various townships, and among the rest, to the inhabitants of Scituate, some of them coming from here. A large tract of land there had also been given to their four London partners, Mr. Sherley, Mr. Beauchamp, Mr. Andrews and Mr. Hatherley. At Mr. Hatherley's request, the locality was fixed upon for himself and them, for the other three had given him power to choose for them. This tract of land extended up to the border-line of their neighbors of Massachusetts, who some years later established a town called Hingham on the land next to it. This now led to great disputes between these two townships about their boundaries, and some meadow lands that lay between them. The inhabitants of Hingham began to allot some of these meadows to their people, measuring and staking them out for that purpose. The people of Scituate pulled up their stakes and threw them away. So it developed into a controversy between the two governments. Many letters passed between them about it, and it hung in suspense for about two years. The Court of Massachusetts appointed men to fix their boundary line according to their patent, and the way they went to work made it include all Scituate itself and I know not how much more. On the other hand, according to the boundary lines of the patent of New Plymouth, theirs would take in Hingham and much more within the bounds they had set.

In the end both courts agreed to choose two commissioners on each side and give them absolute power to settle the boundaries between them, and what they decided was to stand irrevocably. They had one meeting at Hingham, but could not agree; for their commissioners stood stiffly on a certain clause in their grant: that their limits should extend from Charles River or any branch or part thereof and 3 miles further to the southward; or from the most southern part of the Massachusetts Bay, and 3 miles further south. But they chose to adhere to the former limit, for they had found a small river, or brook rather, which a long way inland trended far southward and entered some part of what was taken to be Charles River; and from the most southerly part of this, and 3 miles further southward, they wished to run a line eastwards to the sea, about 20 miles, which would take in a part of New Plymouth itself. Now though the patent and colony of New Plymouth was much the older, the patent for the extension upon which Scituate stood was granted after theirs of Massachusetts; so the latter took first place as regards this extension.

The New Plymouth answer to the deputies of Massachusetts was, they owned that their claims for Scituate could not be based in any way upon their original grant; but on the other hand, neither could the others prove this stream to be a part of Charles River, for they did not know which Charles River was, except so far as the people here, who came first, gave the name to the river upon which Charlestown was afterwards built, believing it to be that which Captain Smith so named. Now those who first named it had best reason to know it, and to explain which it was. But they only termed it Charles River as far as it was navigated by them—that is, as far as a boat could go. But that all the small brooks that should flow into it, far inland, and were all differently named by the natives, should now be made out to be the Charles River, or parts of it, they saw no reason to allow. They gave an instance of the Humber in old England, which had the Trent, Ouse, and many other rivers of lesser note running into it; and again many smaller brooks fell into the Trent and Ouse; but all had their own names. Again it was contended that no mention was made of an east line in their patent; they were to begin at the sea and go west by a line, etc.

At this meeting, however, no conclusion was reached; but things were discussed and well prepared for an issue. Next year the same commissioners were appointed and met at Scituate, and concluded the matter as follows.

The agreement as to the boundaries between New Plymouth and Massachusetts:

Whereas there were two commissioners appointed by the two jurisdictions; the one of Massachusetts Government, appointing John Endicott, gent., and Israel Stoughton, gent.; the other of New Plymouth Government, appointing William Bradford, Governor, and Edward Winslow, gent.; for the setting out and determining the boundaries of the lands between the said jurisdictions, whereby this present age and posterity to come may live peaceably and quietly. And for as much as the said commissioners on both sides have full power so to do, as appears by the record of both jurisdictions, we, the said commissioners above named, do hereby with one consent and agreement conclude, determine, and by these presents declare that all the marshes at Cohasset that lie on the one side of the river next to Hingham shall belong to the jurisdiction of Massachusetts, and all the marshes that lie on the other side of the river next to Scituate shall belong to the jurisdiction of New Plymouth, except sixty acres of marsh land at the mouth of the river on the Scituate side next to the sea, which we do hereby agree, conclude and determine shall belong to the jurisdiction of Massachusetts. And further we do hereby agree, determine and conclude that the boundaries between the said jurisdictions are as follows, viz.: from the mouth of the brook that runs into Cohasset marshes, which we call by the name of Bound Brook, with a straight and direct line to the middle of a great pond that lies on the right hand of the upper path or common way that leads between Weymouth and New Plymouth, close to the path as we go along, which was formerly, and we desire may still be, called Accord Pond,[1] lying about five or six miles from Weymouth, southerly; and from thence with a straight line to the southernmost part of Charles River, and three miles southerly into the country, as expressed in the patent granted by His Majesty to the Company of the Massachusetts Colony. Provided always, and nevertheless concluded and determined by mutual agreement between the said commissioners that if it fall out that the said line from Accord Pond to the southernmost part of Charles River and three miles southerly, restrict or hinder any part of any settlement begun by the Governor of New Plymouth, or hereafter

---

[1] So named because it was the scene of an early treaty of peace between Indians and Pilgrims.

to be begun within ten years after the date of these presents, that then notwithstanding the said line, where it shall so obtrude as aforesaid, so much land as shall make up the quantity of eight square miles, to belong to every settlement so begun, or to be begun as aforesaid; which we agree, determine, and conclude, to appertain and belong to the said Governor of New Plymouth. And whereas the said line from the said brook which runs into Cohasset salt marshes, called by us Bound Brook, and the pond called Accord Pond, lie near the lands belonging to the townships of Scituate and Hingham, we do therefore hereby determine and conclude, that if any divisions already made and accorded by either of the said townships do cross the said line, that then it shall stand and be in force according to the former intents and purposes of the said towns granting them—the marshes formerly agreed upon excepted; and that no town in either jurisdiction shall hereafter exceed, but contain themselves within the said lines expressed.

In witness whereof we, the commissioners of both jurisdictions, do by these presents indented set our hands and seals, the ninth day of the fourth month in the 16th year of our sovereign lord, King Charles, and in the year of Our Lord, 1640.

WILLIAM BRADFORD, Governor JOHN ENDICOTT
EDWARD WINSLOW   ISRAEL STOUGHTON

The extended New Plymouth patent having been taken out in the name of William Bradford, as in trust, ran in these terms: "To him, his heirs, associates, and assigns." But the number of freemen having now greatly increased, and several townships being established and settled in several quarters, such as New Plymouth, Duxbury, Scituate, Taunton, Sandwich, Yarmouth, Barnstable, Marshfield, and not long after Seekonk—afterwards called at the wish of the inhabitants Rehoboth—and Nauset, it was desired by the Court that William Bradford should make surrender of the same into their hands. This he willingly did.

In these two years, they had several letters from England, asking them to send someone over to end the business of the accounts with Mr. Sherley, who now professed he could not make them up without help from them, especially from Mr. Winslow. They had serious thoughts of it, and the majority of the partners here believed it best to send; but they had formerly written such bitter and threatening letters that Mr. Winslow was neither willing to go himself, nor that any other of the partners should do so; for he was convinced that if any of them went, they would be arrested, and an action for such a sum laid upon them that they would be unable to procure bail, and would consequently be imprisoned, and that then the partners there could force them to do whatever they wished. Or else they might be brought into trouble by the archbishop's means, as things then were over there.

But though they were much inclined to send, and Captain Standish was willing to go, they decided, since they could not agree about it and it was of such importance, and the consequences might prove dangerous, to ask Mr. John Winthrop's advice. It seemed the more suitable because Mr. Andrews had in many letters acquainted him with the differences between them, and appointed him his assign to receive his part of the debt; and though they declined to pay anything as a debt till the controversy was ended, they had deposited £110 in money in his hands for Mr. Andrews, to be paid to him in part as soon as he should come to any agreement with the rest.

But Mr. Winthrop was of Mr. Winslow's mind, and dissuaded them from sending; so they abandoned the idea, and returned this answer. That the times were dangerous in England as things stood with them, for they knew how Mr. Winslow had suffered formerly, and for a little thing had been clapped into the Fleet, and how long it had been before he could get out, to his and their great loss; and things were not better but worse in that respect. However, that their honesty might be made manifest to all, they would make them this offer: to refer the case to some gentlemen and merchants at the Bay of Massachusetts, such as they should choose, and were well known to them, as they had many friends and acquaintances there better known to them than to the partners here; and let them be informed of the case by both sides, and receive all the evidence that could be produced, in writing or otherwise. The partners here would then bind themselves to stand by the decision and make good their award, though it should cost them all they had in the world. But this did not please them; they were offended at it. So it came to nothing; and afterwards Mr. Sherley wrote, that if Mr. Winslow would meet him in France, the Low Countries, or Scotland, let him name the place, and he would come to him there. But owing to the troubles that now began to arise in our own nation and other reasons, this did not come to any effect.

What made them especially desirous to bring things to an end was partly to stop the aspersions cast upon them about it—though they believed that they had suffered the greatest wrong and had most cause for complaint; and partly because they feared a fall in the price of cattle, in which the greatest part of their means was invested. This was no vain fear; for it fell indeed before they had reached a conclusion, and so suddenly that the price of a cow which a month before had been at £20, now fell to

£5; and a goat that went at £3 or fifty shillings, would now yield but eight shillings or ten shillings at the most. Everyone had feared a fall in cattle, but it was thought it would be by degrees, and not straight from the highest pitch to the lowest. It was a great loss to many and some were ruined. Another reason why they so much wished to close their accounts was that many of them were growing aged —and indeed it was a rare thing that so many partners should all live together so many years. And they saw many changes were likely to occur, so they were loth to leave these entanglements upon their children and posterity, who might be driven to move their homes as they had done; indeed they themselves might have to do so before they died. However, things had still to be left open; but next year they ripened somewhat, though they were then less able to pay for the reasons mentioned above.

"But ther fell out some difference aboute baptising, he holding it ought only to be by diping, and putting the whole body under water, and that sprinkling was unlawful."

CHAPTER XXI

[*1641*]

Mr. Sherley being weary of this controversy and desirous to end it, wrote to Mr. John Atwood and Mr. William Collier, two of the inhabitants of this place, and special acquaintances of his, and desired them to be intermediaries and advise the partners here as to some way of reaching a composition by mutual agreement. He also wrote to the partners similarly, in part as follows:

James Sherley in England to Governor Bradford at New Plymouth:

Sir, I have written so much concerning the closing of our accounts that I confess I do not know what more to write. If you desire an end, as you seem to do, there are, I think, only two ways: either we can perfect all accounts, from the first to the last, on both sides; or we must do it by compounding, and this way, first or last, we shall have to come to. If we fight about it at law, we shall both only cleave the air, and the lawyers will be the chief gainers. Then let us set to the work one way or another and make an end, so that I may not continue to suffer both in my reputation and my business. Nor are you free in this respect. The gospel suffers by your delay, and causes its followers to be ill spoken of. . . . Do not be afraid to make a fair and reasonable offer; believe me I shall not take advantage of you; or else let Mr. Winslow come over and let him have full power to compound with me. Otherwise, let the accounts be fully made up so that we may close according to the figures. Now, blessed be God, times are so much changed here that I hope to see many of you return to your native country again, and have such freedom and liberty as the word of God prescribes. Our bishops were never so near a downfall as now.[1] God has miraculously confounded them, and brought down all their popish and Machiavellian plots and projects upon their own heads. . . . I pray you take it seriously into consideration; let each give way a little that we may meet. . . . Be you and all yours kindly saluted. So I ever rest,

Your loving friend,
JAMES SHERLEY.

Clapham, May 18th, 1641.

Being urged by this letter, and also by Mr. Atwood's and Mr. Collier's mediation, to bring things to an end, and by none more earnestly than by their own desires, the New Plymouth Partners took this course. They appointed these two men to meet them on a certain day and summoned other friends on both sides, and Mr. Freeman, brother-in-law of Mr. Beauchamp. Having drawn up an inventory of all remaining stock whatsoever, such as housing, boats, the bark, and all implements belonging to them,

---

[1] The troubles of Charles I were mounting; he had been forced to sacrifice his chief minister, the Earl of Strafford, who was beheaded a few days before this letter was written. Cromwell and his Puritan Roundheads were soon to win their first victories.

used during the period of trading; together with the surplus of all commodities, such as beads, knives, hatchets, cloth or anything else, both valueless and saleable; with all debts, both bad and collectable; and having spent several days upon it with the help of all books and papers, either in their hands or those of Josias Winslow, their accountant, they found the total sum on valuation amounted to £1400. They then all of them took a voluntary and solemn oath, in the presence of one another and of all their friends above mentioned now present, that this was all that any of them knew or could remember; and Josias Winslow did the same on his part. But the truth is the valuation was too low; for, as an instance, in reckoning some cattle taken from Mr. Allerton, a cow which had cost £25 was so valued in this account; but she subsequently realized only £4-15-0. Also, being conscientious about their oaths, they included all that they knew of which was owing to the stock, but they did not make such a diligent search concerning what the stock might owe them, so that many scattered debts fell upon them afterwards, which they had not charged in.

However, this done, they drew up certain articles of agreement between Mr. Atwood, on Mr. Sherley's behalf, and themselves.

Articles of Agreement made and concluded on October 15th, 1641:

Whereas there was a partnership[2] for a period of years agreed upon between James Sherley, John Beauchamp,

---

[2] The partnership here dissolved was the one set up in 1627 and 1628 for the purchase of the London adventurers' interest in the colony and the conduct of the colony's trade, as described above, p. 239.

and Richard Andrews, of London, merchants, and William Bradford, Edward Winslow, Thomas Prince, Myles Standish, William Brewster, John Alden, John Howland, and Isaac Allerton, in a trade of beaver skins and other furs from New England; and the term of the said partnership having expired, various consignments of goods having been sent to New England by the said James Sherley, John Beauchamp, Richard Andrews, and many large returns made from New England by the said William Bradford, Edward Winslow, etc.; a dispute arising about the expense incurred for two ships, the one called the *White Angel* of Bristol, and the other the *Friendship* of Barnstable, and a projected voyage in her, etc.; which said ships and their voyages the said William Bradford, etc., consider do not concern the accounts of the partnership; and whereas the accounts of the said partnership are found to be confused and cannot be clearly present, through default of Josias Winslow, the bookkeeper, and whereas the said W. B., etc., have received all their goods for the said trade from the aforesaid James Sherley, and have made most of their returns to him, by consent of the said John Beauchamp and Richard Andrews; and whereas, also, the said James Sherley has given power and authority to Mr. John Atwood, with the advice and consent of William Collier of Duxbury, on his behalf, to put an absolute end to the said partnership, with all and every accounts, reckonings, dues, claims, demands whatsoever, to the said James Sherley, John Beauchamp, and Richard Andrews, from the said W. B., etc., for and concerning the said beaver trade, and also the charge of the said two ships, and their voyages made or projected, whether just or unjust, from the world's beginning to this present, as also for the payment of a purchase of £1800 made by Isaac Allerton, on behalf of the said W. B., etc., and of the joint stock, shares, lands, and adventurers, whatsoever, in New England aforesaid, as appears by a deed bearing the date Nov. 6th, 1627; and also for and from such sum and sums of money or goods as are received by William Bradford, Thomas Prince, and Myles Standish, for the recovery of dues, by accounts between them, the said James Sherley, John Beauchamp, Richard Andrews, and Isaac Allerton, for the ship called the *White Angel*. Now the said John Atwood, with advice of the said William Collier, having had much communication and spent several days in discussion of the said disputes and accounts with the said W. B., etc.; and the said W. B., etc., having also with the said bookkeeper spent much time in collecting and listing the remainder of the stock of partnership for the said trade, and whatsoever has been received, or is due by the said attorneyship before expressed, and all manner of goods, debts and dues, thereunto belonging, which in all amount to the sum of £1400 or thereabout; and for better satisfaction of the said James Sherley, John Beauchamp, and Richard Andrews, the said W. B. and all the rest of the abovesaid partners, together with Josias Winslow the bookkeeper, have taken a voluntary oath that the said sum of £1400 or thereabout includes whatever they know, to the utmost of their remembrance.

In consideration of which, and to the end that a full, absolute, and final end may now be made, and all suits in law may be avoided, and love and peace continued, it is therefore agreed and concluded between the said John Atwood, with the advice and consent of the said William Collier, on behalf of the said James Sherley, to and with the said W. B., etc., in manner and form following: viz., that the said John Atwood shall procure a sufficient release and discharge under the hands and seals of the said James Sherley, John Beauchamp, and Richard Andrews, to be delivered fair and unconcealed to the said William Bradford, etc., at or before the last day of August, next ensuing the date hereof, whereby the said William Bradford, etc., their heirs, executors, and administrators and each of them shall be fully and absolutely acquitted and discharged of all actions, suits, reckonings, accounts, claims, and demands whatsoever, concerning the general stock of beaver trade, payment of the said £1800 for the purchase and all demands, reckonings, accounts, just or unjust, concerning the two ships, *White Angel* and *Friendship* aforesaid, together with whatsoever has been received by the said William Bradford of the goods or estate of Isaac Allerton, for satisfaction of the accounts of the said ship *White Angel* by virtue of a letter of attorney to him, Thomas Prince, and Myles Standish, directed from the said James Sherley, John Beauchamp, and Richard Andrews, for that purpose as aforesaid.

It is also agreed and concluded between the said parties to these presents, that the said W. B., E. W., etc., shall now be bound in £2400 for payment of £1200 in full satisfaction of all demands as aforesaid; to be paid in manner and form following; that is to say, £400 within two months next after the receipt of the aforesaid releases and discharges, £110 whereof is already in the hands of John Winthrop, senior, of Boston, Esquire, by the means of Richard Andrews aforesaid, and 80 lbs. of beaver now deposited in the hands of the said John Atwood, to be both in part payment of the said £400, and the other £800 to be paid £200 per annum to such assigns as shall be appointed, inhabiting either New Plymouth or Massachusetts, in such goods and commodities, and at such rates as the country shall afford at the time of delivery and payment; and in the meantime the said bond of £2400 to be deposited in the hands of the said John Atwood. And it is agreed upon, by and between the said parties to these presents, that if the said John Atwood shall not or cannot procure such said releases and discharges as aforesaid from the said James Sherley, John Beauchamp, and Richard Andrews, at or before the last day of August next ensuing the date hereof, that then the said John Atwood shall, at the said date precisely, redeliver, or cause to be delivered, unto the said W. B., E. W., etc., their said bond of £2400 and the said 80 lbs. of beaver, or the due value thereof, without any fraud or further delay; and for performance of all and each of the covenants and agreements herein contained and expressed, which on the one part and behalf of the said James Sherley are to be observed and performed, shall become bound in the sum of £2400 to them the said William Bradford, Edward Winslow, Thomas Prince, Myles Standish, William Brewster, John Alden, and John Howland. And it is lastly agreed upon between the said parties that these presents shall be left in trust, to be kept for both parties, in the hands of Mr. John Rayner, teacher of New Plymouth. In witness whereof, all the said parties have hereunto severally set their hands, the day and year first above written.

JOHN ATWOOD, WILLIAM BRADFORD, EDWARD WINSLOW, etc.

In the presence of Edmund Freeman, William Thomas, William Paddy, Nathaniel Souther.

Next year this long and tedious business came to an issue, as will appear, though not to a final end with all the parties; but so much for the present.

I had forgotten to insert that the church here had in 1638 invited and sent for Mr. Charles Chauncey, a reverend, godly, and very learned man, who stayed till the latter part of 1645—intending, after a trial, to choose him pastor, for the more convenient performance of the ministry, with Mr. John Rayner, the teacher. But there occurred some differences about baptism, he holding that it ought only to be done by dipping and putting the whole body under water, and that sprinkling was unlawful. The church conceded that immersion or dipping, was lawful, but not so convenient in this cold country. But they could not allow that sprinkling, which nearly all the churches of Christ use to this day, was unlawful and merely a human invention. They were willing to yield to him as far as they could, and to allow him to practice according to his convictions, and granted that when he came to administer the ordinance, he might perform it in that way for any who so desired, provided he allowed Mr. Rayner, when requested, to baptize by sprinkling. But he said he could not yield to this. So the church procured some other ministers to discuss the point with him publicly, such as Mr. Ralph Partridge of Duxbury. But he was not satisfied; so the church sent to several other churches to ask their help and advice in the matter, and with his will and consent sent them his arguments—such as to the church of Boston in Massachusetts, to be communicated to other churches there; and to the churches of Connecticut and New Haven, and many others. They received very able answers from them and other learned ministers, who all concluded against him. Their answers are too long to give here. But Mr. Chauncey was not satisfied. They considered that everything that was proper had been done, so Mr. Chauncey, who had been almost three years here, removed to Scituate, where he is still a minister of the church.

About this time, cattle and other things having fallen greatly in value, people began to be less affluent. Many had already gone to Duxbury, Marshfield, and other places, and amongst them many of the leading men, such as Mr. Winslow, Captain Standish, Mr. Alden. Others dropped away daily, with the result that the place became far less flourishing.

"But it may be demanded how came it to pass that so many wicked persons and profane people should so quickly come over to this land, and mixe them selves amongst them."

CHAPTER XXII

[*1642*]

It was strange to see and consider how wickedness grew and broke forth here in a land where it was so witnessed against, and so resolutely hunted down, and so severely punished when found out; as in no place that I have known or heard of; and to such an extent that they have been somewhat censured for the severity of their punishments. And yet all of this did not suppress the breaking out of sundry notorious sins, of which in this and other years we were given sad examples. There was not only incontinence between unmarried persons, for which many men and women were sharply punished, but also among married persons also. But that which is even worse, sodomy and other sins fearful to name broke out more than once. I say it may be justly marveled at, and cause us to fear and tremble at the thought of our corrupt natures, which are with so much difficulty bridled, subdued, and mortified—nay, and cannot be by any other means save the powerful grace of Christ's spirit. But, besides this, one reason may be that the Devil has a greater spite against the churches of Christ here because of their very determination to preserve holiness and purity and to punish the contrary wherever it arises in church or commonwealth, so that he might cast a blemish or stain upon them in the eyes of the world, which is usually over ready to pass judgment. I would rather think this than, as some have believed, that Satan has more power in these heathen lands than in more Christian nations, especially over the servants of God.

Another reason may be that, as with streams when their waters are stopped or dammed up, when evils find a passage they break forth with more violence, and make more noise and disturbance than when they are suffered to run quietly in their own channels. Wickedness, being here stopped by strict laws and narrowly looked into, so it cannot run its course freely, searches everywhere and at last breaks out when it gets an opening.

A third reason may be, as I am verily persuaded, that there are not more evils of this kind in proportion to our numbers than in other places; but they are here more discovered and seen and made public by search, inquisition, and punishment; for the church examines its members closely, and the civil magistrates too look into these matters more than elsewhere. Besides, the people are few in comparison with other places, where the very numbers make it possible to conceal evil more easily; here it is brought to light and set out plainly to view as on a hill.

But to proceed. A letter came from the Governor of the Bay to those here, touching the aforementioned matters, which, since it may be useful, I shall here insert.

Sir:

Having an opportunity to signify the desires of our General Court in two things of special importance, I willingly take this occasion to impart them to you, that you may seek counsel of your magistrates and elders, and give us your advice thereon. The first is concerning heinous offenses as to uncleanness, the details of the particular cases with the circumstances and questions being herewith enclosed. The second thing concerns the islanders at Aquidneck;[1] seeing that most of them went from here for offenses against church or commonwealth and the rest are of like mind in their rejection of us. And it is no factional dispute which separates them from us, but in very truth they rend themselves from all true churches of Christ, and many of them from civil authority also. We have had some experience here with some of their emissaries who have come among us and defied the magistracy, ministry, churches, and church covenants as anti-Christian; secretly sowing the seeds of Familisme and of Anabaptistry,[2] to infect some and endanger others; so that we are not willing to join with them in any league or confederacy, but would like your advice as to how we may avoid them and keep our people from being infected by them.

Another thing I should mention to you concerns the maintenance of the beaver trade. If there is not a com-

---

[1] This was the Rhode Island settlement, founded by Anne Hutchinson, who with her followers had been driven out of the Massachusetts Bay colony in 1638. The court charges against Mrs. Hutchinson included blasphemy, heresy, and "traducing the ministers."

[2] The Familists were a sect which rejected formal dogma but professed love for all human beings, no matter how depraved; it had adherents in England and Holland in the 16th and early 17th centuries. The Anabaptists were another dissident Protestant sect; they believed in the strict separation of church and state, and hence were particularly unpopular in Boston, which was then the capital of a small theocracy.

pany to control it wherever the English have jurisdiction, so that all will agree as to their way of trade, the Indians will abuse us and the trade will be overthrown. For this reason we have lately put it into order among us, and hope for encouragement from you. Not to trouble you further, I remain with my loving remembrance of yourself,

Your loving friend,
Ri. Bellingham.

The note enclosed follows on the other side.

Worthy and beloved Sir:

Your letter (with questions enclosed) I have communicated to our assistants, and we have referred them to the reverend elders among us, some of whose answers we are enclosing; from the rest we have not received any. The distance between us is the reason for the delay, and this also prevents the elders from taking counsel together.

For ourselves (you know our breeding and abilities), we prefer to have light from you and others to whom God has given greater gifts than to presume to give our judgment in such difficult and important cases. Yet, open to correction and submission to better judgments, we propose this one thing to your prudent consideration: it seems to us, in the case of willful murder, that though a man did smite or wound another with the full purpose or desire to kill him (which is murder in high degree before God) yet if he did not die, the magistrate must not take the other's life. So in other gross and foul sins, though the attempt is made, which in the sight of God is the same as the accomplishment, yet we doubt whether it may be safe for the magistrate to proceed to the death penalty; we think, upon the ground stated, that he may not. . . . Yet we admit the foulness of the circumstances and frequency of the offense darkens the issue, and causes us to desire further light from you, or from anyone else to whom God may give it.

As for the islanders, we have no speech with them, nor desire to have, further than necessity or humanity may require.

As for trade, we have held to an orderly course as far as we could, and have been sorry to see the spoils thereof go to others, and fear it will not be recovered. But in these and other things which concern the common good, we shall be willing to advise and concur with you. Thus with my love to yourself and the rest of our worthy friends, your assistants, I take leave, and rest,

Your loving friend,
W. B.[3]

Plymouth, March 3, 1642.

It may be demanded how so many wicked persons and profane people should so quickly come to this land and mix among the settlers, seeing it was religious men who began the work and they came for religion's sake. I confess this may be marveled at, especially in time to come, when the reasons cannot be fully known; and all the more since here there were so many hardships to be overcome. I shall endeavor to give some answer. And first, as it says in the Gospel, it is ever to be remembered that where the Lord begins to sow good seed, there the envious man endeavors to sow tares. Men who had come over into a wilderness where there was much hard work

---

[3] Following his reply, Bradford inserted the opinions, written mainly in Latin, of the three ministers consulted—Mr. Raynor, Mr. Partridge, and Mr. Chauncey—on the questions which had been under discussion, namely, how much pressure the magistrate can exert to extract a confession; and analyses of the sins of murder, adultery, sodomy, and bestiality, and the punishment therefor, as set forth in the Old Testament and by church authorities.

to be done building and planting had to take what help they could get when they could not get the kind they wanted; thus many undisciplined servants were brought over, both men and women; who, when their time of service had expired, became heads of families, giving increase to this class. Another reason was that men finding so many good people willing to come to these parts began to make a trade of it, to transport passengers and their goods, hiring ships for that end; and then to make up their freight and increase their profits, they filled up their ships with any who had money to pay. And thus the country became pestered with many unworthy persons. Again, since the Lord's blessing usually follows His people in outward as well as spiritual things (though afflictions are mixed in too), many people cling to God's people, as they followed Christ, for the sake of the loaves (John, VI, 26; Exod., XII, 38). Others were sent by their friends in the hope that they would improve themselves; others that they might be freed of such burdens, and freed of the shame of dissolute relatives. And thus, by one means or another, in twenty years' time, it is a question if the greater number have not grown worse.

I now come to the conclusion of the long and tedious business between the partners here and those in England.

James Sherley in England to the partners of New Plymouth:

Loving Friends,—Mr. Bradford, Mr. Winslow, Mr. Prince, Captain Standish, Mr. Brewster, Mr. Alden, and Mr. Howland,

Give me leave to include you all in one letter concerning the final end and conclusion of this tiresome and tedious business, which I think I may truly say is uncomfortable and unprofitable for all. . . . It has pleased God now to show us a way to cease all suits and disputes, and to conclude in peace and love as we began. I am content to make good what Mr. Atwood and you have agreed upon, and for that end have sent him an absolute and general release to you all, and if it lacks anything to make it complete, write it yourselves and it shall be done, provided that you all, either jointly or severally, seal a similar discharge to me. For that purpose I have drawn up a copy and sent it to Mr. Atwood with the one I have sealed for you. Mr. Andrews has sealed an acquittance also and sent it to Mr. Winthrop, with such directions as he thought fit, and, as I hear, has transferred his debt, which he makes £544, to the gentlemen of the Bay. Mr. Weld, Mr. Peters, and Mr. Hibbins have taken a great deal of pains with Mr. Andrews, Mr. Beauchamp, and myself, to bring us to agree, and we have had many meetings and spent much time upon it. Mr. Andrews wished you to have one third of the £1200, and the Bay two thirds; but to do that we three partners here must have agreed to it, which would be a difficult matter now. However, Mr. Weld, Mr. Peters, Mr. Hibbins, and I have agreed, and they are giving you their bond to settle with Mr. Beauchamp and procure his general release, and thus free you from all the trouble and expense that he might put you to. Now our agreement is, that you must pay to the gentlemen of the Bay £900, they to bear all expenses which may in any way arise concerning the free and absolute clearing of you from us three; and you to have the other £300. . . .

Upon receiving my release from you I will send you your bonds for the purchase money. I would have sent them now, but first I want Mr. Beauchamp to release you as well as I, because they bind you to him as well as to me, though I know that if a man is bound to twelve men, when one releases him it is the same as if all did so; so my discharge is to that extent sufficient. So do not doubt but you shall have them and your power of attorney, and anything else that is fit. . . .

Your loving and kind friend in what I may or can,
JAMES SHERLEY.
June 14th, 1642.

Mr. Andrews' discharge was similar to Mr. Sherley's. He was by agreement to have £500 of the money, which he gave to those at the Bay, who brought his discharge and received the money, viz.; one third of the £500 paid down, and the rest in four equal payments, to be paid yearly, for which they gave their bonds. £44 more was demanded, in addition; but they believed they could arrange it with Mr. Andrews, so it was not included in the bond.

But Mr. Beauchamp would give way in nothing, and demanded £400 of the partners here, sending a release to a friend to be delivered to them on receipt of the money. But his release was not perfect, having left out some of the partners' names, with some other defects; and besides, the other partners there gave them to understand he had not nearly so much due to him. So no end was made with him till four years after.

"We therfore doe conceive it our bounden duty, without delay, to enter into a presente consociation amongst ourselves, for mutuall help and strength in all our future concernments."

CHAPTER XXIII

[*1643*]

I must open this year with an event which brought great sadness and mourning to them all. About the 18th of April, died their reverend elder, my dear and loving friend, Mr. William Brewster, a man who had done and suffered much for the Lord Jesus and the gospel's sake, and had borne his part in weal or woe with this poor persecuted church for over thirty-five years in England, Holland, and this wilderness, and had done the Lord and them faithful service in his calling. Notwithstanding the many troubles and sorrows he passed through, the Lord upheld him to a great age; he was nearly fourscore years, if not quite, when he died. He had this blessing added by the Lord to all the rest; he died in his bed in peace, in the midst of his friends, who mourned and wept over him, and gave him what help and comfort they could; and he, too, comforted them whilst he could. His illness was not long, and until the last day he did not keep his bed. His speech continued until about the last half day and then failed him; and at about nine or ten o'clock that evening he died, without any pangs at all. A few hours before, he drew his breath short, and some few minutes from the end he drew it long, as a man fallen into a sound sleep—without any gaspings—and so, sweetly departed this life into a better.

I would ask, was he the worse for any of his former sufferings? What do I say? Worse? Nay; he was surely the better, for now they were added to his honor. "It is a manifest token," says the Apostle (II Thessalonians, 1, 5, 6, 7), "of the righteous judgment of God that ye may be counted worthy of the Kingdom of God, for which ye also suffer; seeing it is a righteous thing with God to recompense tribulation to them that trouble you; and to you who are troubled, rest with us, when the Lord Jesus shall be revealed from Heaven, with His mighty angels." And I Peter, IV, 14: "If you be reproached for the name of Christ, happy are ye, for the spirit of glory and of God resteth upon you." What though he lacked the riches and pleasures of the world in this life, and pompous monuments at his funeral? Yet "the memorial of the just shall be blessed, when the name of the wicked shall rot,"— with their marble monuments (Proverbs, x, 7).

I should say something of his life, if to say a little were not worse than to be silent. But I cannot wholly forbear, though perhaps more may be written at some later time. After he had attained some learning, viz., the knowledge of the Latin tongue and some insight into Greek, and had spent some little time at Cambridge—then being first seasoned with the seeds of grace and virtue—he went to court, and served that religious and godly gentleman, Mr. Davison, for several years, when he was Secretary of State. His master found him so discreet and faithful that he trusted him more than all the others who were round him, and employed him in all matters of greatest trust and secrecy. He esteemed him rather as a son than a servant; and knowing his wisdom and godliness he would converse with him in private more as a friend and familiar than as a master. He accompanied him, when he was sent as ambassador by the Queen into the Low Countries, in the Earl of Leicester's time,[1]—besides other important affairs of state, to receive possession of the cautionary towns,[2] in token of which the keys of Flushing were delivered to him in Her Majesty's name. Mr. Davison held them some time, handing them over to Mr. Brewster, who kept them under his pillow the first night. On his departure, the Netherlands honored Mr. Davison with a gold chain; he gave it into the keeping of Mr. Brewster, and when they arrived in England commanded him to wear it as they rode through the country, until they arrived at court. He remained with him through his troubles, when later, he was dismissed in connection with the death of the Queen of Scots,[3] and for some good time after, doing him much faithful service.

Afterwards Mr. Brewster went and lived in the country, much respected by his friends and the gentlemen of the neighborhood, especially the godly and religious. He did much good there in promoting and furthering religion, not only by his practice and example and the encourage-

---

[1] This was the time when Queen Elizabeth was sending aid to the Dutch in their fight against Spanish rule.
[2] Towns turned over to Elizabeth as security for the performance by the Dutch of their treaty obligations.
[3] The warrant for the execution of Mary Stuart was placed in the hands of Davison, as one of Elizabeth's secretaries of state. Mary was beheaded Feb. 8, 1587. Elizabeth afterward repudiated responsibility for the act and discharged Davison, saying he had been too hasty.

ment of others, but by procuring good preachers for the places thereabouts, and persuading others to help and assist in such work, generally taking most of the expense on himself—sometimes beyond his means. Thus he continued for many years, doing the best he could and walking according to the light he saw, till the Lord revealed Himself further to him. In the end, the tyranny of the bishops against godly preachers and people, in silencing the former and persecuting the latter caused him and many more to look further into things, and to realize the unlawfulness of their episcopal callings, and to feel the burden of their many anti-Christian corruptions, which both he and they endeavored to throw off; in which they succeeded, as the beginning of this treatise shows.

After they had joined themselves together in communion, as was mentioned earlier, he was a special help and support to them. On the Lord's day they generally met at his house, which was a manor of the bishop's, and he entertained them with great kindness when they came, providing for them at heavy expense to himself. He was the leader of those who were captured at Boston, in Lincolnshire, suffering the greatest loss, and was one of the seven who were kept longest in prison and afterwards bound over to the assizes. After he came to Holland, he suffered much hardship, having spent most of his means, with a large family to support, and being from his breeding and previous mode of life not so fit for such laborious employment as others were. But he always bore his troubles with much cheerfulness and content.

Towards the latter part of those twelve years spent in Holland, his circumstances improved, and he lived well and plentifully; for through his knowledge of Latin he was able to teach many foreign students English. By his method they acquired it quickly and with great fluency, for he drew up rules to learn it by, after the manner of teaching Latin; and many gentlemen, both Danes and Germans, came to him, some of them being sons of distinguished men. By the help of some friends he also had means to set up a printing press, and thus had employment enough, and owing to many books being forbidden to be printed in England, they might have had more work than they could do. But on moving to this country all these things were laid aside again, and a new way of living must be framed, in which he was in no way unwilling to take his part and bear his burden with the rest, living often for many months without corn or bread, with nothing but fish to eat, and often not even that. He drank nothing but water for many years, indeed until five or six years before his death; and yet by the blessing of God he lived in health to a very old age. He labored in the fields as long as he was able; yet when the church had no other minister, he taught twice every Sabbath, and that both powerfully and profitably, to the great edification and comfort of his hearers, many being brought to God by his ministry. He did more in this way in a single year than many who have their hundreds a year do in all their lives.

As for his personal qualities, he was favored above many; he was wise and discreet and well-spoken, having a grave and deliberate utterance, with a very cheerful spirit. He was very sociable and pleasant among his friends, of an humble and modest mind and a peaceable disposition, under-valuing himself and his own abilities and sometimes over-valuing others. He was innocent in his life and conversation, which gained him the love of those without as well as those within; nevertheless, he would tell them plainly of their faults, both public and privately, but in such a way that it was usually well taken. He was tender-hearted and compassionate with those in misery, especially when they were of good birth and rank and had fallen into want and poverty, either for religion's sake or through the oppression of others; he would always say that of all men such deserved to be most pitied. None displeased him more than those who would haughtily and proudly exalt themselves, having risen from nothing, and having little else to commend them than a few fine clothes or more means than others. When preaching, he deeply moved and stirred the affections, and he was very plain and direct in what he taught, being thereby the more profitable to his hearers. He had a singularly good gift of prayer, both public and private, in ripping up the heart and conscience before God, in the humble confession of sin and begging the mercies of God in Christ for the pardon of it. He always thought it better for ministers to pray oftener and divide their prayers, than to be long and tedious—except on special occasions, such as days of humiliation and the like; because he believed that heart and spirit, especially in the weak, could with difficulty continue so long to stand bent, as it were, towards God—as is meet in prayer—without flagging and failing. In the government of the church, which was proper to his office as elder, he was careful to preserve good order and purity both in doctrine and communion, and to suppress any error or contention that might begin to arise; and accordingly God gave success to his endeavors in this, all his days, and he was given to see the fruit of his labors. But I must break off, though I have only touched the heads of a few things.

I cannot but take occasion here to wonder at the marvelous providence of God, that, notwithstanding the many changes these people went through, and the many enemies they had and the difficulties they met with, so many of them should live to a very old age. It was not only their reverend elder—for one swallow makes no summer, as they say—but many more of them, some dying about and before this time and some still living, who reached sixty or sixty-five years of age, others seventy and over, and some nearly eighty, as he was. It must needs be accounted for by more than natural reasons, for it is found in experience that change of air, hunger, unwholesome food, much drinking of water, sorrows and troubles, etc., are all enemies to health, causing many diseases, loss of natural vigor and shortness of life. Yet all those unfavorable conditions were their lot. They went from England to Holland, where they found both worse air and diet than where they came from; thence, enduring a long imprisonment, as it were, aboard ship, they came to New England; and their way of living here has already been shown, and what crosses, troubles, fears, wants, and sorrows, they were liable to. In a sense they may say with the Apostle (II Corinthians, XI, 26, 27) that they were "in journeyings often, in perils of water, in perils of robbers, in perils by their own nation, in perils by the heathen, in perils in the wilderness, in perils on the sea, in perils among false brethren; in weariness and painfulness, in watchings often, in hunger and thirst, in fastings often, in cold and nakedness." What was it then that upheld them? It was God's visitation that preserved their spirits—(Job, X, 12): "Thou hast granted me life and favor, and thy visitation hath preserved my spirits." He that upheld the Apostle upheld them: they were "persecuted, but not forsaken; cast down, but not destroyed;"—(II Corinthians,

IV, 9)—"as unknown, and yet well known; as dying and behold we live; as chastened and not killed" (II Corinthians, VI, 9). God, it seems, would have all men behold and observe such mercies and works of His providence as towards His people, that they in like cases might be encouraged to depend upon God in their trials, and also bless His name when they see His goodness towards others. Man lives not by bread alone. It is not by good and dainty fare, by peace and rest and heart's ease, in enjoying the contentment and good things of this world only, that health is preserved and life prolonged. God in such examples would have the world see and behold that He can do it without them; and if the world will shut its eyes and take no notice of it, yet He would have his people see and consider it. Daniel was better off with pulse than others with the king's dainties. Jacob, though he went from his own nation to another people, and passed through famine, fear, and many afflictions, yet lived till old age, and died sweetly and rested in the Lord, as numberless other of God's servants have done, and still shall do through God's goodness, notwithstanding all the malice of their enemies: "When the branch of the wicked shall be cut off before his day"—(Job, XV, 32)—"and bloody and deceitful men shall not live out half their days." (Psalms, LV, 23.)

Owing to the plotting of the Narragansetts, ever since the Pequot war, the Indians had formed a general conspiracy against the English in all parts, as was partly discovered the year before, and now confirmed by various discoveries and the free confessions of several Indians from different places. They therefore sought means to prevent the trouble and secure themselves, which ultimately resulted in the formation of closer union and confederation, defined by articles from which the following extracts are taken.

Articles of Confederation between the Colonies under the Governments of Massachusetts, New Plymouth, Connecticut, New Haven, and those in combination therewith.[4]

Whereas we all came into these parts of America with one and the same end and aim, namely to advance the kingdom of Our Lord Jesus Christ and to enjoy the liberties of the Gospel in purity and peace; and whereas in our settling, by a wise providence of God, we find ourselves further dispersed along the seacoasts and rivers than was at first intended, so that we cannot, as desired, conveniently live under one government and jurisdiction; and whereas we live surrounded by people of several tribes and strange languages, who may hereafter prove injurious to us and our posterity, . . . we therefore conceive it our bounden duty without delay to enter into an immediate consociation among ourselves for mutual help and strength in our future concerns, so that in national and religious affairs, as in other respects, we may be and continue one, according to the tenor and true meaning of the ensuing articles.

1. Wherefore it is fully agreed and concluded by and between the parties or jurisdictions above named and they jointly and severally by these presents do conclude and agree, that they all be, and henceforth be called by the name of the United Colonies of New England.

---

[4] Roger Williams was told that his colony of Rhode Island was not eligible as an independent unit and that he must join forces with a neighboring colony in order to be admitted. Maine and New Hampshire were also excluded. Maine was now a vast grant held by Sir Ferdinand Gorges.

2. The said United Colonies, for themselves and their posterity jointly and severally, hereby enter into a firm and perpetual league of friendship and amity, for offense and defense, mutual advice and succor, upon all just occasions, both for preserving and propagating the truth of the Gospel, and for their own mutual safety and welfare.

3. It is further agreed that the colonies which at present are or hereafter shall be begun within the limits of Massachusetts shall be forever under Massachusetts, and shall have separate jurisdiction among themselves in all cases as a complete body; and that New Plymouth, Connecticut, and New Haven shall each of them similarly have separate jurisdiction and government within their limits. . . .

4. It is by these confederates agreed that the expense of all just wars, whether offensive or defensive, upon what party or member of this confederation soever they fall, shall, both in men, provisions, and all other disbursements, be borne by all the parties of this confederation, in different proportions, according to their different abilities, . . . according to the different numbers which from time to time shall be found in each jurisdiction upon a true and just count, . . . and that according to the different expenses of each jurisdiction and colony, the whole advantage of the war—if it please God to bless their endeavors—whether in lands, goods, or persons, shall be proportionately divided amongst the said confederates.

5. It is further agreed that if these jurisdictions, or any colony under or in combination with them be invaded by any enemy whatsoever, upon notice and request of any three magistrates of the jurisdiction so invaded, the rest of the confederates without any further meeting or expostulation shall forthwith send aid to the confederate in danger, but in different proportions; viz., Massachusetts a hundred men sufficiently armed and provided, and

each of the rest forty-five so armed and provided, or any lesser number if less be required, according to this proportion; . . . but none of the jurisdictions to exceed these numbers till by a meeting of the commissioners for this confederation further aid appear necessary; and this proportion to continue till upon knowledge of greater numbers in each jurisdiction, which shall be brought before the next meeting, some other proportion be ordered. . . .

6. It is also agreed that for the management of all affairs concerning the whole confederation, two commissioners shall be chosen by and out of each of these four jurisdictions; namely, two for Massachusetts, two for New Plymouth, two for Connecticut, and two for New Haven, being all in church fellowship with us, who shall bring full power from their General Courts respectively to hear, examine, weigh, and determine all affairs of war or peace, leagues, aids, expenses, etc., . . . not intermeddling with the government of any of the jurisdictions, which by the third article is reserved entirely to themselves. But if these eight commissioners when they meet shall not all agree, any six of the eight agreeing shall have power to settle and determine the business in question. But if six do not agree, then such propositions, with their reasons, so far as they have been debated, shall be referred to the four General Courts, viz.: Massachusetts, New Plymouth, Connecticut, and New Haven; and if at all the said General Courts the business so referred be concluded, then it shall be prosecuted by the confederates and all their members. It is further agreed that these eight commissioners shall meet once every year, besides special meetings, to consider and conclude all affairs belonging to this confederation, which meeting shall always be on the first Thursday in September; and that the next meeting after the date of these presents, which shall be accounted the second meeting, shall be at Boston in Massachusetts, the

third at Hartford, the fourth at New Haven, the fifth at New Plymouth, and so on, successively—if in the meantime some central place be not agreed upon as more convenient for all the jurisdictions.

7. It is further agreed that at each meeting of these eight commissioners, whether ordinary or extraordinary, six of them agreeing may choose a president from among themselves, whose duty shall be to direct the proceedings of that particular meeting; but he shall be invested with no such power or respect as might hinder the propounding or progress of any business, or in any way turn the scales, otherwise than in the preceding article is agreed.

8. It is also agreed that the commissioners for this confederation hereafter at their meetings, whether ordinary or extraordinary, as they may have commission or opportunity, shall endeavor to frame agreements in cases of a civil nature, in which all the colonies are interested, for the preservation of peace among themselves, and preventing as much as possible all causes of war or dispute with others. . . .

9. And since the justest wars may have dangerous consequences, especially for the smaller settlements in these United Colonies, it is agreed that neither Massachusetts, New Plymouth, Connecticut, nor New Haven, nor any member of any of them, shall at any time hereafter begin, undertake, or engage themselves, or this confederation or any part thereof, in any way whatsoever (sudden exigencies excepted), without the consent and agreement of six of the forementioned eight commissioners. . . .

10. That on special occasions, when meetings are summoned by three magistrates of any jurisdiction, if any of the commissioners do not come, due notice having been given or sent, it is agreed that four of the commissioners shall have power to direct a war which cannot be delayed, and to send for due proportions of men out of each jurisdiction; but not less than six shall determine the justice of

the war, or allow the demands or bills of expenses, or cause any levies to be made for it.

11. It is further agreed, that if any of the confederates shall hereafter break any of these articles of agreement, or in any way injure any one of the other jurisdictions, such breach of agreement or injury shall be duly considered by the commissioners for the other jurisdictions; that both peace and this present confederation may be entirely preserved without violation.

12. Lastly, this perpetual confederation and its several articles, being read and seriously considered both by the General Court of Massachusetts and by the commissioners for New Plymouth, Connecticut, and New Haven, is fully allowed and confirmed by three of the afore-named confederates, viz., Massachusetts, Connecticut, and New Haven; the commissioners for New Plymouth, having no commission to conclude, request time to advise with their General Court. . . .

At a meeting of the commissioners for the confederation held at Boston on the 7th of September, it appearing that the General Court of New Plymouth, and the several townships thereof, have read, considered, and approved these articles of confederation, as appears by commission from their General Court bearing date the 29th of August, 1643, to Mr. Edward Winslow and Mr. William Collier, to ratify and confirm the same on their behalfs; we therefore the commissioners for Massachusetts, Connecticut, and New Haven, do also, for our several governments subscribe to them.

JOHN WINTHROP, Gov. of Mass.	GEORGE FENWICK
THOMAS DUDLEY	EDWARD HOPKINS
THEOPH. EATON	THOMAS GREGSON

At their first meeting held at Boston on the above mentioned date, amongst other things they had the following matter of great importance to consider. The Narragansetts, after subduing the Pequots, thought they were going to rule over all the Indians round them; but the English, especially those of Connecticut, were friendly with Uncas, sachem of the Monhigg tribe, which lived near them, as the Narragansetts did near those of Massachusetts. Uncas had been faithful to them in the Pequot war, and they had agreed to support him in his just liberties, and were willing that such of the surviving Pequots as had submitted to him, should remain with him and live quietly under his protection. This greatly increased his power and importance, and the Narragansetts could not endure to see it. So Miantinomo, their chief sachem, an ambitious man, tried secretly and by treachery according to the Indian way, to make away with him, hiring someone to kill him. They tried to poison him; that not succeeding, they planned to knock him on the head in the night in his house, or to shoot him—and such like devices.

But none of these plots taking effect, Miantinomo made open war upon Uncas, though it was contrary to his agreements with the English and the Monhiggs. He suddenly came upon him with 900 or 1000 men, without proclaiming war. Uncas at that time had not half so many; but it pleased God to give him the victory, and he slew many of the Narragansetts, and wounded many more; but most important of all, he took Miantinomo prisoner. But as he was a great man, and the Narragansetts a powerful people who would be sure to seek revenge, he did nothing until he had taken the advice of the English; so by the help and direction of those of Connecticut, he kept him prisoner until this meeting of the confederation.

The commissioners weighed the cause between Uncas and Miantinomo, and the evidence being duly considered, the commissioners saw that Uncas would not be safe while Miantinomo lived. So they concluded that he might justly put such a false and blood-thirsty enemy to death; but in his own jurisdiction, not on English ground. They advised that in his execution all mercy and toleration should be shown, contrary to the practice of the Indians who use tortures and all kinds of cruelty. Furthermore, as Uncas had hitherto shown himself a friend to the English, and had consulted them in this, if the Narragansett Indians, or others, unjustly attacked Uncas for this execution, the commissioners promised that the English would assist and protect him as far as they could against violence, upon notice and request. Uncas followed this advice, and accordingly executed Miantinomo,[5] in a fair manner, with due respect for the honor of his position. But what followed on the Narragansetts' part will appear later.

---

[5] Miantinomo was killed by a blow on his head from a hatchet. A stone monument to him now stands on the scene of his capture, near Norwich, Connecticut.

"And thus was this poore church left like an anciente mother, growne old, and forsaken of her children . . ."

CHAPTER XXIV

[*1644*]

M*r*. Edward Winslow was chosen governor this year.

Many having left here, owing to the district being so limited and barren, and their finding better accommodation elsewhere—and several others looking for opportunity to go, the church began seriously to consider whether it were not better to remove jointly to some other place, than to be thus weakened, and, as it were, insensibly dissolved. Much consultation took place, and opinions varied. Some were for staying together here, arguing that people could live here, if only they were content, and that it was not so much for necessity that they removed as for enriching themselves. Others were resolute upon removal, and signified that here they could not stay and that if the church did not remove they must. This swayed many to agree to removal rather than that there should be a total dissolution, if a place could be found suitable to accommodate the whole body more conveniently and comfortably and with room for development, should others join them for their greater strength and better subsistence.

With these provisos, the majority consented to removal to a place called Nauset, which had been superficially viewed, and the good-will of the owners obtained. They began too late to see the error of their previous policy, for they found they had already given away the best and most convenient places to others and now were in want of such situations themselves; for Nauset was about fifty miles from here, on the outskirts of the country, and remote from all society. Furthermore, on closer examination, they found it would prove so limited that it would not suffice to accommodate the whole body, much less be capable of any expansion. So in a short time they would be worse off there than they were now. This made them change their resolution; but such as were resolved upon removal took advantage of the agreement made, and went on notwithstanding; nor could the rest hinder them, since they had already made some beginning.

Thus was this poor church left like an ancient mother, grown old and forsaken of her children—though not in their affections, yet as regards their bodily presence and personal helpfulness. Her ancient members being most of them worn away by death, and those of later times being, like children, transferred to other families, she, like a widow, was left only to trust in God. Thus she who had made many rich, herself became poor.

Soon another broil was begun by the Narragansetts. Though they had unjustly made war upon Uncas, as before described, the winter before this, they earnestly urged the Governor of Massachusetts to permit them to make war again in revenge for the death of their sagamore, claiming that Uncas had first received and accepted ransom for Miantinomo, and then put him to death. But the Governor refused the presents they brought, and told them it was they themselves who had done wrong and broken the conditions of peace; neither he nor any of the English would allow them to make any further war upon

Uncas, and that if they did so the English must assist him and oppose them; but if when the commissioners met, the matter having had a fair hearing, it could be proved that he had received this ransom, they would make Uncas return it.

Notwithstanding this, at the spring of the year they gathered in great power, and fell upon Uncas, killing many of his men and wounding more, besides receiving some loss themselves. Uncas then called for aid from the English. They told him the Narragansetts' charges; he denied them. They told him it must come to trial, and if he was innocent, should the Narragansetts refuse to desist, they would assist him. So at this meeting they sent both to Uncas and the Narragansetts, and required their sagamores to come or send deputies to the commissioners, who had now met at Hartford, promising a fair and impartial hearing of all their grievances, and that all wrongs should be redressed. They also promised that they should come and return without any danger or molestation.

Upon which the Narragansetts sent one sagamore and some other deputies, with full power to do what was thought right. Uncas came in person, accompanied by some of his chiefs. After discussion, the commissioners made the following declaration to the Narragansett deputies:

1. That they did not find any proof of a ransom being agreed upon.
2. It did not appear that any wampum had been paid as a ransom, or any part of a ransom for Miantinomo's life.
3. That, had they in any way proved their charge against Uncas, the commissioners would have required him to make due satisfaction.

4. That if hereafter they could produce satisfactory proof, the English would consider it and proceed accordingly.

5. The commissioners required that neither they nor their allies, the Nyanticks, should make war or injurious assault upon Uncas or any of his tribe, until they could show proof of the ransom being given, unless he should first attack them.

6. That if they attacked Uncas, the English had undertaken to assist him.

Hereupon the Narragansett sachem, consulting with the other deputies, undertook on behalf of the Narragansetts and Nyanticks that no hostile acts should be committed upon Uncas or any of his tribe till after the next planting of corn; and that thereafter, before they made war they would give thirty days' notice to the Governor of Massachusetts or Connecticut. The commissioners, approving of this offer, required Uncas, as he expected the continuance of the favor of the English, to observe the same terms of peace with the Narragansetts and their people.

The foregoing conclusions were then subscribed by the commissioners for the several jurisdictions, on the 19th of Sept., 1644: Edward Hopkins, President; Simon Bradstreet, William Hathorne, Edward Winslow, John Brown, George Fenwick, Theoph. Eaton, Thomas Gregson.

The Narragansett deputies further promised that if, contrary to this agreement, any of the Nyantick Pequots made any attack upon Uncas or any of his people, they would deliver them to the English for punishment, and that they would not attempt to incite the Mohawks against Uncas during this truce. Their names were subscribed with their marks: Weetowish, Pampiamett, Chinnough, Pummunish.

"*Thus whilst the commissioners in care of the publick peace sought to quench the fire kindled amongst the Indeans these children of strife breath out threatenings, provocations, and warr against the English them selves.*"

CHAPTER XXV

[*1645*]

This year the commissioners were summoned to meet at Boston before their ordinary time, partly in regard to some differences between the French and the government of Massachusetts, about their aiding Governor La Tour against Monsieur d'Aulney; and partly about the Indians, who had broken the agreements of peace concluded last year. This meeting was held at Boston on July 28th.

Besides some underhand attacks made on both sides, the Narragansetts gathered a great power and fell upon Uncas and killed many of his men and wounded many more, far exceeding him in number, and having got a large number of arms. They did this without the knowledge and consent of the English, contrary to the former agreement, and were determined to continue the war, notwithstanding anything the English said or did. So, encouraged by their recent victory, and by a promise of assistance from the Mohawks—a strong, warlike, and desperate tribe—

they had already devoured Uncas and his people in their hopes, and would surely have done so in fact if the English had not quickly gone to his aid. But the English of Connecticut sent him forty men, as a garrison for him,[1] till the commissioners could meet and take further steps.

Having thus met, they forthwith sent three messengers, Sergeant John Davis, Benedict Arnold, and Francis Smith, with full and ample instructions both to the Narragansetts and Uncas, requiring them either to come in person or send qualified deputies; and if they refused or delayed, to warn them that the English were determined to oppose these hostile invasions, and that they had sent their men to defend Uncas, and to know of the Narragansetts whether they would stand by the former peace.

The messengers returned from the Narragansetts, not only with slights, but with a threatening answer. They also brought a letter from Mr. Roger Williams, assuring them that war would shortly break out, and the whole country would be aflame; and that the sachems of the Narragansetts had concluded a neutrality with the English of Providence and Aquidneck Island. Whereupon the commissioners, considering the great danger and provocations offered, and the necessity we should be put to of making war on the Narragansetts, and being cautious to have the way clear in a matter of such wide public concern to all the colonies, thought fit to advise with such of the magistrates and elders of Massachusetts as were at hand, and also with some of the chief military commanders there; who being assembled, it was then agreed:

---

[1] Uncas had a fort on a point of land running out into the Thames River, then called the Pequot River.

1. That our engagement bound us to aid and defend Uncas.

2. That this aid could not be confined to defense of him and his fort or habitation, but must be extended to the security of his liberty and property.

3. That this aid must be speedy, lest he should be swallowed up in the meantime.

4. The justice of the war being clear to ourselves and the rest then present, it was thought meet that the case should be stated, and the reasons and grounds of the war declared and published.

5. That a day of humiliation should be appointed, which was the fifth day of the week following.

6. It was also agreed by the commissioners that the total number of men to be raised throughout the colonies should be 300—Massachusetts 190, New Plymouth 40,[2] Connecticut 40, New Haven 30; and that considering Uncas was in instant danger, 40 men should forthwith be sent from Massachusetts for his relief—for the 40 previously sent from Connecticut had orders to stay only one month, and their time having expired, they returned; and the Narragansetts hearing of it, took the advantage and came suddenly upon him and gave him another blow, to his further loss, and were ready to do so again; but the 40 men from Massachusetts having arrived, they drew off.

The declaration of war which they published I shall not transcribe, as it is very long and is already in print. I will only note the insolent reception of it by the Narragansetts, and the answers to the three messengers sent from the commissioners to deliver it. They received them with scorn and contempt, and told them they resolved to have no

---

[2] These figures would indicate that Massachusetts Bay Colony was now almost five times as strong as Plymouth.

peace without the head of Uncas; that it mattered not who began the war, they were determined to continue it; that if the English did not withdraw their garrison from Uncas, they would procure the Mohawks against them. Ultimately they threatened that they would lay the English cattle in heaps as high as their houses, and that no Englishman should stir outside his door so much as to relieve himself, but he should be killed. When the messengers demanded guides to pass on through their country to deliver the message of the commissioners to Uncas, they refused them, and in scorn offered them an old Pequot woman. Nay, the messengers personally were in danger; for while the interpreter was speaking with them about the answer he should take back, some natives came and stood behind him with hatchets, according to their murderous manner; but one of his comrades gave him warning, and so all three broke off and came away. These and similar affronts so terrified the Indians they had with them, that they ran away, and left them to get home as best they could.

So the confederation hastened the preparations, according to the agreement, and sent to New Plymouth to despatch their forty men with all speed, to be stationed at Seekonk, lest it should be in danger before the rest were ready. They were all well armed with snaphance [3] guns, under command of Captain Standish. Those from other places were also led by able commanders, such as Captain Mason for Connecticut, etc. Major Gibbons [4] was made General, with such commissions and instructions as were proper.

---

[3] An old-time musket with a spring lock.
[4] Major Edward Gibbons was commander of the Massachusetts troops. He had formerly been with Morton at Merry Mount.

Everything being ready—some of the soldiers already started and the rest ready to march—the commissioners thought it right before any hostile act was committed, to return a present which had previously been sent to the Governor of Massachusetts from the Narragansett sachems, and though not accepted by him, had been laid by to be accepted or refused according to their behavior. So it was sent back by two messengers and an interpreter, who were further instructed to inform the Narragansetts that the men the English had already sent to Uncas and other parts, had express orders, so far, only to stand upon his or their defense, and not to attempt any invasion of the Narragansetts' country; and that even yet, if they made due reparation for what had past, and gave good security for the future, they should find that the English were as desirous of peace and as tender of Narragansett blood as ever. If therefore Pessecuss, Jenemo, with the other sachems, would without further delay come with them to Boston, the commissioners promised and assured them free liberty to come and return without molestation. But deputies would not now serve, nor would the preparations on hand be stayed or the directions recalled till the aforementioned sagamores came, and further consultation had taken place. If, on the other hand, they would have nothing but war, the English were ready, and would proceed accordingly.

Pessecuss, Mixano, and Weetowish, three principal sachems of the Narragansett Indians, and Awasequin, deputy for the Nyanticks, with a large train of men, a few days after, came to Boston. To omit all other circumstances, and the discussion which took place between them and the commissioners, they came to the following conclusion.

1. It is agreed between the commissioners of the United Colonies and the Narragansett and Nyantick sagamores, that the latter shall pay or cause to be paid at Boston to the Massachusetts commissioners the full sum of 2000 fathom of good white wampum, or a third part of black wampum, in four payments; namely, 500 fathom within 20 days, 500 fathom within four months, 500 fathom at or before next corn planting time, and 500 fathom within two years from the date of these presents; which 2000 fathom the commissioners accept as satisfaction for former expenses defrayed.

2. The aforesaid sagamores and deputy, on behalf of the Narragansett and Nyantick Indians, hereby promise and covenant that upon demand and proof they will restore to Uncas, the Monhigg sagamore, all captives both men, women, and children; all canoes, which they or any of their men have taken, or as many Narragansett canoes, in good condition, in place of them; and will give full satisfaction for all such corn as they or any of their men have destroyed of his or his men's, since last planting-time; and the English commissioners hereby promise that Uncas shall do likewise.

3. Whereas there are various disputes and grievances between the Narragansett and Nyantick Indians, and Uncas and his men, which in the absence of Uncas cannot now be determined, it is hereby agreed that the Narragansett and Nyantick sagamores either come themselves or send their deputies to the meeting of the commissioners for the Colonies, either at New Haven in September, 1646—or sooner, upon due notice, if the said commissioners meet sooner—fully instructed to make due proof of their injuries, and to submit to the judgment of the commissioners in giving or receiving satisfaction; and the said commissioners, not doubting but Uncas will either come himself or send his deputies, promise to give full hearing to both parties impartially, according to their allegations and proofs.

4. The said Narragansett and Nyantick sagamores and deputies do hereby promise and covenant to maintain a firm and perpetual peace, both with all the English United Colonies and their successors, and with Uncas, the Monhigg sachem, and his men; with Ossamequine, Pumham, Sokanoke, Cutshamakin, Shoanan, Passaconaway, and all other sagamores and their tribes who are in friendship with or subject to any of the English; hereby engaging themselves, that they will not at any time hereafter, disturb the peace of the country by any attacks, hostile attempts, invasions, or other injuries to any of the United Colonies or their successors, or to the aforesaid Indians, either in their persons, buildings, cattle, or goods, directly or indirectly; nor will they combine with any other enemy against them; and if they know of any Indians or others who are conspiring or intend harm to the said English or any Indians subject to or in friendship with them, they will without delay acquaint and give notice thereof to the English commissioners, or some of them. Or if any questions or disputes shall at any time hereafter arise between them and Uncas, or any Indians mentioned above, they will, according to former engagements which they hereby confirm and ratify, first acquaint the English and request their judgment and advice therein, and will not attempt or begin any war or hostile invasion, till they have liberty and permission from the Commissioners of the United Colonies so to do.

5. The said Narragansett and Nyantick sagamores and deputies do hereby promise that they will forthwith deliver and restore all such Indian fugitives or captives as have at any time fled from the English, and are now living among them, or give due satisfaction for them to the commissioners for Massachusetts; and further, that they will without delay pay or cause to be paid a yearly tribute, a month before harvest, every year after this, at Boston, to

the English Colonies, for all such Pequots as live among them, according to the former treaty and agreement made at Hartford, 1638, namely one fathom of white wampum for every Pequot man, and half a fathom for each Pequot youth, and one hand length for each male child; and if Weequashcooke refuse to pay this tribute for any Pequots with him, the Narragansett sagamores promise to assist the English against him. And they further undertake that they will resign and yield up the whole Pequot country and every part of it to the English Colonies, as due to them by conquest.

6. The said Narragansett and Nyantick sagamores and deputy do hereby promise and covenant that within 14 days, they will bring and deliver to the Massachusetts commissioners on behalf of the Colonies, four of their children, viz., the eldest son of Pessecuss, the son of Tassaquanawite, the brother of Pessecuss, the son of Awashawe, and the son of Ewangso, a Nyantick, to be kept as hostages or pledges by the English, till the aforementioned 2000 fathom of wampum has been paid at the times appointed, and the differences between themselves and Uncas have been heard and settled, and until these articles have been underwritten at Boston by Jenemo and Wipetock. And further, they hereby promise and covenant that if at any time hereafter any of the said children shall escape or be taken away from the English, before the promises be fully accomplished, they will either bring back and deliver to the Massachusetts commissioners the same children, or if they cannot be found, such and so many other children as shall be chosen by the commissioners for the United Colonies or their assigns, within twenty days after demand; and in the meantime, until the said four children be delivered as hostages, the Narragansett and Nyantick sagamores and deputy do freely and of their own accord leave with the Massachusetts commissioners, as pledges for pres-

ent security, four Indians, viz., Weetowish, Pummunish, Jawashoe, Waughwamino, who also freely consent and offer themselves to stay as pledges, till the aforesaid children are delivered.

7. The commissioners for the United Colonies do hereby promise and agree that the four Indians now left as pledges shall be provided for at the expense of the United Colonies, and that the four children to be delivered as hostages shall be kept and maintained at the same expense; that they will require Uncas and his men, with all other Indian sagamores before named, to forbear all acts of hostility against the Narragansett and Nyantick Indians for the future, and further, all the promises being duly observed and kept by the Narragansetts and Nyanticks and their tribes, they will at the end of the two years restore the said children delivered as hostages, and maintain a firm peace with the Narragansett and Nyantick Indians and their successors.

8. It is fully agreed by and between the said parties that if any hostile attempts be made while this treaty is in hand, or before notice of this agreement can be given, such attempts and the consequences thereof shall on neither part be counted a violation of this treaty, nor a breach of the peace here made and concluded.

9. The Narragansett and Nyantick sagamores and deputy hereby agree and covenant to and with the commissioners of the United Colonies that henceforth they will neither give, grant, sell, nor in any way alienate any part of their country, nor any parcel of land therein to any of the English or others, without consent and permission of the commissioners.

10. Lastly, they promise that if any Pequot or other Indians be found among them who have in time of peace murdered any of the English, they shall be delivered to just punishment.

In witness whereof the parties above named have interchangeably subscribed these presents, the day and year above written.

JOHN WINTHROP, President	PESSECUSS his mark
HERBERT PELHAM	MEEKESANO his mark
THOMAS PRINCE	WEETOWISH his mark
JOHN BROWN	AWASEQUIN his mark
GEORGE FENWICK	ABDAS his mark
EDWARD HOPKINS	PUMMUNISH his mark
THEOPH. EATON	CUTSHAMAKIN his mark
STEPHEN GOODYEAR	

In drawing up this treaty and agreement between the commissioners of the United Colonies and the sagamores and deputy of the Narragansett and Nyantick Indians, Benedict Arnold was interpreter, upon his oath; Sergeant Callicote, and his man, an Indian, were present; and Josias and Cutshamakin, two Indians acquainted with the English language, assisted—making the whole treaty and every article clear to the sagamores and deputy present. Thus was the war pending at this time prevented.

"Some discontented persons under the governmente of the Massachusets sought to trouble their peace, and disturbe, if not innovate, their governmente, by laying many scandals upon them."

CHAPTER XXVI

[*1646*]

About the middle of May this year, three men of war entered the harbor. The Captain's name was Thomas Cromwell, and he had captured several prizes from the Spaniards in the West Indies. He had a commission from the Earl of Warwick.[1] Aboard his vessel were about eighty strong young fellows, but very unruly, who, when they came ashore, so distempered themselves with drink that they became like madmen; and though some of them were punished and imprisoned, they could hardly be restrained; but in the end they became more moderate and orderly. They remained here about a month or six weeks, then going on to Massachusetts; in the meantime scattering a great deal of money among the people—and even more sin than money, I fear, notwithstanding all the care taken to prevent it.

---

[1] As president of the New England Company, Warwick was closely associated with various colonial ventures of the time; he was a leader of the Puritan party in England.

While they were here, a sad accident occurred. One desperate fellow amongst them started wrangling with some of his comrades. Captain Cromwell commanded him to be quiet and cease his quarreling; but he would not, and reviled him with bad language, and in the end half drew his rapier intending to run at him; but the captain closed with him and snatched the rapier from him and gave him a box on the ear; even then he would not give over, but continued to assault him. Whereupon the captain gave him a blow with the hilt of the rapier, just as it was in the scabbard. It chanced to hit his head, and the small end of the bar of the rapier-hilt piercing his skull, he died a few days after. But the captain was exonerated by court martial, for it appeared that the fellow was so quarrelsome that he had several times been chained under hatches to prevent him from hurting his comrades, to which they testified.

This Captain Cromwell made another voyage to the West Indies from the Bay of Massachusetts, well manned and provisioned. He was out three years and took many prizes, and returned rich to Massachusetts. The same summer he had a fall from his horse; he fell on his rapier hilt and bruised himself so badly that he died shortly after. It was remarked by some that this might show the hand of God, and that as one of his men had died of the blow he gave him with the rapier hilt, so his own death was caused by similar means.

This year Mr. Edward Winslow went to England. Some discontented persons in Massachusetts had endeavored to disturb the peace and to undermine if not upset their government, by uttering many slanders about them, and even intended to prosecute them in England by petitioning and complaining to Parliament.[2] Samuel Gorton and his people also made complaints against them. So they chose Mr. Winslow, as their agent, to defend them, and gave him commission and instructions to that end. He managed things so well for them that he cleared them of all blame and dishonor, and disgraced their opponents. But owing to the great upheavals in the government there, he was detained longer than was expected, and later he met with other employments there, so that he has now been absent for four years, which has been much to the loss of this government.[3]

---

[2] The reference is to the efforts of members of the Church of England and the Church of Scotland to undermine the Independent Churches and establish their own ecclesiastical system in New England. Parliament was controlled by a Presbyterian majority, which favored these schemes—a fact which makes Winslow's success all the more remarkable.

[3] Winslow remained in England, and never returned to Plymouth, though he wrote pamphlets in defense of the Pilgrims. Later he was to become one of Cromwell's most trusted councillors.

APPENDIX

The names of those who came over first in the *Mayflower*, in the year 1620 and were by the blessing of God the first beginners and founders of the Settlements and Colonies of New England, with their families: written down A. D. 1650.[1]

JOHN CARVER; Katherine, his wife; DESIRE MINTER; two men-servants, JOHN HOWLAND and ROGER WILDER; a boy, WILLIAM LATHAM; a maid-servant; a child who was put under his charge, called JASPER MORE.

    Mr. and Mrs. Carver, Wilder, and Jasper More all died here during the first general sickness. Desire Minter returned to England; Latham stayed twenty years and then returned; the maid-servant married here, and died a year or two after. Howland married Elizabeth Tillie. Both are living. They had ten children.

WILLIAM BREWSTER; Mary, his wife; two sons, Love and Wrestling; a boy in his charge called Richard More, and another of his brothers.

    The rest of his children were left behind, and came over afterwards. Mr. Brewster lived here 23 or 24 years, being about 80 when he died. His wife died some time before. Wrestling died unmarried. Love had four children, and died in 1650. The eldest son, who came after, had nine children, and is still living; and the daughters, who came with him, married, and are dead. The brother of Richard More died the first winter. Richard married and has four or five children.

EDWARD WINSLOW; Elizabeth, his wife; two men-servants, GEORGE SOWLE and ELIAS STORY; a little girl in his charge, ELLEN, sister of Richard More.

---

[1] The list of *Mayflower* passengers appeared at the end of Bradford's chronicle, followed by an account of what subsequently happened to each one. For the reader's convenience, this latter data, slightly abridged, is set after each name on the original list.

Mr. Winslow's wife died the first winter. He married later the widow of Mr. White, and has two children living. Story and Ellen More died soon after the ship's arrival. George Sowle is living and has eight children.

WILLIAM BRADFORD; Dorothy, his wife.

Their only child, a son, was left behind, and came over after. Mrs. Bradford died soon after their arrival. Mr. Bradford married again, and had four children.

ISAAC ALLERTON; Mary, his wife; three children, Bartholomew, Remember, and Mary; a servant boy, JOHN HOOK.

Mrs. Allerton, and the boy, Hook, died in the first general sickness. Bartholomew married in England. His daughter, Remember, married at Salem and has three or four children living. Mary married here and has four children. Mr. Allerton married, secondly, a daughter of William Brewster, and had one son; he married a third time, and left this place long ago.

SAMUEL FULLER; a servant, WILLIAM BUTTON.

His wife and a child were left behind, and came over afterwards. Two more children were born here, and are living. Button died at sea. Mr. Fuller died 15 years ago.

JOHN CRACKSTON; his son, John.

John Crackston died in the first sickness. His son died 5 or 6 years after; he lost himself in the woods in winter, and his feet were frozen, which brought on fever.

MYLES STANDISH; Rose, his wife.

Mrs. Standish died in the first sickness. Captain Standish married again, and has four sons living.

CHRISTOPHER MARTIN; his wife, two servants, SOLOMON PROWER and JOHN LANGMORE.

All these died in the first sickness, soon after their arrival.

WILLIAM MULLINS; his wife; two children, Joseph and Priscilla; a servant, ROBERT CARTER.

All but Priscilla died in the first sickness. She married John Alden; both are living. They have eleven children.

WILLIAM WHITE; Susanna, his wife; one son, Resolved; and one born aboard ship called Peregrine; two servants, WILLIAM HOLBECK and EDWARD THOMSON.

Mr. White and his two servants died soon after their landing. His widow married Mr. Winslow. His two sons are living.

STEPHEN HOPKINS; Elizabeth, his wife; two children by a former wife, Giles and Constanta; and two by this wife, Damaris and Oceanus—the latter born on the voyage; two servants, EDWARD DOTY and EDWARD LISTER.

Mr. and Mrs. Hopkins lived here over twenty years, and had one son and four daughters born here. Doty is living, and has seven children by a second wife. Lister went to Virginia and died there.

RICHARD WARREN.

His wife and four daughters were left behind and came afterwards, and two more were born here. Mr. Warren lived some four or five years here.

JOHN BILLINGTON; Ellen, his wife; two sons, John and Francis. Billington was executed after he had been here ten years. His eldest son died before him; his second is married.

EDWARD TILLIE; Anne, his wife; two children (their cousins), HENRY SAMSON and HUMILITY COOPER.

Mr. and Mrs. Edward Tillie died soon after their arrival. Humility Cooper returned to England and died there. Henry Samson is living and has seven children.

JOHN TILLIE; his wife; their daughter, Elizabeth.

Mr. and Mrs. John Tillie died soon after their arrival. Elizabeth married John Howland (see above).

FRANCIS COOK; his son, John.

Mrs. Cook and other children came over afterwards. Three more children were born here. His son, John, is married. Mr. Cook is a very old man, and has seen his children's children have children.

THOMAS ROGERS; Joseph, his son.

Mr. Rogers died in the first sickness. His son, Joseph, is living and has six children. The rest of his children came over afterwards, and are married, and have many children.

THOMAS TINKER; his wife; their son.

All died in the first sickness.

JOHN RIGDALE; Alice, his wife.

Both died in the first sickness.

JAMES CHILTON; his wife; their daughter, Mary.

Another daughter, who was married, came after. Mr. and Mrs. Chilton died in the first sickness. Mary Chilton married, and has nine children.

EDWARD FULLER; his wife; their son, Samuel.

Mr. and Mrs. Fuller died soon after they came ashore. Samuel Fuller is living, and has four children, or more.

JOHN TURNER; two sons.

All died in the first sickness. His daughter came some years after to Salem, and is married.

FRANCIS EATON; Sarah, his wife; their baby, Samuel.

Mrs. Eaton died in the general sickness. Mr. Eaton married

a second and third time, having three children by his third wife. Samuel is married and has a child.

MOSES FLETCHER; JOHN GOODMAN; THOMAS WILLIAMS; DIGERIE PRIEST; EDMUND MARGESON; RICHARD BRITTERIDGE; RICHARD CLARK; RICHARD GARDNER; PETER BROWN; GILBERT WINSLOW.

The first seven died in the general sickness. Digerie Priest's wife and children came afterwards, she being Mrs. Allerton's sister. Gardner became a sailor, and died in England, or at sea. Peter Brown married twice, leaving four children; he died about sixteen years since. Gilbert Winslow, after several years here, returned to England and died there.

JOHN ALDEN.

Mr. Alden was hired at Southampton as a cooper. Being a likely young man, he was desirable as a settler; but it was left to his own choice to stay here or return to England; he stayed, and married Priscilla Mullins (see above).

JOHN ALLERTON; THOMAS ENGLISH; WILLIAM TREVOR; and one ELY. The first two were hired as sailors, the one to stay here with the shallop, the other to go back and help over those left behind; but both died here before the *Mayflower* returned. The last two were hired to stay here a year; both returned when their time was out.

Of these 100 or so of persons who came over first, more than half died in the first general sickness. Of those that remained, some were too old to have children. Nevertheless in those thirty years there have sprung up from that stock over 160 persons now living in this year 1650; and of the old stock itself nearly thirty persons still survive. Let the Lord have the praise, Who is the High Preserver of men.